Kierkegaard and the New Nationalism

New Kierkegaard Research

Antony Aumann, Northern Michigan University,
and Adam Buben, Leiden University

Advisory Board: John J. Davenport, Fordham University;
Rick Anthony Furtak, Colorado College;
Sheridan Hough, College of Charleston; Noreen Khawaja, Yale University;
Sharon Krishek, Hebrew University of Jerusalem;
John Lippitt, University of Notre Dame Australia;
Jon Stewart, Slovak Academy of Sciences; Patrick Stokes, Deakin University

New Kierkegaard Research promotes scholarship on all aspects of Kierkegaard's thought and its legacy. The series includes volumes dedicated to the careful exegesis of Kierkegaard's writings, as well as ones that bring his ideas into dialogue with other thinkers. It also serves as an outlet for books drawing inspiration from Kierkegaard to address current questions in philosophy, religion, and other disciplines.

New Kierkegaard Research is pluralistic in nature. It welcomes proposals from scholars approaching Kierkegaard from either analytic or continental philosophical backgrounds, as well as from those adopting historical, contemporary, or comparative frameworks. Emphasis is placed on philosophical engagement with Kierkegaard's ideas, but the series publishes books by authors working in a variety of academic fields.

Titles in the series

Kierkegaard and the New Nationalism: A Contemporary Reinterpretation of the Attack upon Christendom, by Thomas J. Millay
Ethical Silence: Kierkegaard on Communication, Education, and Humility, by Sergia Hay

Kierkegaard and the New Nationalism

A Contemporary Reinterpretation of the Attack upon Christendom

Thomas J. Millay

LEXINGTON BOOKS
Lanham • Boulder • New York • London

Published by Lexington Books
An imprint of The Rowman & Littlefield Publishing Group, Inc.
4501 Forbes Boulevard, Suite 200, Lanham, Maryland 20706
www.rowman.com

86-90 Paul Street, London EC2A 4NE

Copyright © 2022 by The Rowman & Littlefield Publishing Group, Inc.

All rights reserved. No part of this book may be reproduced in any form or by any electronic or mechanical means, including information storage and retrieval systems, without written permission from the publisher, except by a reviewer who may quote passages in a review.

British Library Cataloguing in Publication Information Available

Library of Congress Cataloging-in-Publication Data

Names: Millay, Thomas J., author.
Title: Kierkegaard and the new nationalism : a contemporary
   reinterpretation of the attack upon Christendom / Thomas J. Millay.
Description: Lanham : Lexington Books, [2021] | Series: New Kierkegaard
   research | Includes bibliographical references and index. | Summary:
   "Kierkegaard and the New Nationalism argues for the relevance of
   Kierkegaard's "attack upon Christendom" within our current situation of
   resurgent nationalism. Kierkegaard's ascetic voice calls his readers not
   simply to critique nationalism, but to renounce it, thereby striking at
   nationalism's self-assertive core"— Provided by publisher.
Identifiers: LCCN 2021044291 (print) | LCCN 2021044292 (ebook) | ISBN
   9781793640338 (cloth) | ISBN 9781793640352 (paper) | ISBN 9781793640345
   (ebook)
Subjects: LCSH: Kierkegaard, Søren, 1813-1855. | Nationalism. |
   Kierkegaard, Søren, 1813-1855. Indøvelse i Christendom.
Classification: LCC B4377 .M49 2021 (print) | LCC B4377 (ebook) | DDC
   198/.9—dc23
LC record available at https://lccn.loc.gov/2021044291
LC ebook record available at https://lccn.loc.gov/2021044292

To: The Millay Men Book Club
. . . a sign of hope in troubled times . . .

Contents

Preface	ix
Acknowledgments	xvii
Abbreviations	xix
1 The Attack: History and Context	1
2 Concepts: The Truth-Witness, New Testament Christianity, and Denmark	55
3 An Evolving Martyrdom	69
4 Asceticism in the Streets	89
5 Kierkegaard's Critique of Nationalism Reconsidered	103
6 Some Perspectives on Destruction: Kierkegaard, Cone, and Third World Theology	123
Conclusion: The Attack as a Work of Love: Kierkegaard and Contemporary Political Theology	141
Bibliography	155
Index	161
About the Author	165

Preface

In the fall of 2017, I found myself walking toward an AAR (American Academy of Religion) seminar room. I was filled with a greater than ordinary sense of anticipation. I am a lover of all things Kierkegaard, but especially of his late and last writings. Much of the scholarship on Kierkegaard focuses on his earlier works: *Fear and Trembling* (1843), *Philosophical Fragments* (1844), *Concluding Unscientific Postscript* (1846)—everything up to and including his *Works of Love* (1848). Yet this AAR session was titled "Kierkegaard's Attack upon Christendom: Then and Now." The "attack upon Christendom" is the label typically given to Kierkegaard's final outburst of publications (1854–1855), which take aim at the Danish society of his age in way that is often both harsh and hilarious. Finally, I thought, here is a slice of scholarship which will be focused on these writings I love.

I arrived early to the seminar room, made myself a coffee out in the hallway, and settled into my seat, making sure to have pen and paper ready. The session commenced. As the presenters made their observations and arguments, I noticed something strange happening. To a person, none of the participants discussed Kierkegaard's attack upon Christendom at all. Each took "attack" in a kind of allegorical sense, referring to Kierkegaard's critique of various aspects of Christian culture, whether that be social conformity, hypocrisy, or other such vices. The papers were highly accomplished and interesting in their own right. But I couldn't help feeling a little puzzled.

Eventually I raised my hand and asked about this curious absence: Why, in a session on "The Attack upon Christendom," was there no discussion of Kierkegaard's attack upon Christendom? The answers were revealing. At the risk of misrepresenting the panelists, I believe their responses to my question can be adequately summarized as follows: "We are interested in a Kierkegaard who is still relevant as a contemporary theological resource. Yet the late

Kierkegaard, with his relentless mockery of clergy, his calls to cease attending church, his rejection of any possibility of Christian community, and his general rancor against just about everything, is not amenable to a present-day appropriation."

I am sympathetic to this answer. I too believe scholars of Kierkegaard should have an eye toward relevance. Two recent edited volumes are explicitly dedicated to this premise, and I hold this to be a salutary trend.[1] If the attack upon Christendom can only be of historical interest, then it should be consigned to being of secondary importance (at most). After all, any investigation into Kierkegaard which is solely a matter of historical curiosity is alien to the spirit of Kierkegaard himself, who was always pressing his audience to consider how his words might change their lives.[2]

In a certain sense, then, I agree with the panelists: whatever cannot be used for contemporary purposes should be set to one side. However, where I dissent from the panelists is in seeing Kierkegaard's attack upon Christendom in such a way. The following book was written out of the contrarian conviction that the works of the late Kierkegaard are in fact the most relevant of any of his writings to our current situation.

That current situation is one of resurgent nationalisms. This is the case, for example, in my own country: the United States of America. In fact, we do not need scholars to establish that the still popular 45th president of the United States was a nationalist. The former president openly and proudly admitted as much, saying at a rally in Houston in October of 2018, "You know what? They have a word, it sort of became old fashioned, it's called a 'nationalist.' And I say 'really, we're not supposed to use that word?' You know what I am? I'm a nationalist."

Yet America is not alone in its embrace of nationalist leadership. Nationalism is a globally resurgent phenomenon. Britain's Brexit, for example, built upon decades of resentment following World War II to affirm a broadly popular England-first ideology, as Fintan O'Toole has argued in his book *The Politics of Pain*.[3] India's Prime Minister Narendra Modi's Hindutva ideology replicates the same national self-assertion in a different guise, as his Bharatiya Janata Party (or BJP) tries to enforce a majoritarian state by increasingly excluding non-Hindus.[4] And, lest they feel left out, there is another nation that does perhaps deserve to be included: namely, Denmark. Though it is still too early to tell exactly how this will play out, it seems the ascendant Social Democratic party in Denmark (led by Mette Frederiksen) has achieved its victory through appropriating some of the nationalistic fervor previously whipped up by the Dansk Folkeparti, a fervor most vividly evident in cartoonish figures like Qur'an desecrator Rasmus Paludan.[5] Further, Denmark's situation shows that it is not only the political Right who is drawing on the sentiments of nationalism; refusing to be outdone, the Left can also be found mobilizing anti-immigrant rhetoric.

If we take this situation of resurgent nationalism as the context within which Kierkegaard is currently being read, the relevance of the attack upon Christendom quickly becomes apparent. Earlier writings from Kierkegaard's pen were carefully calibrated to cultivate individual inward transformation. As of 1851, Kierkegaard publicly says he does not wish to make any change in externals; internal renewal is the goal of his authorship,[6] and he disapproves of his message being "in any way vainly externalized by proposing external changes in the established order" (PC 301/*Pap*. X-5 B 40).[7] As we will see, it is only in the attack literature that Kierkegaard begins to advocate the real structural dismantling of Christendom, a demolishing which would include a variety of external changes, such as separating the financial apparatus of the church from that of the state.[8]

Still, we may ask the question: why are these writings relevant, especially in a country like the United States, which has already separated church and state? Yet it is clear the separation of church and state in the United States is only true at a formal and financial level. Christianity continues to be deeply imbricated in the maintenance and expansion of American empire. To this entanglement, the attack literature provides a direct challenge. I will argue that, in Kierkegaard's attack, we see a conjunction between Christianity and an ascetic political theology which fundamentally challenges the self-assertive core of nationalism.

For Kierkegaard, Christianity is a doctrine of self-renunciation. The Christian life begins with self-denial and continues by working out the consequences of this initial moment. That much is already clear in Kierkegaard's second authorship, especially in *Practice in Christianity*. In the attack, Kierkegaard joins together his ascetic interpretation of Christianity with a proposal for what the political consequences of such a vision might be. He argues forcefully and repeatedly that Christianity cannot be joined together with the self-assertive practices of the modern nation-state. Just as at the beginning of his authorship, he gives us an either/or: either we will be Christians, or we will live in a great nation—we cannot have both.

The context for Kierkegaard's ascetic political theology is Golden Age Denmark (ca. 1800–1850). Denmark's ascendancy in this period was marked by self-assertions of many kinds, not least extractive colonialism.[9] This self-assertion made possible the relatively comfortable life of the 19th century Danish bourgeoisie, whose lives were newly filled with consumer goods (cigars, coffee), modern conveniences (running tap water), and modern entertainment (Tivoli Gardens).

Kierkegaard has no critique of this self-assertion, considered in itself. But he does say: you cannot have all this *and* be a Christian. If the condition of material happiness in this world is self-assertion (as Kierkegaard believes it to be), he argues that you cannot be happy in this world and also save your soul.

The lie of Christendom, so far as Kierkegaard understood it, was to tell the itching ears of its audience that precisely the opposite was the case: that in fact you could have it all, that you could be happy in this life and the next. Such a lie thrives only when complicity with the evil which rules this world is (consciously or unconsciously) accepted, for it is that evil which makes earthly comforts available. Kierkegaard is here to remind us that the true Christian cannot accept such complicity; she lives in solidarity with the abased Christ.

The true Christian's life is marked by suffering: it begins in the renunciation of this world, which includes a thumbing of one's nose at one's nation, especially insofar as one's nation has pretensions to greatness. This renunciation of the self-assertion required of worldly happiness works itself out in concrete forms, often taking the traditional markers of poverty, chastity, and obedience, as we shall see. The Christian life is a renunciation, then, of the comfortable and happy life which the thriving modern nation-state promises and can on occasion deliver. It is marked by the sufferings inherent in such a renunciation. But, as Kierkegaard's stark voice reminds us, these sufferings are a small price to pay when salvation is at stake.

It should now be clearer why the attack literature is particularly relevant to our current situation of resurgent nationalisms. In these writings, Kierkegaard takes direct aim at the political conjuncture of Christianity and self-assertion. Insofar as Christianity has been coopted into the project of nationalism, Kierkegaard offers a counter-path of disjunctive resistance. To the current preoccupation with flourishing, Kierkegaard responds: 'No. What we need to embrace is suffering. *Askēsis* is the only path that will lead us toward faithfulness to the essence of Christianity.'

In the writings of the attack and in his own personal life, Kierkegaard set standards of renunciative suffering which clarify what a life of exemption from the status quo looks like. The Golden Age had handed Kierkegaard a ticket which guaranteed him entrance to a life of earthly goodness: a beautiful wife, a happy family, membership in elite aesthetic salons, and a position within a respected and well-funded clergy establishment. For no easily calculable reason—for reasons which seemed to benefit no one, least of all himself—Kierkegaard rescinded the ticket he was offered. To a modernity which is above all committed to making people happier, Kierkegaard's ascetic vision makes no sense. That is precisely why it is a vision worthy of exploration.

A full exploration of the late Kierkegaard's ascetic vision requires patient labor. Several elements are required: historical context, close readings of key texts, a sense of how the attack literature evolves over time, an assessment of the political ramifications of Kierkegaard's polemic, and an argument for the possibility of contemporary appropriation of the attack which respects the inherent complexity of this task. When these elements are gathered together, an understanding of the attack in-and-for-itself can be united to an appreciation of its continuing relevance. The purpose of this book is to lay out these elements with that end goal in mind.

Chapter 1 of *Kierkegaard and the New Nationalism* unfolds in four stages. First, it tells the story of the attack, providing a narrative overview of its key characters and events. Second, portraits of the principal figures Jakob Peter Mynster and Hans Lassen Martensen are joined with a summary sketch of Golden Age society. Third, chapter 1 gives a retrospective précis of themes in Kierkegaard's authorship that led him to see his attack upon Christendom as a necessary course of action. Finally, an overview of Kierkegaard's voluminous journal entries in the years 1851–1854, penned between the publication of his final book (*For Self-Examination*) and the beginning of the attack, will then show how Kierkegaard gradually selects certain themes for expanded consideration, a selection which then gives shape to the attack. Rather than a break from his prior authorship, the attack should be seen as the amplification of previous tendencies. This initial chapter thus provides a narrative of the events of the attack and the context within which those events took place.

Chapters 2 and 3 build on the multiple contexts developed in the first chapter in order to provide an in-depth reading of the attack literature itself. Chapter 2 focuses on the crucial concepts of the attack: the truth-witness, New Testament Christianity, and Denmark, showing how these concepts extend and modify aforementioned Kierkegaardian themes. Chapter 3 charts an authorial development often neglected in scholarship on the attack, namely the evolving nature of Kierkegaard's positions. Kierkegaard does not openly advocate the institutional dismantling of Christendom right at the beginning of the attack. Instead, he works toward this position over time. Chapter 3 maps this development and argues that the ultimate aim of Kierkegaard's attack is the demolition of Danish society as constituted at that time.

Chapter 4 takes the results of the first three chapters and argues for a specific global interpretation of the late Kierkegaard: namely, as an ascetic, as someone whose writings evince a commitment to poverty, chastity, and obedience, and whose life to some degree manifested these theoretical commitments. There has been a good deal of recent scholarship tying Kierkegaard to mystical traditions and showing how—through themes such as rest, trust, and unity with God—Kierkegaard reflects those traditions and is in some sense a mystic himself.[10] I appreciate this scholarship, but I also believe it leaves open the possibility of blunting the sharpness of Kierkegaard's vision. My advocacy of an ascetic Kierkegaard intentionally keeps our focus on themes such as suffering, renunciation, and the rejection of the world.

Chapter 5 then argues that Kierkegaard's ascetic vision should be interpreted as an anti-nationalistic *praxis* of resistance. Kierkegaard's is no quietistic asceticism; instead, its political consequences include the very real effect of no longer considering Denmark to be a Christian nation. Furthermore, in this chapter I argue that it is precisely as an ascetic vision that Kierkegaard makes an important contribution to the current discourse surrounding nationalism. In a critical engagement with Benedict Anderson and Stephen Backhouse, chapter 6 argues for *askēsis* as a more consequential mode of resistance to nationalism than ideology critique. The latter mode of critique, while important, does not address the fundamental desire that gives birth to nationalism. In addition, to point out that national identities are incoherently fabricated does little to undermine those whose concern is not truth but an empowering mythology. Evidence for the critical position I take here is found in the new nationalism currently rearing its monstrous head across the globe, especially through an engagement with the American white nationalist Richard Spencer and white evangelical American Christianity. I then show how Kierkegaard's asceticism is perfectly calibrated to address the root cause of nationalist mythologies: namely, desire. It is only in the practice of daily renunciations that desire can be changed. When desire shifts to the valence of self-denial and *then* is yoked to a theoretical account of Christian resistance to nationalism (such as one finds in Backhouse's Kierkegaard)—at that point, true change, true critique with both words and life, becomes possible.

I believe a full appreciation of Kierkegaard's attack upon Christendom will provide effective tools for the critique of new nationalisms; however, that does not mean we should be uncritical when appropriating these writings for our present context. Chapter 6 complicates Kierkegaard's denunciation of self-assertion and advocacy of self-renunciation by looking to the writing of James H. Cone, who wrote primarily for an audience which is not in the dominant subject position which Kierkegaard's generally elite Danish clientele occupied. Cone's work suggests that Kierkegaard's advocacy of *askēsis* cannot be recommended without the use of practical reason, a form of analysis that can make distinctions between positions of power in the current arrangement of our world. At the same time, reading Kierkegaard with Cone leads to an underlining of a moment in Cone's own career when Cone moved toward black renunciation of American power in solidarity with what was then called the Third World. Reading Kierkegaard and Cone together thus both complicates Kierkegaard and highlights a specific moment within Cone's developing corpus as a crucial inflection point.

Finally, the conclusion synthesizes the multiple threads of *Kierkegaard and the New Nationalism* to argue for the continuing relevance of a discourse of renunciation and suffering within the domain of political theology. Ultimately, I argue, Kierkegaard is right: renouncing the world will cost us something. The kind of Christianity that supports nationalism is sustained by the belief that one can have it all: dominance in this world, glory in the next. Kierkegaard returns us to a fundamental choice: either this world, or the world to come. It is only in the facing of this choice—both at a theoretical level and at the level of daily ascetic practice—that nationalism can be confronted and undermined.

The writings of the late Kierkegaard are characterized by extremity: pastors are described as cannibals, Christendom as the abolition of Christianity, and procreation as a sin. My conviction is that this extremity—outlandish though it may at times be—is precisely the wake-up call our age of extremisms requires. We need to make the stakes clear for ourselves. Either we are going to make peace with the powers of this world and achieve a measure of earthly happiness, or we are going to be Christians. There is no in-between. The writings of the late Kierkegaard give us conceptual awareness of this fact, and then ask us: Which will you choose?

The more one realizes the apostasy inherent in Christian nationalism, the greater one's appreciation for the late Kierkegaard. The attack upon Christendom is relevant precisely because it asks of us the major questions of our times: Will you ally yourself with the forces of this world, or not? If not, how will you renounce them? And what will such renunciation cost you? Through all the historical reckoning with Kierkegaard's attack in what follows, these contemporary questions will guide and shape our inquiry. If you agree with me that any focus on Kierkegaard must include an emphasis on contemporary appropriation, I hope by the end of this book you will be persuaded that it is precisely these texts—the literature of the attack—which deserve our full attention.

NOTES

1. Paul Martens and C. Stephen Evans, eds., *Kierkegaard and Christian Faith* (Waco: Baylor University Press, 2016); James Lorentzen and Gordon Marino, eds., *Taking Kierkegaard Personally: First Person Responses* (Macon: Mercer University Press, 2020).

2. See Thomas J. Millay, *You Must Change Your Life: Søren Kierkegaard's Philosophy of Reading* (Eugene: Cascade, 2020).

3. Fintan O'Toole, *The Politics of Pain: Postwar England and the Rise of Nationalism* (New York, NY: Liveright Publishing Company, 2019).

4. See Angana P. Chatterji, Thomas Blom Hansen, and Christophe Jaffrelot, eds., *Majoritarian State: How Hindu Nationalism is Changing India* (Oxford: Oxford University Press, 2019).

5. Sune Haugbolle, "Did the Left Really Win in Denmark?" *Foreign Policy*, June 7, 2019.

6. See "An Open Letter: Prompted by a Reference to me by Dr. Rudelbach" (COR 51–60/SKS 14:111–116).

7. See also an interesting journal entry from 1854, where Kierkegaard states that "at least for the time being" (!), his task "is not to change the state of things, but to take stock"; Mynster's task, on the other hand, was to "conceal" the state of things (KJN 11:357/SKS 27:651).

8. With reference to the situation after Denmark's shift to constitutional (rather than absolute) monarchy, Bruce H. Kirmmse writes: "In the end, there was very little change from the absolutist period. Despite the 1849 Constitution and the triumph of liberalism, liberal secularism was never even attempted. The Church remained bound to the state administration more tightly than ever, and the cabinet portfolio of *Kultusminister* was established to oversee the Church, education, museums, the ballet and opera, and culture generally—which ought to give a fair idea of how, and in what categories, Christianity was construed by governing circles" (*Kierkegaard and Golden Age Denmark* [Bloomington: Indiana University Press, 1990], 76).

9. See *Danmark og kolonierne*, 5 Volumes (Copenhagen: Gads, 2017).

10. See especially the work of Christopher Barnett, *From Despair to Faith: The Spirituality of Søren Kierkegaard* (Minneapolis: Fortress, 2014), and Simon Podmore, *Anatomy of the Abyss: Kierkegaard and the Self before God* (Bloomington: Indiana University Press, 2011).

Acknowledgments

There are six people who have been crucial to this project who must be thanked.

First, Paul Martens. It is your insights into both the continuity and the brilliance of the late attack literature which has guided me throughout my writing.

Second, Marcia Robinson. Your incisive questions have been on my mind for years now, and this material is much improved as a result.

Third, Tyler Davis. You have served as my guide to the works of James Cone and much else besides.

Fourth, Gordon Marino. Thank you, Gordon, for believing in me enough to make me a Senior Research Fellow at the Hong Kierkegaard Library—and for the invitation to deliver the Julia Watkin Memorial lecture in the summer 2020, which was the occasion for developing chapter 5 of this book, "Kierkegaard's Critique of Nationalism Reconsidered."

Fifth and sixth, Adam Buben and Antony Aumann: Thank you both for believing in this project and improving its quality through your editorial guidance.

Finally, I must thank:

Routledge, for permission to use material from Copyright 2019 Thomas J. Millay, "Kierkegaard, Hegel, and Augustine on Love" from *The Kierkegaardian Mind* edited by Adam Buben, Eleanor Helms, and Patrick Stokes. Reproduced by permission of Taylor and Francis Group, LLC, a division of Informa plc. Permission conveyed through Copyright Clearance Center, Inc. A chapter in this edited volume formed an earlier version of the conclusion of this book.

And also: Princeton University Press, for permission to use extracts from: Kierkegaard's Writings, Volume 16: *Works of Love*, translated by Howard

V. Hong and Edna H. Hong, Princeton: Princeton University Press, 1995; Kierkegaard's Writings, Volume 23: The Moment and *Late Writings*, translated by Howard V. Hong and Edna H. Hong, Princeton: Princeton University Press, 1998; reprinted with permission.

Abbreviations

References to Kierkegaard's writings in English will use the following abbreviations, adapted from Mercer University Press's *International Kierkegaard Commentary* series:

CI   *The Concept of Irony, with Continual Reference to Socrates; Notes of Schelling's Berlin Lectures*, edited and translated by Howard V. Hong and Edna H. Hong, Kierkegaard's Writings, vol. II (Princeton: Princeton University Press, 1989).

COR   *The Corsair Affair and Articles Related to the Writings*, edited and translated by Howard V. Hong and Edna H. Hong, Kierkegaard's Writings, vol. XIII (Princeton: Princeton University Press, 1982).

CUP   *Concluding Unscientific Postscript to Philosophical Fragments, Volume I: Text*, edited and translated by Howard V. Hong and Edna H. Hong, Kierkegaard's Writings, vol. XII:1 (Princeton: Princeton University Press, 1992).

EOI   *Either/Or, Part I*, edited and translated by Howard V. Hong and Edna H. Hong, Kierkegaard's Writings, vol. III (Princeton: Princeton University Press, 1987).

EOII   *Either/Or, Part II*, edited and translated by Howard V. Hong and Edna H. Hong, Kierkegaard's Writings, vol. IV (Princeton: Princeton University Press, 1987).

FSE *For Self-Examination*, in *For Self-Examination; Judge for Yourself!* edited and translated by Howard V. Hong and Edna H. Hong, Kierkegaard's Writings, vol. XXI (Princeton: Princeton University Press, 1990).

FT *Fear and Trembling*, in *Fear and Trembling; Repetition*, edited and translated by Howard V. Hong and Edna H. Hong, Kierkegaard's Writings, vol. VI (Princeton: Princeton University Press, 1983).

JP *Søren Kierkegaard's Journals and Papers*, edited and translated by Howard V. Hong and Edna H. Hong, assisted by Gregor Malantschuk, vols. 1–6 (Bloomington: Indiana University Press, 1967–1978).

KJN *Kierkegaard's Journals and Notebooks*, ed. Niels Jørgen Cappelørn, Alastair Hannay, David Kangas, Bruce H. Kirmmse, George Pattison, Vanessa Rumble, and K. Brian Söderquist, vols. 1–11 (Princeton: Princeton University Press, 2007ff.).

Pap. *Søren Kierkegaards Papirer*, ed. P. A. Heiberg, V. Kuhr, and E. Torsting, vols. I–XI-3 (Copenhagen: Gyldendal, 1909–1948).

PC *Practice in Christianity*, edited and translated by Howard V. Hong and Edna H. Hong, Kierkegaard's Writings, vol. XX (Princeton: Princeton University Press, 1991).

PF *Philosophical Fragments*, edited and translated by Howard V. Hong and Edna H. Hong, Kierkegaard's Writings, vol. VII (Princeton: Princeton University Press, 1998).

SKS *Søren Kierkegaards Skrifter*, ed. Niels Jørgen Cappelørn, Joakim Garff, Jette Knudsen, and Johnny Kondrup, vols. 1–28, K1–K28 (Copenhagen: Gads Forlag, 1997–2013).

SLW *Stages on Life's Way*, edited and translated by Howard V. Hong and Edna H. Hong, Kierkegaard's Writings, vol. XI (Princeton: Princeton University Press, 1988).

TM *The Moment and Late Writings*, edited and translated by Howard V. Hong and Edna H. Hong, Kierkegaard's Writings, vol. XXIII (Princeton: Princeton University Press, 1998).

UDVS   *Upbuilding Discourses in Various Spirits*, edited and translated by Howard V. Hong and Edna H. Hong, Kierkegaard's Writings, vol. XV (Princeton: Princeton University Press, 1993).

WL   *Works of Love*, edited and translated by Howard V. Hong and Edna H. Hong, Kierkegaard's Writings, vol. XVI (Princeton: Princeton University Press, 1995).

The corresponding volume and page number in *Søren Kierkegaards Skrifter* (Copenhagen: Gads Forlag) has been provided whenever possible:

SKS 2   *Enten–Eller. Første del*, ed. Niels Jørgen Cappelørn, Joakim Garff, Johnny Kondrup, and Finn Hauberg Moretensen (Copenhagen: Gads, 1997).

SKS 3   *Enten–Eller. Anden del*, Niels Jørgen Cappelørn, Joakim Garff, Johnny Kondrup, and Finn Hauberg Moretensen (Copenhagen: Gads, 1997).

SKS 4   *Gjentagelsen; Frygt og Bæven; Philosophiske Smuler; Begrebet Angest; Forord,* ed. Niels Jørgen Cappelørn, Joakim Garff, Johnny Kondrup, and Finn Hauberg Mortensen (Copenhagen: Gads, 1997).

SKS 6   *Stadier paa Livets Vei*, ed. Niels Jørgen Cappelørn, Joakim Garff, Jette Knudsen, Johnny Kondrup, and Finn Hauberg Mortensen (Copenagen: Gads, 1999).

SKS 7   *Afsluttende uvidenskabelig Efterskrift*, ed. Niels Jørgen Cappelørn, Joakim Garff, Jette Knudsen, and Johnny Kondrup (Copenhagen: Gads, 2002).

SKS 8   *En literair Anmeldelse; Opbyggelige Taler I forskjellig Aand*, ed. Niels Jørgen Cappelørn, Joakim Garff, and Johnny Kondrup (Copenhagen: Gads, 2004).

SKS 9   *Kjerlighedens Gjerninger*, ed. Niels Jørgen Cappelørn, Joakim Garff, and Johnny Kondrup (Copenhagen: Gads, 2004).

SKS 12 *Indøvelse i Christendom; En obyggelig Tale; To Taler ved Altergangen om Fredagen*, ed. Niels Jørgen Cappelørn, Joakim Garff, Anne Mette Hansen, and Johnny Kondrup (Copenhagen: Gads, 2008).

SKS 13 *On min Forfatter-Virksomhed, Til Selvprøvelse Samtiden anbefalet, Dette skal gies; saa være det da sagt, Hvad Christus dømmer om official Christendom, Guds Uforanderlighed, Øieblikket nr. 1–10*, ed. Niels Jørgen Cappelørn, Joakim Garff, Johnny Kondrup, Tonny Aagaard Olesen, and Steen Tullberg (Copenhagen: Gads, 2009).

SKS 14 *Bladartikler*, ed. Niels Jørgen Cappelørn, Joakim Garff, Johnny Kondrup, Tonny Aagaard Olesen, and Steen Tullberg (Copenhagen: Gads, 2010).

SKS 19 *Notesbøgerne 1–15*, ed. Niels Jørgen Cappelørn, Joakim Garff, Jette Knudsen, and Johnny Kondrup (Copenhagen: Gads, 2001).

SKS 20 *Journalerne NB–NB5*, ed. Niels Jørgen Cappelørn, Joakim Garff, Jette Knudsen, and Johnny Kondrup (Copenhagen: Gads, 2003).

SKS 21 *Journalerne NB6–NB10*, ed. Niels Jørgen Cappelørn, Joakim Garff, Jette Knudsen, and Johnny Kondrup (Copenhagen: Gads, 2003).

SKS 22 *Journalerne NB11–NB14*, ed. Niels Jørgen Cappelørn, Joakim Garff, Anne Mette Hansen, and Johnny Kondrup (Copenhagen: Gads, 2007).

SKS 23 *Journalerne NB15–NB20*, ed. Niels Jørgen Cappelørn, Joakim Garff, Anne Mette Hansen, and Johnny Kondrup (Copenhagen: Gads, 2007).

SKS 24 *Journalerne NB21–NB25*, ed. Niels Jørgen Cappelørn, Joakim Garff, Anne Mette Hansen, and Johnny Kondrup (Copenhagen: Gads, 2007).

SKS 25 *Journalerne NB26–NB30*, ed. Niels Jørgen Cappelørn, Joakim Garff, Anne Mette Hansen, and Johnny Kondrup (Copenhagen: Gads, 2008).

SKS 26   *Journalerne NB31–NB36*, ed. Niels Jørgen Cappelørn, Joakim Garff, Anne Mette Hansen, and Johnny Kondrup (Copenhagen: Gads, 2009).

SKS 27   *Løse Papirer*, ed. Niels Jørgen Cappelørn, Joakim Garff, Anne Mette Hansen, and Johnny Kondrup (Copenhagen: Gads, 2013).

Other abbreviations:

IKC   *International Kierkegaard Commentary*, edited by Robert L. Perkins, vols. 1–24 (Macon: Mercer University Press, 1984–2010).

KRSRR   *Kierkegaard Research: Sources, Reception and Resources*, ed. Jon Stewart, vols. 1–21 (Aldershot: Ashgate; London: Routledge, 2007–2017).

KSYB   *Kierkegaard Studies Yearbook*, Years 1998–2018, ed. Niels Jørgen Cappeljørn et al. (Berlin: Walter de Gruyter, 1998ff).

Chapter One

The Attack

History and Context

The majority of *Kierkegaard and the New Nationalism* is devoted to an in-depth reading of Kierkegaard's attack upon Christendom and to the subsequent analysis of this literature in the light of both historical and contemporary manifestations of nationalism. In order to set this reading and analysis on firm ground, however, a number of preliminary elements are required. The current chapter provides: a summary narrative of the attack, beginning with an explanation of why the attack began in 1854 and not 1848; an unfolding of the context of the attack, both at a more granular level by attending to two particular individuals (Bishops Mynster and Martensen), and at the larger scale of the society of Golden Age Denmark; a retrospective reading of Kierkegaard's authorship prior to the attack which argues for interpreting previous writings as in fundamental continuity with these last publications; and finally a glimpse at Kierkegaard's journals from 1851–1854, which explain how he finally arrives at the decision to attack. Putting these elements in place will set the reading and interpretation of the attack on solid contextual ground, and in later chapters I will frequently make recourse to the background for the attack as laid out here.

SUSPENDED SENTENCE

To speak about the historical development of Kierkegaard's attack upon Christendom is to speak about delay. *Practice in Christianity*—which was written in 1848 and published in 1850—contains *in nuce* the whole of the attack, as Kierkegaard himself openly acknowledged in the twentieth newspaper article of the attack literature (TM 69–70/SKS 14:213). *Practice in Christianity* has two essential theses: (1) Christianity should be defined as suffering or self-denial; (2) Insofar as it is successful in combining the label "Christian" with a life of comfort and ease, Christendom is the abolition of Christianity. The task *Practice in Christianity* performs is one of conceptual clarification, leading us from the confusion sown in (2) back to a clear vision of (1). *Practice in Christianity* undoes the work of Christendom by reminding us of the true definition of Christ, as one who is abased, poor, a criminal and an outcast, recalling us to the true following of Christ, which entails taking these existential conditions upon oneself.

Describing it as productive of illusions which undermine a true following of Christ, *Practice in Christianity* harbors a negative estimate of Christendom, to say the least. At the same time, the framing device for *Practice in Christianity* prevents it from being interpreted as a direct assault upon Christendom. In the Preface to *Practice in Christianity* No. I, Kierkegaard states that the purpose of the text is to provoke its readers to "a personal admission," a "confession," and a greater reliance upon "*grace*" (PC 7/SKS 12:15).[1] This message is then repeated at the beginning of Nos. II and III (PC 73, 149/SKS 12:85, 153). Furthermore, it is expanded upon in the "The Moral," found at the end of No. I of *Practice in Christianity*:

> "And what does all this mean?" It means that each individual in quiet inwardness before God is to humble himself under what it means in the strictest sense to be a Christian, is to confess honestly before God where he is so that he still might worthily accept the grace that is offered to every imperfect person—that is, to everyone. And then nothing further; then, as for the rest, let him do his work and rejoice in it, love his wife and rejoice in her, joyfully bring up his children, love his fellow beings, rejoice in life. If anything more is required of him, God will surely let him understand. (PC 67/SKS 12:79)

With these framing passages in mind, it appears that the purpose of *Practice in Christianity* is the maintenance of the status quo, with one important difference: the status quo must admit that it is not equivalent to the ideal of Christianity, and that it has departed from the Christian ideal precisely to the extent that the lives lived within it are comfortable ones.

To summarize the practical import of *Practice in Christianity*, everything is to remain in place, structurally speaking; however, an admission of inadequacy is to be made. The leaders of Christianity are to openly admit their lives are not accurate guides as to what the essential nature of Christianity is supposed to be. The message of the "Moral" of *Practice* thus accords with Kierkegaard's 1851 "Open Letter" to Dr. Rudelbach, where Kierkegaard states that the purpose of his writing has nothing to do with any sort of external change, and is aimed only at provoking inward, individual transformation.[2]

With this framing, *Practice* can—and, according to Kierkegaard, *should*—be considered a last possible defense of Christendom (TM 69/SKS 14:213). Therefore, due to *Practice in Christianity*'s Preface and "Moral," this writing cannot properly be considered an attack upon Christendom.

After publishing *Practice in Christianity*, and a kind of companion piece titled *For Self-Examination* (which supplements *Practice in Christianity*'s Christology with an ascetic pneumatology), Kierkegaard fell silent for several years, from September 21, 1851, to December 17, 1854. Though prepared in all its conceptual elements, Kierkegaard waited to unleash his polemic upon the public, and he did so for three principle reasons: (1) Respect for Jakob Peter Mynster, which translated into a respectfully patient waiting upon Mynster's response to Kierkegaard's charges against Danish Christendom and against Mynster himself; (2) A desire not to interfere with the election of the next Bishop of Sjælland; (3) A desire not to be sued by the rather heavy-handed Ørsted administration. Let's take a moment to unpack these three reasons.

(1) Kierkegaard had enormous respect for Jakob Peter Mynster, Bishop of Sjælland from 1834–1854. In fact, Kierkegaard states that he was "devoted to him with a hypochondriacal passion" (KJN 8:509/SKS 24:500). Mynster was Kierkegaard's boyhood pastor,[3] and it seems that for Kierkegaard, piety toward Mynster and piety toward his father were inseparable.[4] Couched within this general human and personal respect, however, was a growing conviction that Mynster's version of Christianity—with its emphases on comfort, duty, and the social maintenance of good order—was a betrayal.

These competing positions led Kierkegaard to the place he arrived in *Practice in Christianity*. He decided resolutely to critique Christendom, and fairly explicitly to critique Mynster.[5] At the same time, Kierkegaard would not call for the sacking of Mynster nor for the dismantling of Christendom. Instead, Kierkegaard would wait for Mynster to confess his inadequacy in comparison to the Christian ideal—the ideal of which *Practice in Christianity*, with its abased, lowly Christ, had reminded its readers. Kierkegaard would wait, in other words, for honesty.

Respect for Mynster did not prevent Kierkegaard from directing critical remarks at him in a published work. However, Kierkegaard's respect for the bishop did lead him to limit his criticism, thus to (a) not explicitly mention Mynster by name, and to (b) give Mynster's good will the benefit of the doubt, allowing him time to respond in an authentic way to the charges made in *Practice in Christianity*.

As Kierkegaard understood it, the only possible authentic response from Mynster would be a "confession" (*Tilstaaelse*). Furthermore, Kierkegaard was willing to extend a measure of trust and believe in the possibility that Mynster would make a confession. As Kirmmse summarizes:

> [T]hroughout the early 1850's, SK nourished the faint hope that Mynster might make some kind of concession before he died, while at the same time SK was storing up polemical material for use in the event that he did not.[6]

Kirmmse's assessment is supported by an 1854 journal entry penned soon after Mynster's death:

> Now he is dead.
> If he could have been moved to end his life by confessing to Xnty that what he has represented was not rlly Xnty but a lenient version of it, it would have been extremely desirable, for he bore an entire age.
> Therefore, the possibility of a confession of this sort had to be held open until the end—indeed, until the end—in case he might possibly make it on his deathbed. That is why he was never to be attacked; that is why I had to put up with everything, even when he did so desperate a thing as that involving Goldschmidt,[7] for of course no one could know whether that might not perhaps move him so that he would come forward with that admission after all.
> Dead without that confession, everything is changed: now the only thing left is that he preached Xnty firmly into an illusion.[8] (KJN 9:264/*SKS* 25:262 [March 1, 1854])

Part of the narrative of delay is therefore the natural course of Jakob Peter Mynster's life. The timing of the attack depended on the amount of time Mynster lived. Kierkegaard's ambivalent relation to Mynster—in which he privately held incisive criticisms of the bishop but was also constrained by a pious devotion to the man that was intertwined with Kierkegaard's childhood and his respect for his father—led him to delay the attack until after Mynster's death. Indeed, the first newspaper article of the attack was written soon after Mynster's passing. With Kierkegaard's concern for upsetting the bishop now a non-factor, it would seem the way was paved for the attack to begin. However, the article Kierkegaard wrote about Mynster was not published right away. Why not?

(2) After Mynster's death in January of 1854, it was necessary to select his successor. Jockeying for the spot began immediately, with H. N. Clausen and Hans Lassen Martensen emerging as major contenders. Martensen was not immune from direct participation in the struggle, nor from trying to tip matters in his direction. On February 5, 1854—two days before Mynster's funeral—Martensen gave a memorial sermon eulogizing Bishop Mynster at Christiansborg Castle Church. He then had the sermon published soon after, the piece being advertised for purchase in the February 13th edition of

Berlingske Tidende.[9] Due to the speech's rapid publication and its content (a paean for Mynster which presents Martensen as a capable judge in such matters, able to decide who for this age is a "truth-witness"), it seems safe to conclude Martensen's speech is an effort to position himself as rightful successor to Mynster's throne. Martensen had long been an object of Kierkegaard's ire,[10] and the prospective nominee giving this particularly fawning sermon was simply too much for Kierkegaard. He decided Martensen must be folded into the attack as well.

However, the very fact that Martensen was up for the episcopal chair complicated the matter. Kierkegaard did not want to appear as if he was speaking out of a personal vendetta against Martensen. This kind of personal attack could be easily dismissed as a petty carping. Kierkegaard wanted instead to speak about Martensen, but also to connect him to larger problems with Christendom. The problems of which Kierkegaard spoke were exemplified by Martensen, but not limited to him. In order to avoid confusion on this score, Kierkegaard delayed the publication of the initial article of the attack, as he himself attests:

> This article has, as may be seen from its date, lain ready for some time.
>
> As long as the appointment to the bishopric of Sjælland was in question, I thought that I ought to leave Professor Martensen out of public discussion, since, whether or not he became bishop, he in any case was a candidate for this office, and no doubt desired, while it was pending, that as far as possible nothing pertaining to him would happen.
>
> With Prof. Martensen's appointment as bishop, this consideration dropped out. (TM 7/SKS 14:125)

Again, we have an issue of ambivalent respect, although this time it is likely for different reasons. Rather than any personal fondness for Martensen, it seems Kierkegaard maintained a strategic public respect for the potential bishop. This maneuver was intended to prevent confusion as to the stakes of Kierkegaard's attack. It is not as if Kierkegaard wished to prevent Martensen from becoming the Bishop of Sjælland, favoring another candidate instead. Rather, as would become clear in the course of the attack, Kierkegaard wished for there to be no Bishop of Sjælland at all. It is the office and the structure which are the true targets of the attack, with Mynster and Martensen serving only as useful, well-known examples of the problem. This, at least, was how Kierkegaard perceived the purpose of the attack. And to give him the benefit of the doubt, Kierkegaard's issues with Christendom were truly conceptual in nature; to reduce the whole attack to a personal grudge would indeed be to minimize the force of Kierkegaard's arguments, which possess a logic that is not dependent on his individual and contingent animus toward particular figures.

With the appointment of Martensen to the position of Bishop of Sjælland in June of 1854, the source of potential confusion which worried Kierkegaard was eliminated. However, the first article of the attack was not published right after Martensen's ascension to the episcopal throne. Why not?

(3) To answer that question, let's return to the passage previously cited and read a bit further:

> With Prof. Martensen's appointment as bishop, this consideration dropped out. But since under the circumstances the article could not appear and therefore did not appear right away, I decided that, after all, there was no reason to hurry. Then, too, Bishop Martensen's appointment provoked attack on him from other sides and of a completely different kind; I most definitely did not want to join in with that attack. So I waited. (TM 7/SKS 14:125)

The second explanation here is clearer than the first. There was in April of 1854 a politically motivated opposition to Martensen's appointment by members of the National-Liberal party, who supported a different candidate (namely, the aforementioned H.N. Clausen). This opposition took the form of published critique, for example in the pages of the newspaper *Dagbladet*.[11]

While the second explanation is fairly clear, the first explanation remains vague. What does Kierkegaard mean when he says, "under the circumstances the article could not appear"? Given the specific timing of the eventual publication of the first newspaper article of the attack, Bruce Kirmmse gives a plausible reading of the "circumstances" under which "the article could not appear":

> SK did not immediately publish his reply to Martensen, partly because he did not want to be encumbered with a lawsuit by Martensen for having attempted to interfere with Martensen's chances for the episcopal chair, and partly because he did not wish to be involved in a libel or blasphemy suit brought by the extremely conservative A.S. Ørsted ministry which was then in power. A lawsuit by either Martensen or the government would likely have been a long-drawn-out affair and would have obscured the broader and deeper intent of SK's assault, namely to alter the entire ordering of boundaries between the spiritual and political realms. Thus SK spent most of 1854 writing pieces that he would use in the campaign when it finally came, and he waited, first, for the bishopric question to be settled, and second, for the Ørsted ministry to be replaced by a liberal regime which took a more generous view of freedom of the press. . . . A new, liberal ministry took office on December 18, 1854, and on the same day SK opened his 'attack on Christendom' in the columns of the liberal daily *The Fatherland* [*Fædrelandet*], which was Denmark's leading serious newspaper. The simultaneity of the beginning of SK's attack and the installation of a new liberal ministry was thus anything but a coincidence.[12]

Given the simultaneity of the new regime and the publication of the initial attack article, Kirmmse's reasoning is persuasive: Kierkegaard had been waiting to speak his mind so as to avoid any legal wrangling. With the accession of Peter Georg Bang to the position of prime minister, who supported a moderate freedom of the press, all three obstacles to the publication of Kierkegaard's attack literature were eliminated, and Kierkegaard began the attack immediately thereafter.

By that time, the waiting game had gone on for upward for three years. However, that did not bother Kierkegaard: "So I waited; I thought, as stated, that there was no reason at all to hurry and nothing at all to be lost by waiting. Someone might even find that something was gained, find that such a slow emergence of the objection has a deeper significance" (TM 7/SKS 14:125). Time was not a problem for Kierkegaard. Rather, this long delay assisted the points he wanted to make. It is not as if he just didn't 'like' Bishops Mynster or Martensen. It is that he thought the office they occupied was a fundamentally unchristian position. Whomever was in that spot would be brought over into the league of that which was anti-Christ. Time helped to clarify that it was not—or not only—personal animosity which motivated the attack, but a genuinely theological conviction that the Danish ecclesial system, with the Bishop of Sjælland at its head, was a betrayal and perversion of true Christianity.

The reasons for Kierkegaard's fear of being misunderstood are clear. For the first time in his writing career, he would be saying in print things like "this is why I have said of Bishop Mynster that he, seen in the light of a truth-witness and Christianly evaluated, was self-indulgent" (TM 18/SKS 14:138) and "Dr. Martensen is too subaltern a personality to be able to be impressive" (TM 10n./SKS 14:129n.), instead of restricting his critique to pastors in general as elegant men, dressed in silk, who pretend to speak in the place of a poor and abased human known as Jesus Christ (PC 38/SKS 12:51). Kierkegaard had spent his life as an author constructing a rich and multifaceted critique of Christianity as it was practiced in the Denmark of his age. He did not want all that orchestrated labor to be dismissed as the bitter ravings of a slighted theological licentiate. He wished it to be seen for what it was, and what in retrospect I believe we can see it to be: a profound and thoroughgoing critique of modern Christendoms as betrayals of Christianity.

THE FIRST PHASE OF THE ATTACK: *FÆDRELANDET*

Once all three causes of delay had worked themselves out, Kierkegaard began his attack. As mentioned, the concepts which supported the attack had largely been articulated in *Practice in Christianity*. Now those concepts—previously developed in a long and at times challenging book—would be worked out in a public way, in a major newspaper, with a linguistic flair intended to draw as much attention to the charges being made as possible.[13]

So it was that on December 18, 1854, Kierkegaard stopped waiting. He published an article in the newspaper *Fædrelandet* titled "Was Bishop Mynster a 'Truth-Witness,' One of 'the Authentic Truth-Witnesses'—*Is This the Truth?*" (TM 3–8/SKS 14:123–126). The article is scathing, judging that Bishop Mynster was decidedly not a "truth-witness," describing Mynster's own version of Christianity as "dubious," and presenting Martensen's February 5th memorial for Mynster as a worldly-wise and thinly veiled bid for his own occupancy of the bishopric. Alongside these negative elements, there is also an extended definition of what it really means to be a "truth-witness" and an invocation of "the Christianity of the New Testament"—both important phrases, conceptually speaking, which we will return to in the next chapter.

Following upon this initial article were some twenty further pieces. Although many were written in 1854 (as Kirmmse indicated, above),[14] these articles were mainly published in 1855 at the rate of one every few days until May 26th of that year. Highlights include the anti-social nature of Christianity (TM 10/SKS 14:130); the petty worldliness of pastors (TM 20–21/SKS 14:141–142)—or, to be more luridly descriptive, the wealthy, banal, berobed, merchant class, police-state-endorsing nature of pastors, who after all are just in it for the money (TM 31, 43, 61, 85/SKS 14:155, 174, 201, 220). There is yet more: the claim that boozing, stealing, and murdering is better than being an earnest Christian of the Martensen variety (TM 21/SKS 14:142); the claim that "official Christianity, the proclamation of official Christianity, is not in any sense the Christianity of the New Testament" but is instead an "illusion" (TM 28/SKS 14:151); the claim that true Christianity burns everything down (TM 51/SKS 14:189); the claim that Martensen is an effeminate, worldly-wise, "obtuse-sagacious," soulless-mindless bureaucrat (TM 79–85/SKS 14:217–221); the claim that there is no Christianity in modern Denmark (TM 35–38/SKS 14:163–165); and a profound pessimism about whether—given the bending of the arc of history toward apostasy—there are even any human beings around anymore who could possibly be Christians (TM 33–34/SKS 14:159).

Kierkegaard certainly did not pull any punches. The conviction articulated in *Practice in Christianity*—that Christendom had abolished Christianity (PC 36/SKS 12:49)—is conceptually developed in a rigorous public theology, one that asks readers to clarify their definition of a truth-witness and to open their New Testaments and compare the Christianity there with the Christianity in Denmark. The attack literature is in this way a tantalizing mixture of bawdy rhetoric and demanding conceptual content. To truly understand what Kierkegaard is doing, a reader would have to follow his line of reasoning, which deconstructed contemporary Christianity by looking to Christianity's construction in the first century. At the same moment such conceptual rigor is being employed, Kierkegaard's use of flamboyant rhetoric, and his employment of an *ad hominem* style unafraid to explicitly name the person being attacked, certainly did stir his audience, either for or against him (mostly against).

Fædrelandet was a serious newspaper with a substantial audience of subscribers.[15] Kierkegaard was hoping his articles would be read and produce a reaction,[16] and they did. The newly elected Bishop, Hans Lassen Martensen, was one of the first to respond, with an article in *Berlingske Tidende* published on December 28, 1854, just ten days after Kierkegaard's initial article. Martensen is to be commended for his response, in that he did not complain about Kierkegaard's lack of personal respect for him. Apart from a few insults, Martensen generally focused on the issue at hand: the definition of a truth-witness.

Martensen takes issue with how Kierkegaard defines the truth-witness, and in explaining his disagreement Martensen perceptively focuses on the real difference between himself and Kierkegaard: their opposing philosophies of history. Martensen embraced a progressive-dialectical view of history which was shaped by G. W. F. Hegel. In this view, the truth of Christianity remained the same over the centuries, but the form in which truth was embodied shifted and developed over time. Once there was an age of martyrdom, and that was an appropriate form of embodied truth for that time. By contrast, now—given how Christianity has over the centuries infused itself into culture—it is cultural leaders who are the truest representatives; they are the ones whose lives most evidently embody Christian truth.

In his own words, Martensen expresses his disagreement with Kierkegaard as follows:

> And then what can it be that justifies his casting a false light upon my statement that there stretches from the days of the apostles until our day a chain of truth-witnesses, as if I thereby had said that the Christian truth-witnesses in our day should as a matter of course be compared to those in the apostolic age, although I have expressly added what he fraudulently omits—that while the Lord and the Spirit are the same, there is a difference in the times, the gifts, and the instruments. . . . But it assuredly will not do to forget, because of the great difference in the various developmental stages of the Church, what must be the same in all ages, unless we want to give up the article in our catechism: I believe in one holy universal Church. Those who believe this article know also that there is in the Church from generation to generation a propagating truth-witness, and that there also are those in every age and in every generation, both in the congregation and among the teachers, who bear this witness, who vitally and personally testify to the great fact of Christianity. If this had not been the case, the unity

of the Church would have been broken over the years. Of course, it is useless to make such observations to Dr. S. Kierkegaard, whose Christianity is without Church and without history, and who seeks Christ only in the "desert" and in "private rooms."[17]

In these words, Martensen expresses a Hegelian view of organic historical development: there is an essence of Christianity, such that it is one phenomenon over time, but that essence progressively changes and develops over the centuries. In that way, it is like a plant which goes through different stages of development, but all according to its original *physis*. For Martensen, this view simply *is* what it means to have a philosophy of history; thus, from his perspective, he is correct to say that Kierkegaard simply has no "history" whatsoever.

Furthermore, when we supplement these words with what we know of Martensen's understanding of history from his other works, we see exactly the view briefly stated above: while Christianity was once expressed in opposition to the state and thus underwent persecution, now Christianity has suffused the nation-state; in fact, the nation-state and its ecclesial officers play a crucial role in the continuing existence of Christianity, in that they provide the doctrinal essence—the truth—which each individual is then required to appropriate for themselves.[18] It is therefore precisely someone like Mynster— someone in the upper echelons of the state who preserves and hands along the essence of Christian teaching—who fits the definition of "truth-witness." As we will see further in the next chapter, Martensen is exactly right in his assessment of Kierkegaard's understanding of the truth-witnesses: for how a truth-witnesses was defined in the first century must still be how a truth-witnesses is defined, according to Kierkegaard's counter-philosophy of history.

The disagreement between Martensen and Kierkegaard is therefore not merely a matter of personal animosity (though there was plenty of that). There is a genuine conceptual difference between the two when it comes to how the truth-witness is to be defined, and this difference is grounded in an even more basic disagreement with respect to how history is to be understood: is history a theater in which truth is progressively realized, or is it a static realm into which the eternal truth invaded in a moment, but in such a way that the truth remains punctiliar (i.e., it is never able to be absorbed into historical development)?

Elite response to this battle generally sided with Martensen. For example, the poet and hymn-writer B. S. Ingemann agreed with H. L. Martensen's critical response to Kierkegaard, and told him so in a letter written on January 28, 1855:

I have been greatly angered and offended by Søren Sophist's unseemly antics on Mynster's grave. Your rebuke was harsh, but just and fitting. . . . In my view, unbounded pride and vanity and a great deal of other baseness peep out through the ascetic rags and holes with which he adorns himself. . . . It is a shame that his talent made it impossible to ignore the scandal in the graveyard! The most painful punishment for him would have been to have taken no notice of it.[19]

Notice what has happened in Ingemann's remarks: the issue has been transferred from a conceptual disagreement over definitions to a matter of respect for cultural institutions and figureheads such as Mynster and Martensen. By attacking authority figures, Kierkegaard has shown his "unbounded pride and vanity." This issue appears as a minor thesis in Martensen's article as well,[20] but to Ingemann it is the major issue at stake.

Lack of respect in fact seems to be what angered the Copenhagen elite the most about Kierkegaard's attack. Debate about Kierkegaard's attack ruined otherwise pleasurable evenings among socialites, as August Bournonville informs us in the pages of his diary: "Evening party, *Høedt*, *Paullis*, S. Phiseldeck. We had a pleasant time, but Høedt displeases me by defending Søren Kierkegaard's vile attack on Münster."[21] In a back-and-forth exchange of letters in March of 1855, B. S. Ingemann and Carsten Hauch agree that the attack is disrespectful and, insofar as it rails against the proper authorities, is a sign of the times:

Ingemann to Hauch, March 9, 1855: The little war around here, which is probably over by now—the graveyard scandal on Mynster's grave—has made me very angry, mostly because of the support that the impudence and shamelessness of this sophistry has found among young people, to whom this cruel clowning with the truth seems brilliant.

***

Hauch to Ingemann, March 25, 1855: I am in complete agreement with your judgment of Kierkegaard's behavior. And it is remarkable how quickly unbelief and leveling sansculottism have used him in support of their views about tearing down what rises above the level of the ordinary. All reverence is to be uprooted from the heart: if nothing on earth be respected, nothing in heaven need be respected either. How unfortunate is the younger generation, which is educated and grows up under these auspices.[22]

To these chorus of voices concerned about respect and authority, we can add Meïr Aron Goldschmidt. He was less concerned about respect than the above authors, but he also diagnosed the attack literature as the self-glorifying pabulum of a wannabe reformer.²³ There were also positive responses to the attack, but the general tenor of elite response was negative: a reaction which makes sense, on account of the fact that they were the intended object of the invective.

Considering these responses, we can reasonably conclude Kierkegaard was hitting his mark. He was stirring blood and setting passion in motion (TM 12/ SKS 14:131); he was attacking in such a way that the attack felt like an attack to those who were attacked. With these criteria, it is clear the newspaper phase of the attack was a success. What is less clear is whether Kierkegaard had successfully inculcated a new conceptual awareness among his audience with respect to how true Christian witness was to be defined. Yet Kierkegaard's efforts were not finished.

THE SECOND PHASE OF THE ATTACK: *THE MOMENT*

For many years, Kierkegaard contemplated starting a subscription service for those who truly valued his writings. In 1849 he wrote:

> From the very beginning of my being an author in Denmark I have noticed that I have some few purchasers who definitely buy every book I publish. The number is not very great, and I will not have any particular pecuniary advantage from being an author for them. Yet if it is agreeable to them I will continue being an author, but only for them. In other words, I am hereby inviting subscription to a series of books to be published, some of which are ready.²⁴ (PC 298/*Pap*. X 5 B 35)

Initially, nothing came of these plans. Yet in May of 1855, after having published twenty newspaper articles of incendiary rhetoric and offensive theology,²⁵ Kierkegaard did just as he was previously planning to do: he started a subscription service, and the product he was delivering was titled *The Moment*.²⁶ Rather than the at times rather large tomes of his previous authorship, *The Moment* consists of brief pamphlets which bind together several articles, with titles such as "'Take an emetic!'," "How Fortunate That Not All of Us Are Pastors!," "True Christians/Many Christians," "A Dose of Life-Weariness," and "That the Pastors Are Cannibals, and in the Most Abominable Way."

Although they engage in less *ad hominem* than the newspaper articles, these pamphlets certainly lack the grace and sophistication of masterpieces such as *Concluding Unscientific Postscript* and *Works of Love*. Indeed, Kierkegaard himself says he regrets departing from his usual writing practice, but unfortunately God has called him to do so. He calls his new writing practice 'working in the moment':

> [T]o work in the moment—God knows there is nothing I dislike more.
>   To be an author—well, yes, this appeals to me. If I am to be honest, I must indeed say that I have been in love with being productive—but, please note, in the way I want it. And what I have loved is exactly the opposite of working in the moment; what I have loved is precisely the distance from the moment, the distance in which I, like a lover, can tag after the thoughts and, just like an artist in love with his instrument, I can converse with the language, draw forth the expressions just as the thought requires them—blissful pastime!—throughout an eternity I could not become weary of this occupation! (TM 91/SKS 13:129–130)

Kierkegaard then goes on to say that he is taking leave of his "beloved distance" because he understands it as his duty, religiously speaking, to write in the moment in order to prosecute his case before as large a contemporary audience as possible (TM 92/SKS 13:130).

It is possible to oversell the distinction being making here; *The Moment* is artistic in its own fashion.[27] It may not have the intricacy of *Upbuilding Discourses in Various Spirits*, but it is consistently funny, entertaining, and outrageous in a purposeful way. Beyond that, it retains importance as a public display of ascetic theology orchestrated so as to undermine and destroy the society to which it was speaking. As Bruce Kirmmse summarizes near the beginning of his monumental *Kierkegaard in Golden Age Denmark*:

> He called for nothing less than the total dismantling of the traditional aristocratic-conservative synthesis known as 'Christendom' or 'Christian culture,' which was the time-honored and comfortable marriage of the 'horizontal' element of traditional society and the 'vertical' element of religious transcendence, a synthesis in which religion had served as the guarantor of social stability, 'moral values,' and personal significance. This very Christendom which was the target of Kierkegaard's final authorship was the matrix in which the luxuriant cultural life of the Golden Age had blossomed, and without which it quickly withered.[28]

That the attack was public and aimed at the destruction of Christendom is clear. However, why have I described the attack literature as a manifestation of 'ascetic theology'? According to the literature of the attack, the dismantling of Christendom was to happen through renunciation. This is why it is correct to speak of the attack as a public display of ascetic theology. Whereas Christian asceticism can often be confined to an elite audience of highly committed individuals, this was asceticism in the streets, so to speak.

Kierkegaard was recommending an *askēsis* to all Danish citizens, and this *askēsis*—if implemented—would cause a wholesale change in their society: Denmark would revoke its status as a Christian nation and confess to be what it actually was, a worldly project striving—by whatever means necessary—to achieve comfortable lives for a small sub-set of its citizens. If Kierkegaard's message took hold, the urban elite would renounce the web of relations which maintained their material status, seeing it as inextricably connected to a false and indeed impossible synthesis of the worldly and the Christian; at the same time, the rural peasant would recognize the religion of her country as being orchestrated to cosset the souls of the well-off, and she too would refuse to think of Denmark as a Christian nation. If Denmark is to be defined as a total endeavor, an attempt to provide complete happiness of soul and body—at least for those "rare few"[29] who could achieve elite status—then the attack on Christendom was an invitation to reject the project that was modern Denmark. It was an embrace of misery born out of the recognition that worldly happiness is false.

All this will receive a more in-depth treatment in subsequent chapters, including a closer look at how the attack evolved over time, asking for different actions from its readers at different points along its development. Before turning to this evolution, we must bring the late Kierkegaard's story to a close, as well as broaden our gaze to the context within which his story takes place.

COMING TO AN END

The ninth issue of *The Moment* was published September 24, 1855. This publication would be Kierkegaard's last. There was a tenth issue of *The Moment* in preparation for typesetting, but Kierkegaard could not be present to oversee these matters, and the issue would be published only posthumously. On September 25, 1855, Kierkegaard wrote his final journal entry. On October 2, he checked himself into hospital. He would not emerge.[30]

Fittingly, there was controversy at Kierkegaard's funeral. Kierkegaard was given a church burial with customary honors, which it must be admitted is rather odd, given his expressly stated position in his final days. At the graveside, Kierkegaard's nephew, Henrik Lund, vocally pointed out this oddity:

> I protest viewing our presence here as participation in the worship of God sponsored by 'official Christianity,' because he has been brought here against his repeatedly expressed will, and has in a way been violated.[31]

Lund interrupted the service to exclaim these words. It was seen as yet another act of impropriety attached to the scandalous life of the late Kierkegaard.

Lund's provocative act of resistance retains importance for us today. We still want to appropriate Kierkegaard and make him a part of mainstream, bourgeois cultural institutions. Though we may wish to eulogize him and to make him into a genial 'Christian thinker for our time,' a Christian poet-philosopher who helps us recover our inward passion amid outwardly normal lives, Lund's protest helps remind us that here was a man who died refusing communion and breaking with just about everything his society considered 'normal.'[32]

Before we move onto a deeper consideration of the attack literature in later chapters, it is useful at this point to gain a better understanding of what Kierkegaard was attacking. True, Kierkegaard detested 'the normal'—but what exactly are the norms he was attacking? How was 'the normal' understood in his age? A few broad strokes can illuminate a great deal; thus, the two focused treatments that follow.

BISHOPS

Now that we know the general narrative of the attack, we can spend some time deepening our knowledge of these events by reflecting on the people and the society caught up in Kierkegaard's searing polemic. In this way, multiple layers will be added beneath the story told thus far, increasing our understanding of the attack literature and the motivation behind its production.

For a deeper understanding of the attack, no persons are more important than its two principal targets: Bishops Mynster and Martensen. I should note that the treatment of the two bishops that follows contains only a sliver of the possible information about them that could be given. The accounts that follow are limited to a sympathetic explanation of each bishop's social role, while at the same time suggesting how even a sympathetic account—wherein one respects each participants' intentions and self-understanding in regard to the narrative of their life—shows precisely why Kierkegaard felt compelled to attack these two figures.

Jakob Peter Mynster (1775–1854) was the flashpoint for the beginning of the attack. Mynster was an accomplished man in many respects, being a gifted author, orator, and administrator. For our purposes, there are two perspectives on Mynster which are essential to grasp: one is Mynster's own perspective on himself, the other is Kierkegaard's evaluation of the bishop. Mynster saw himself as an embattled standard-bearer for Christianity amidst the hostile climate of modernity. Kierkegaard, on the other hand, saw Mynster as living the most settled of lives, ensconced in respect and assured of high position. The key to understanding Bishop Mynster is to realize how both these perspectives are correct.

As Mynster was coming of age in early Golden Age Denmark, the chief battle in the sphere of religion was between traditional Christian belief and skepticism.[33] Orthodox beliefs such as affirming the divinity of Christ and the historicity of the gospel accounts were challenged in the 18th century, with leading figures such as the Royal Confessor Christian Bastholm (1740–1819) arguing that a moralistic interpretation of Christ's importance (i.e., Christ as moral exemplar rather than divine savior) should take the place of traditional belief in the modern world. This battle would play out within the soul of Mynster himself. Kirmmse provides a portrait of the buffeted young man: "Mynster seems to have been an uncertain and insecure youth who was not wholly satisfied by the politics or religion of the radical Enlightenment, but who was also haunted by a feeling that he was unable to give himself wholly to Christianity."[34] Thus we have a man who was neither hot nor cold. He was precisely the kind of person God spits out of the divine mouth (Rev 3:16), and it seems Mynster shared this revulsion at himself.

As time went on, Mynster found himself preaching traditional Christian doctrine from the pulpit, affirming the historicity of the biblical accounts. However, he did so out of respect for the "humble souls" he was called to "shepherd," rather than any personal belief in these things.[35] His spirit continued to be troubled by this evident hypocrisy. This inner turmoil, which was causing a good deal of suffering for Mynster, was finally resolved by—Christianity itself. It seems Mynster arrived at a point of true desperation, and it was there the message of the gospel first really engaged him. These words—the words of the Gospels—became true for him when he needed them to be true; that is, when he could not go on with his life otherwise.[36] When his back was against the wall, when he was in despair over himself and his hypocrisy, Mynster took comfort in Christianity, in the message that God loves human beings and offers them a fundamental acceptance.

When Mynster thereafter spoke to a skeptical age, he spoke as one who knew—personally—what he was speaking about. He had been through the kind of crisis precipitated by rationalism and come out the other side. To be sure, Mynster's understanding of Christianity was not completely traditional; as Kristoffer Olesen Larsen puts it, his religion was essentially "bourgeois humanism which has been united with a faith in Providence and dressed in orthodox expressions."[37] At the same time, he did openly and with confidence endorse Christianity, thus meeting the basic (and perhaps the only) condition of traditionalist Danes who wanted to preserve their nation and culture as a Christian nation and culture.

From this point in his life, wherein he was able to fully and confidently assert the truth of Christianity, Mynster would be elevated further and further in the ecclesiastical world, until he reached the absolute highest point possible for a Danish pastor: Bishop of Sjælland, the head of the Danish Lutheran Church.[38] Yet this elevation should be seen not just as victory, but also as embattlement. For as he advanced, Mynster was taking a true and actual Christian faith—personally felt and personally appropriated—into the highest realms of elite society. He was taking his newfound faith right to where the skeptics were: the halls of power, where what counted as rationality or enlightenment was adjudicated and defined. Mynster therefore functioned as a kind of Danish Schleiermacher, preaching on the continued relevance of Christian truth amidst an environment of cultured despisers.

According to his own viewpoint, Mynster was a standard-bearer for the Christian faith amidst the hostile environment of elite urban skepticism. Of course, from another viewpoint, Mynster's residence among the elite of society was not as an embattled culture warrior, but as a cosseted aesthete who embraced all the pleasures of life: wine, food, dance, education, conversation, secure finances, and most of all the pleasure of being respected for keeping the faith. It is apparent that Kierkegaard, despite his personal respect for Mynster which stretched back to his boyhood relation to him, holds this other viewpoint.

We can give Mynster the benefit of the doubt and understand him on his own terms, while at the same time acknowledging Kierkegaard's alternative perspective: for Mynster's defense of Christianity required precisely its vindication at the highest levels of power and the widest reaches of application. Mynster showed Christianity to be worthy of the allegiance of a whole nation, even amidst skeptical modernity. The success of Mynster in defending the continuing cultural authority of Christianity is precisely that with which Kierkegaard is taking issue, for Kierkegaard did not believe Christianity could become cultural without betraying itself. That is, Christianity could not become the animating spirit of a nation—its moral compass, its ground for deciding right action, its basis for determining military engagement and its underlying framework for social policies—without completely departing from its essence. As we will see in following chapters, this is because Kierkegaard believed nations, and human cultures generally, are grounded in self-assertion, while Christianity is based in self-denial.

It is in this way that Mynster's self-interpretation and Kierkegaard's interpretation of Mynster are both true. Mynster had brought a personally appropriated Christian faith into the halls of urban elite power, and in so doing was in an embattled position. At the same time, Mynster's victorious preservation of Christian faith at the heart of the Christian nation of Denmark was exactly what Kierkegaard considered to be a complete departure from true Christian teaching.

Just as Mynster had directly confronted the philosophy of his age and showed how it could be lived through and overcome by an earnest yet

Christian intellectual, so also Hans Lassen Martensen (1808–1884) absorbed the philosophy of his age—Hegelianism—and demonstrated its compatibility with Christianity. Beginning in the second half of the 1820s with the rise of J. L. Heiberg, Hegelianism became *the* fashionable philosophy in Denmark, attracting attention and discussion from nearly every significant intellectual at the time.[39] Martensen was only one of a group of thinkers who fully endorsed Hegel and endeavored to popularize his philosophy within Denmark.

Martensen thus parallels Mynster in being engaged philosophically and thus being able to "satisfy the demands of the times."[40] Yet Martensen in fact went much further than Mynster in showing how his philosophy could be synthesized with Christianity. Whereas Mynster showed how one could live through skepticism and Enlightenment and still honestly retain Christian belief, Martensen showed how Christian belief was in fact the culmination of the Hegelian philosophy.

Martensen's vindication of Christianity also went further than Mynster's, for the Christian belief affirmed in his writings was not just some individual, private, inward devotion: no, in both his early *Outlines of Moral Philosophy* and his later *Christian Ethics*, Martensen demonstrated at an epic length how it was the Christian nation—not simply individual Christian believers—that was the absolute highest development of history, an unsurpassable realization of God's kingdom come on earth.[41] In this sense, Martensen had gone beyond Hegel and shown the true culmination of history to be modern Denmark. Martensen's Denmark preserved John Locke's secular imperative to put the material needs of its people first and foremost,[42] while also ensuring the salvation of their souls. The Danish Christian nation fulfilled every concern of the human person. While this new world—modernity—might seem challenging to Christianity for an uninformed observer, Martensen arrived to tell us otherwise. Modernity was in fact not the defeat of Christianity, but its apotheosis: the good of the body and the good of the soul could now be united in the total project of the modern nation-state. (At this point it is worth noting that, like many 'progressive' 19th century intellectuals, Martensen thought that Jews had no place within this total project.[43])

If the role of Bishop of Sjælland was to show how the developments of modernity and modern philosophy did not invalidate Christian belief, then Martensen was the exactly right person for the job. Like Mynster, he had peered deeply into the well of modern secularity and still decided to be Christian. In him one could see a still victorious Christianity, which we may propose was exactly the sign of hope those who elected him wanted to see.

Martensen's Christianity was defined precisely by its victory within this world. The ability of the Christian nation to provide everything for its citizens was quite simply the point of Martensen's Christianity; a Christian faith that included no aspect of worldly triumph was neglecting its duty to the whole person. Further, Martensen's personal triumph was a small though significant sign of Christianity's larger victory in the world.

These triumphant features, which from Martensen's own viewpoint should be highly valued as the march of the Kingdom into this world, were exactly what Kierkegaard rejected and attacked. For the latter, Christianity was defined by its hatred and renunciation of the world. It was defined by defeat: by abasement, poverty, persecution, marginality, and ultimately death. According to his own criteria, worked out at length in numerous theoretical works, Martensen was thoroughly successful. Because of his different criteria, Kierkegaard viewed this success as the loss of a true relation to Christianity.

The preceding description of Jakob Peter Mynster and Hans Lassen Martensen, alongside the brief words on Kierkegaard's critique of these two men, generates a suggestive hypothesis that must await further confirmation in later chapters. The hypothesis is that Kierkegaard's attack was accurate. By 'accurate,' I mean that the attack does not prosecute any description of Mynster or Martensen with which the two would disagree. They would concur with Kierkegaard that they were honored figures who stood at the heart of their cultures. They would also acknowledge they stood for accepted Christian truths at the highest levels of society, thereby preserving Denmark's status as a Christian nation. The disagreement with Mynster and Martensen does not have to do with who these figures were, but on how their characters were to be evaluated in light of Christian truth.

Mynster and Martensen were the gilding on a golden age. As already emphasized, these two figures were in a sense simply figureheads: they were emblems of what their society wanted. Now that we have covered these two gentlemen in some depth, we can turn to that wider society, and to its desires.

THE DANISH GOLDEN AGE: A SELECTIVE HISTORY

The years 1800–1850 are known as the Danish Golden Age. It was a period of intense artistic creativity from the greatest writers Denmark has produced. At the beginning of the period, Adam Oehlenschläger (1779–1850) connected Denmark to the burgeoning movement of Romantic poetry;[44] his verse celebrates the re-enchantment of nature with a sense of divine spirit.[45] Later, Johan Ludvig Heiberg would establish and maintain a remarkably intellectual theatre environment, while at the same time producing entertaining vaudevilles. In the 1830s, Hans Christian Andersen was penning his well-known fables such as "The Ugly Duckling" and "The Little Mermaid." Of course, there is Kierkegaard himself, who in the early- to mid-1840s was writing the works that would earn him the title 'the father of existentialism.' This explosion of brilliant literature is not even to mention innovations in science, of which the best known are those of Hans Christian Ørsted, who in 1820 discovered electromagnetism.[46] There are some exceptions to the rule, with Vilhelm Hammershøi painting in the early 1900s and Tove Ditlevsen writing her memoirs in the later 20th century.[47] For the most part, however, Denmark's greatest cultural contributions come from these golden years.

The cultural flourishing of the 19th century was preceded by the Danish economic boom of the 18th century. This period is essential to understanding the origin of the comfortable, bourgeois society Kierkegaard addresses in his attack. The wealth came from a particular tactic. In a war-ravaged 18th-century Europe, Denmark was notable for its neutrality, refusing to take sides in combat. And the Danes made money off this refusal, as Bruce Kirmmse summarizes:

> The eighteenth century was a time of stability and prosperity for Denmark, whose neutrality in the numerous petty wars of the period enabled the commercial patriciate to bring home enormous profits from the shipping trade, in which Danish ships carried goods to and from the various belligerents. This century of commercial splendor built up and reinforced a high urban culture[.][48]

While everyone else was fighting, Denmark was making money. Selling to all sides, Denmark raked in profits and elevated a sizable portion of its population to a bourgeois level.

Of course, the success of Denmark's economic growth involved more than its neutrality, as reading Kirmmse alone might suggest. It also involved the slave trade and colonialism. Because of its relatively small size (and the relatively small size of its colonies), it is easy to overlook Denmark's entanglement in the European colonial project. Yet it was significant:

> Its colonies were small in terms of population and, with the notable exception of Greenland, territory. But Denmark was an active partner in virtually all aspects of European imperialism, from exploration to trading posts, colonial administrations to slave possession; particularly in the second half of the 1700s it developed a lucrative trade in goods and slaves in the shadow of the larger European powers' engagement in major warfare over colonial possessions and monopolies on trade[.][49]

Indeed, Erik Gøbel estimates that Danish ships transported some 85,000 enslaved persons across the Atlantic.[50] When Kierkegaard effectively says to Danish society, 'burn it all down,' it is important to keep this context in mind. If the wealth of Danish society was built in the 18th century, this building activity was inextricably connected to all the brutalities inherent in colonial extraction and the slave trade. These sordid entanglements were also connected to the consumer goods enjoyed by the urban elite of the 18th and 19th century: cigars, coffee, and sugar being only some of the products which were rapidly embraced.[51]

The economic boon of 18th century Denmark would be severely challenged by catastrophic developments in the early years of the 19th century.[52] In the early 1800s, neutrality became an untenable position. England and Napoleon's France were locked in increasingly tense combat, and eventually England decided to force the issue, demanding allegiance from Denmark and bombarding the city of Copenhagen when it was not given. The bombardment began on August 16, 1807, and by September 6th Denmark had surrendered its entire fleet of ships over to the British. In the course of the following years of crisis, inflation took root, and the Danish currency was rapidly devalued. In January of 1813—the very year Kierkegaard was born—the Danish state declared bankruptcy. The recovery from this nadir of catastrophe was slow in its arrival, only really bursting forth in the final years of the Golden Age.

Ironically, this severe economic crisis did not tank Denmark's culture. There was enough material excess remaining to support an elite aesthetic culture; it was as if a cultural flourishing replaced the once dominant economic sphere. In fact, "This brilliant elite shone all the more brightly in the first half of the nineteenth century, as if in spite of the fact that the social and economic bases which had enabled it to play a leading role in commercial, political, and clerical affairs were now shattered or severely eroded."[53] The Golden Age was a belated cultural efflorescence of the once-great Danish economy.

The cultural excess known as the Golden Age took a specifically articulated shape. It was not a Golden Age for everyone. Seeing whom the Golden Age was for will further illuminate Kierkegaard's attack, for his polemic is essentially aimed at those who were able to partake in the Golden Age's gilding. Kirmmse helpfully lays out the restricted character of the Golden Age for us as follows:

> For whom was this a Golden Age? First and foremost, it must be noted that it was not a literary Golden Age for the peasants. That portion of the population who were engaged in agriculture (approximately three-fourths of the total) generally had no real literature of their own excepting religious tracts, almanacs, the Bible, and a hymnal.[54]

If the Golden Age was not for the peasants, who then was it for?

> As the historian of literature Svend Møller Kristensen has demonstrated in his analysis of the subscription lists for works by important Golden Age authors, it was the very narrow social group of academically educated men and,

particularly, the upper levels of the absolutist bureaucracy, a group centered almost exclusively in Copenhagen, which was principally responsible for determining tastes, and which constituted the backbone of the public of the high culture of the Golden Age.[55]

Further helpful distinctions are also subsequently added to this picture:

> Møller Kristensen divides the literate class into three more or less distinct groups. At the apex of the social scale there was a small aristocracy of high nobility, the owners of great estates, and the very rich merchant families. Next came the much broader—and for determining literary taste much more important—academically educated portion of the upper bourgeoisie. And, finally, there was the less distinct and much larger uneducated portion of the bourgeoisie, extending from better-off shopkeepers to well-to-do craftsmen. Of these three groups, which constituted virtually the entirety of the reading public for Golden Age literature, it was generally the middle, academic-bourgeois group, which determined the taste and set the tone for the other two groups....
>
> Thus, although this public was nominally bourgeois in social make-up, its orientation was predominantly academic and bureaucratic rather than commercial. It is thus no surprise that the literature of the Golden Age is for the most part anti-bourgeois, stressing poetry at the expense of prose, and is essentially aristocratic and conservative in its social and political outlook, appealing to the standards of the absolutist *ancien régime*.[56]

As Kirmmse goes on to specify, the typical reading audience for a work of Golden Age literature was around 1,000 people, with successful works selling "only 500–1000 copies."[57] Truly, this fits the definition of an elite audience!

These happy few, sustained in blessed *otium* by the once burgeoning Danish economy, had concerns specific to themselves. They dictated the fixations of Golden Age literature, since after all they were both its consumers and producers. They were above all concerned with good order, which included the notion of the preservation of rank. Look, for example, at Oehlenschläger's devotion to "the rare few"[58] and Mynster's endorsement of "good taste" in religious matters, which entailed disapproval of lay enthusiasm in religion.[59] Or take Hans Christian Andersen's sunny view of royalty.[60] In addition, for Heiberg there were only a few exalted individuals (such as Goethe) who could not only catch but also direct the spirit of the age.[61] Some human beings were capable of intellectual refinement and the enjoyment of higher pleasures, and it was to these persons culture should be dedicated. These were the persons to whom the sensual pleasures of life were owed, because they were able to take them and transmute them into objects of common delight. In sum, the Golden Age believed in nobility; it believed in refinement; it believed in church as a space in which God's good ordering of society was proclaimed; and it promulgated these beliefs in the splendid cultural artifacts it produced. When Kierkegaard attacks "Christendom," it is against all this that he takes a stand.

KIERKEGAARD'S DEVELOPMENT

Kierkegaard did indeed attack Christendom; but he did not do so, at least not explicitly, until the very end of his life. What convictions led him to this point? Were these last writings a major departure from his previous authorship, or were they the culmination of what he was saying all along? Before taking a deeper dive into the attack literature, it will be useful to see what preceded it. In this brief summary retrospective, we will have an eye not only toward the works at hand, but also toward two further considerations: (1) the critical element of these writings, directed at the society just outlined; (2) the eventual conceptual content of the attack literature. I will argue that, although shifting the envisioned consequence of his writings toward a large-scale societal change, the attack is consistent with Kierkegaard's earlier social criticism and is essentially a continuation of previous authorial themes.

This approach will be especially useful in resisting interpretations of the attack upon Christendom which desire to seal this period off from the rest of Kierkegaard's writings. In fact, the "attack" literature has frequently been dismissed as a departure from Kierkegaard's earlier authorship that is essentially irrelevant to interpreting the claims of that earlier authorship. In this interpretive pattern, these late writings can be safely left to one side, being of little value in comparison to better Kierkegaardian texts such as *The Sickness unto Death* and *Works of Love*, the attack literature thus being of only negative value in relation to the interpretation of Kierkegaard, as the later texts distort the earlier material and thus confuse the reader.

One example of the scholarly dismissal of Kierkegaard's attack literature will suffice to indicate the contours of this interpretive trend. The example comes from Sylvia Walsh, and it is a sophisticated rebuttal of considering these late writings as equally normative for the interpretation of Kierkegaard. Walsh's position is sophisticated because other scholars either simply ignore these texts, issuing their negative judgment by implication,[62] or write off the late writings as the work of a deranged mind.[63] In the final chapter of her introduction to Kierkegaard, Walsh writes:

> These extremely negative viewpoints expressed in Kierkegaard's final attack on Christendom have led many critics, both in his time and ours, to dismiss this last phase of his theological reflection and critique of Christendom altogether. Clearly, in certain respects it does represent a radical departure from some of the views expressed earlier in his authorship. This suggests, however, that these

writings do not so much constitute the logical conclusion of Kierkegaard's theological reflection as a relaxing of the dialectical balance that characterizes the large body of religious writings produced during the second period of his literary activity from 1847–51. Theologically, it is primarily this second or middle phase of his authorship that should be regarded as normative for the interpretation of Kierkegaard's theology, although his thought undergoes considerable development even in the course of these writings as a result of his personal encounter with the *Corsair* and the political changes of 1848. But there is also a good deal of continuity between the attack literature and this body of writings. For example, Kierkegaard never departs from the conviction that God is love, evidenced by the fact that shortly before his death in 1855 he published the discourse on the changelessness of God's love written in 1851. Nor does he repudiate Christianity's leniency and promise of a resort to grace. Moreover, the attack on Christendom itself, which began somewhat covertly in Kierkegaard's early pseudonymous works and continued to gather steam with increasing emphasis and directness in the later religious writings, reaches its culmination in these late writings. Many of the charges lodged against the established order and present age in these writings, such as the spiritlessness and worldliness of both church and society, are not new, but they do become shriller and more specific as Kierkegaard zeros in on the illusions and practices of the state church in dead earnest. What is different is the fact that he has now given up on the church as an institution, finding it completely indefensible and encouraging others to join him in ceasing to participate in it. But he has not given up on Christianity itself, and that is what distinguishes him most profoundly from other nineteenth-century critics of religion such as Feuerbach, Marx, and Nietzsche.[64]

There are several matters to unpack in this compact assessment of the late authorship, and Walsh is to be commended for allowing that there is continuity between the attack literature and the second authorship.[65] Rather than attending to all the possible issues of interpretation, however, I will focus in on one assertion and attempt to contest it: namely, Walsh's claim that although there are certain continuities between the attack and the earlier authorship, Kierkegaard's theology has changed such that we can isolate an earlier, more fruitful version of it ("Theologically, it is primarily this second or middle phase of his authorship that should be regarded as normative for the interpretation of Kierkegaard's theology"). Rather, the theology of the attack—the whole series of concepts that drive the critique of Mynster, Martensen, and Danish Christendom in its entirety—is the same theology which was present all along.

Arguing for this position is a complex endeavor and will take time. Right now, I will give a succinct overview of concepts from Kierkegaard's previous works. In subsequent chapters, I will show how what we find in the attack literature relates back to the concepts articulated in Kierkegaard's previous authorship and here summarized.

When recounting the themes and concepts that presage the attack, we can go all the way back to Kierkegaard's dissertation, *On the Concept of Irony with Constant Reference to Socrates*, which was completed and defended in 1841.[66] Most of Kierkegaard's dissertation is an extended engagement with the texts of Plato (though also treating Xenophon and Aristophanes), an engagement which argues for a particular interpretation of the 'historical Socrates' as a figure of relentless negativity whose irony functioned to undermine any positive affirmation of truth. However, the final section of the dissertation turns to the subject of irony in contemporary thought. There one finds Kierkegaard's commentary on the prominent German Romantic author Friedrich Schlegel. It is not difficult to see a Golden Age preoccupation with sensual pleasure and aesthetics behind Kierkegaard's critical assessment of Schlegel. With this background in mind, we can turn to the text itself.

In 1799, Friedrich Schlegel published his most famous work of fiction, *Lucinde. Ein Roman*, which caused a literary scandal for its laudatory depiction of an extramarital affair. In his dissertation, Kierkegaard judges the novel an aesthetic and a philosophical failure; furthermore, he argues that the novel's aesthetic failure is a result of its philosophical failure.

The aesthetic failure Kierkegaard most vividly highlights is *Lucinde*'s fragmentary character; it demonstrates, he writes, "the most complete confusion of construction" (CI 292/SKS 1:326).[67] The novel begins with a mythological prologue and subsequently cycles through an epistolary romance, an "Allegory of Impudence" featuring various colorful and reptilian monsters that represent public opinion and wit, and then concludes with the abrupt suicide of its titular character.[68] Kierkegaard recognizes that the confusing construction of the novel is intentional on Schlegel's part, that it is a result of Schlegel's commitment to breaking conventional norms of both aesthetic and ethical character. At the same time, Kierkegaard rejects this as a justification of the novel's aesthetic form because he judges the philosophical stance that sustains Schlegel's aesthetic of fragments to be fundamentally untenable. *Lucinde* is a bad novel because it is based on bad philosophy.

The philosophical mistake at the heart of *Lucinde* is to take a religious approach to aesthetic life, that is, to invest the pleasures of temporal life with infinite meaning. In short, *Lucinde* exalts sensual pleasure as if it could completely satisfy every desire of the human being; the breaking of any ethical bonds that attempt to limit total pursuit of sensual pleasure is the result of exalting sensual pleasure above everything else. To grant Schlegel his premise for the moment, nothing should rein in pursuit of sensual pleasure if it is the most important thing in life. Unfortunately, Schlegel's premise is incorrect; the pleasures temporality affords in the domain of the senses simply cannot bear such weight. All such pleasures are fleeting and will eventually be drained of worth. They are like salt thrown out on the street, which after a time can no longer enhance flavor and so must be trashed. If one wants to live poetically and thereby enjoy oneself, Kierkegaard writes, the only way to really do so is religiously, by inwardly placing one's faith in a space of enjoyment outside of temporality (namely, the eternal).[69] To live poetically through an absolute commitment to sensual-temporal pleasures is, by contrast, to doom oneself to disappointment and eventual despair. Sylvia Walsh offers an apt summary of this dynamic: "The irony of [Schlegel's] philosophy of enjoyment is that, absolutized and carried to its limits, it collapses into just the opposite, revealing itself to be a wholly unsatisfactory way of living esthetically or poetically inasmuch as it has no real present, past, or future but exists only momentarily and meaninglessly in the temporal realm without any relation to the eternal."[70]

In sum, Schlegel's philosophical mistake is that he mischaracterizes the nature of temporality. He takes it for a space of plenitude, capable of sustaining infinite investment. Instead, temporality is a space of poverty, where no individual reality nor the whole of temporal reality itself can bear complete investment. Because of its impoverished nature, temporal reality is not consistently able to return dividends on the kind of investment Schlegel would have us make.

Two selections from the first volume of *Either/Or* (1843) can serve to corroborate this reading of a fragment from *The Concept of Irony*. First, the mini-treatise "Rotation of Crops," subtitled "A Venture in a Theory of Social Prudence," which begins with an analysis of "boredom" (*Kjedsommelighed*) (EOI 285/SKS 2: 275). According to the pseudonymous aesthete who writes "Rotation of Crops,"[71] boredom is an ambivalent reality: it is "evil" or "corrupting" and, at the same time, it possesses "infinite momentum for making discoveries" (EOI 285/SKS 2:275). Boredom is on the one hand a lethargic state of disgust with respect to whatever object of pleasure one was recently enjoying; on the other hand, boredom impels one to move on from that object and seek new possibilities of titillation.[72] Thus, "boredom advances and boredom is the root of all evil" (EOI 286/SKS 2:276). Boredom itself is an unpleasant experience best avoided by an aesthete, yet it is precisely in the effort to avoid boredom that the discovery of new enjoyments is made.

According to the aesthete, the reflective hedonist does not have to sit around waiting for boredom to threaten one's enjoyment and only at that moment seek new recreation. Rather, recognizing the omnipresence of boredom's possibility within an aesthetic lifestyle, the aesthete develops a method to consistently combat boredom before it has the chance to rear its ugly head. That method is the rotation of crops.

Immediately upon introducing this notion, the aesthete makes an important qualification. When hearing the phrase "rotation of crops" within this context, it is easy to have a "vulgar" notion of what is meant (EOI 291/SKS 2:281). In this vulgar notion, "One is weary of living in the country and moves to the city; one is weary of one's native land and goes abroad; one is *europamüde* [weary of Europe] and goes to America. . . . One is weary of eating on porcelain and eats on silver; wearying of that, one eats on gold," etc. (EOI 291–292/SKS 2:281). Such an extensive method will end in failure, in the aesthete's mind, principally because one easily develops an *a priori* disgust for every external object of enjoyment;[73] all external objects participate in the essential shabbiness of this world. Instead, the aesthete recommends to his readers "that principle that seeks relief not through extensity but through intensity" (EOI 292/SKS 2:282).

The intensive method of rotating crops involves the art of balancing immediate sensual enjoyment with the imaginative possibilities of forgetting and recollecting. In short, one should indulge one's sensual appetites, but always with the powers of forgetting and recollecting on reserve. Thus: taking a modicum of pleasure from the object of enjoyment at hand, as soon as one senses boredom or overindulgence approaching, one breaks off extensive enjoyment through at once forgetting about this pleasure and substituting recollection of a previous pleasure in its place. One is able to make this conscious break from the present object of enjoyment precisely because one is aware in advance that the pleasure it can give is limited; the greatest danger for the aesthete is thus to get carried away in an extensive pleasure, placing too much hope in an external object of enjoyment.[74] This hope will always be disappointed; boredom will win the day. Thus, the aesthete "indulges with a certain mistrust" always ready to break off his experience and escape into realms of poetic-imaginative reverie (EOI 293/SKS 2:283). By this method, the aesthete concludes, a person "is then able to play shuttlecock with all existence," triumphing over the shabbiness of external pleasure through the inventive capacities of the imagination (EOI 294/SKS 2:283). Yet this imaginative capacity does seem limited in some manner not fully acknowledged by the aesthete; it is not as if, on account of the superior potential of enjoyment found in poetic recollection, he is recommending one altogether cease seeking external pleasures. Rather, one's imaginative capacity appears to be supplementary in nature; it helps to smooth out the transition from one object of sensual enjoyment to the next.

The aesthete makes an important philosophical insight in this brief manifesto, one not present in *Lucinde*: namely, all pleasures are fleeting and possession of any object of enjoyment for an extended length of time will gradually diminish the pleasure gleaned from this object until it is stale and tasteless. Yet the aesthete's response of rotation, wherein one constantly cycles through an endless variety of sensual pleasures, breaking off from one object after another and attempting to smooth over this disjunctive experience via the power of poetic recollection, only serves to stave off the inevitable. The fact that a given temporal pleasure ends should point the individual toward desiring something other than temporal pleasures; yet, for the committed aesthete, this conclusion is not reached. She or he never comes to the decisive moment of renouncing temporal pleasure as a whole, preferring instead to renounce the particular pleasure in front of her in favor of another temporal pleasure that presumably will do the job, at least for now. The aesthete refuses to confront the fact of death: there will be an end to the cycle of finite pleasures. Readers of Balzac's *La Cousine Bette* can recognize the absurdity of Baron Hulot, who is still pursuing affairs with teenage women well into his veritable dotage. Surely it should be evident to Hulot that this pleasure is going to have to end someday soon. Yet Kierkegaard is trying to teach us that it is possible to have this recognition of the emptiness of sensual pleasure at any point in our lives, if only we seriously consider the nature of the reality at hand; that is, if only we admit to ourselves the poverty of temporality.

The point of "Rotation of Crops" is briefly summed up by an anecdote from the "Diapsalmata" (a collection of aphorisms at the beginning of *Either/Or, Part I*):

> How much the same human nature is! With what innate genius a little child can often show us a vivid picture of the larger scale. I was really amused today by little Ludvig. He sat in his tiny chair and looked around with visible delight. Then the nursemaid, Maren, walked through the room. "Maren!" he shouted. "Yes, little Ludvig," she answered with her customary friendliness and came over to him. He tilted his big head to one side a bit, fastened his enormous eyes on her with a certain roguishness and then said quite phlegmatically, "Not this Maren; it was another Maren." What do we adults do? We shout to the whole world, and when it approaches us in a friendly manner, we say, "It was not this Maren." (EOI 35/SKS 2:44)

I take the lesson of this narrative to be that our intentional expectations of receiving pleasure from the world will always be disappointed. What we hoped some object of enjoyment would be, it never is: truly, Maren never appears. Furthermore, as the aesthete implicitly acknowledges in "Rotation of Crops," the *poesis* of recollection can never provide a sufficiently secure substitute for these "vulgar" external enjoyments. The shuttlecock will always fall. For that reason, the aesthete is in despair, even if he is not conscious of that fact. Phenomenologically, the aesthete may still believe he can find happiness in this world, but in actuality we know that such a pursuit is doomed. We know this because *Either/Or, Part I* acquaints us with the texture of temporal life, and it is one of perpetual disappointment. The inevitability of disappointment with temporality is the philosophical point *Either/Or, Part I* makes; after finishing the book, the reader, instead of hoping and waiting to see if temporality will fulfill her expectations, should be able to make the global conclusion that it will not do so. It is not necessary to live out one's whole life in aesthetic hope to realize it will never fulfill such expectations. Instead, because we know something of the character of temporal reality, we can make a decision about it right now.

Simply put, temporality will never be able to give the aesthete what he desires; it is too poor, in comparison to the infinite nature of human desire, to provide such satisfactions. Poverty is temporality's character. The *eros* of the aesthete always exceeds the limited enjoyment temporal existence furnishes him. And not only *does* it exceed it; it *will always* exceed it. This last, philosophical point is Kierkegaard's way of making us see the necessity of progressing beyond the aesthetic sphere of life. It cannot give us what we are looking for.

The points Kierkegaard is making are philosophical, but one only grasps the critical force of these writings if one is aware of Golden Age Denmark as a space of aesthetic enjoyment, one which combined the consumption of luxury goods (many, such as cigars, newly available at this time) with the consumption of artistic products meant to stimulate their admirers and produce enjoyment in them. The urban elite which constituted the Golden Age audience were a consuming class. Kierkegaard responds that at the heart of all that consumption, after every last object is exhausted, is nothingness. The aesthetic life, considered on its own terms within its own immanent telos, is fundamentally empty.

Perhaps the ethical life can give what the aesthetic life could not. After all, one of the flaws of the aesthetic life is its fragmentary nature; it is perpetually attempting to avoid despair by distracting itself with a new pleasure. Ethical life, by contrast, is characterized precisely by its continuity. The pseudonymous author of *Either/Or, Part II* is a fictional Danish civil servant named Judge William, and Judge William's theory is that ethical life can sustain enjoyment over a long period of time because it takes immediate sensual pleasure and adds to it a sense of duty (EOII 254–255, 266/SKS 3:242–243, 253). The Judge explicitly connects this sense of duty to inwardness (EOII 152/SKS 3:150), and in inwardness—given its relative independence from external reality—one can develop a personal commitment to the object of enjoyment that is able to constantly renew itself (EOII 10, 96–97/SKS 3:19–20, 98–99). The ultimate example of this synthesis of sensual enjoyment and ethical duty is marriage. In a proper marriage, according to the Judge, sensual pleasure harnesses itself to duty and thus can extend far beyond the ephemeral flings of the aesthete, even to one's entire life (EOII 8/SKS 3:18). The combination of pleasure sustained over time through duty makes marriage the most beautiful of all lives (EOII 96/SKS 3:98–99).

Given the critique of aesthetic life rehearsed above, the reader may be tempted to believe that Judge William represents Kierkegaard's definitive response to the deficiencies of the aesthetic sphere. Yet those who are familiar with his dissertation will already know that this is not the case. At the same time as he condemns *Lucinde*'s exaltation of temporal pleasure, Kierkegaard affirms *Lucinde*'s critique of the institution of marriage, writing:

> Lest an injustice be done to Schlegel, one must bear in mind the many degradations that have crept into a multitude of life's relationships and have been especially indefatigable in making love as tame, as housebroken, as sluggish, as dull, as useful as possible. To that extent, we would be very obligated to Schlegel if he should succeed in finding a way out. (CI 286/SKS 1:321)

Of course, Kierkegaard does not believe Schlegel has found a way out; but that is a criticism of Schlegel's positive solution to the problem that in no way applies to his diagnosis of the problem itself, a diagnosis Kierkegaard endorses. Carl Hughes offers a succinct summary of this theme in *The Concept of Irony*: "Although he [i.e., Kierkegaard] hardly subscribes to the novel's [i.e., *Lucinde*'s] absolutization of sensuality, he sees contentment with bourgeois institutions as equally dangerous."[75]

As Hughes demonstrates, there is ample reason to apply the critique of marriage found in *The Concept of Irony* to Judge William's marriage in *Either/Or, Part II*. If his marriage completely satisfies Judge William's desire, it is because Judge William himself is a tame, housebroken, sluggish, dull, useful person. The sharp edge of Judge William's desire has been sanded off to the point where it can be fully met by earthly realities. This is not a virtue in Kierkegaard's mind. Instead, the sluggishness of the Judge's desire leads to a mistaken perception of absolute happiness as being potentially present in time through the institution of marriage, as Hughes points out.[76] The mistakenness of the Judge's perception becomes especially evident in a scene from *Stages on Life's Way*, which reveals that what is absolutized by Judge William is actually simply a cozy, comfortable, traditionally patriarchal domestic life, where his wife brings him tea presumably into eternity.[77] The fact that the Judge could consider this life to be absolute bliss does not make him into the ideal answer to the aesthete's problematic life. Instead, it shows him to be precisely the "boring" person that the aesthete vehemently abhors. Hughes furthermore shows how Kierkegaard's critique of Judge William as an insufferable bore works its way into the rhetoric of *Either/Or, Part II*, in that the work is at some level intentionally boring to read. The phenomenological experience of the reader, Hughes insists, is tied to the message the Judge is attempting to get across: "[a]s the soporific tone of his writing makes clear, he views Christianity as the quieting of yearning rather than its incitement."[78] The end result is "a deathly earnest defense of first love,"[79] a dull moralism with no desire for the truly absolute, resulting in the equation of an ideal life with a bland celebration of societal norms.[80]

Whereas the aesthete at least attempted to escape boredom, Judge William represents a full-on embrace of it, which he artificially inflates as the best of all possible worlds. In the end, Hughes comes to the surprising conclusion that the aesthete is actually closer to the religious than the Judge, in that the aesthete's desire—like that of the religious person—is not satisfied by earthly realities.[81] Though an interesting point, I think we must admit that the Judge is at least trying to relate to the eternal, and in that way is an advance in comparison to the aesthete. Still, Hughes is absolutely correct that the purpose of the character "Judge William" is to enable readers to see that a life which ends in comfortable moralism is dull; it idealizes what is in actual fact ordinary and bland, and we should not be satisfied with it.

To say that we should not be satisfied with Judge William is to say at the same time that we should not be satisfied with *Sittlichkeit*. Translated into Danish as *Sædelighed*, *Sittlichkeit* is a Hegelian concept—used by both Hegel and the Danish Hegelians—that refers to social morality.[82] As opposed to an abstract sense of duty (*Moralität*), *Sittlichkeit* encompasses the concrete obligations one has as a member of one's particular society. Morality in terms of *Sittlichkeit* consists of faithfully discharging one's obligations as a husband, a bourgeois,[83] and a member of the Danish civil service, at least in the case of Judge William. Placing this concept in conversation with Hughes's reading, the Judge's error is to collapse all the spheres of life into *Sittlichkeit*. To think that all of one's desires can be met within *Sittlichkeit* is not to desire women nor God very much. It is also to equate being a "useful," productive, rule-following member of society with religious life. There is nothing more to religious life, in Judge William's mind, than being a good citizen; he finds the whole meaning of his life in the fulfillment of his finite obligations. A conflict between his finite obligations and an infinite duty to God would be, precisely thereby, unthinkable.

Kierkegaard's next work, *Fear and Trembling* (1843), takes this collapse of *Sittlichkeit* and religious life head on as an object of explicit critique. Whereas *Either/Or, Part II* constitutes a critique of the position that the ethical can completely subsume the aesthetic—in that the reading experience of Judge Williams's letters becomes repetitive and boring, replicating a life which is totally devoted only to fulfilling societal duties—*Fear and Trembling* is a different kind of critique of Judge William and the Hegelians' elevation of the ethical life, in that it aims to show that ethical life (*Sittlichkeit*) not only cannot completely contain but is at times even in conflict with religious life.

Once again we see that the ethical life cannot be all that Judge William and the Hegelians want it to be, in that it cannot completely subsume religious life within its boundaries. The example Kierkegaard's pseudonym Johannes *de silentio* chooses to illustrate this incapacity of the ethical is Abraham, the father of faith. With Abraham, an intolerable contradiction comes into the discussion of the interrelations of the ethical and religious spheres. From the ethical point of view, Abraham is a murderer; from the religious point of view, he is the father of faith.[84] Either arch-villain or exalted exemplar: the reader who encounters Abraham must make a choice.

Kierkegaard appreciates the honesty of Immanuel Kant, who emphatically made his choice for the ethical sphere and denounced Abraham as a murderer.[85] What Kierkegaard and his pseudonym Johannes *de silentio* will not tolerate, however, is the Hegelian position which tries to smooth over the contradiction between the ethical and religious understandings of Abraham. Since the Hegelian position is that these understandings must always end in an ultimate harmony, Hegel's explanation of Abraham attempts to demonstrate that whatever contradiction may appear to occur in Abraham is overcome in the course of history.[86] The significance of this interpretation of Abraham is that, according to Hegel, individual faith is ultimately harmonizable with the concerns of wider society.

The ultimate import of Hegel's position is to retain the elevation of society and societal ethics to the highest principle, able to incorporate and integrate every human concern. If there is no contradiction between the ethical and the religious, this fact means that society can continue to have the last word with respect to what the significance of religion is. Religion is thereby annexed into a societal project of living a holistic, flourishing temporal life.[87]

As Merold Westphal and Paul Martens argue, *Fear and Trembling* represents a rejection of Hegel's position, arguing instead that faith constitutes "an absolute relation to the absolute" (FT 56/SKS 4:150).[88] Johannes *de silentio* acknowledges that it is possible God will ask an individual to do something that her society labels "anti-social," and he believes that the person of faith will respond to God's request in obedience. In *de silentio*'s understanding, the person of faith does not have a relative relation to God, obeying God's will only when it happens to coincide with societal norms and expectations. An absolute relation to the absolute means the person of faith will not place the purposes of her society over her relation to the divine, and that—when the two are in conflict—she will choose God's will over society's demands.[89]

Thus Johannes *de silentio*'s response to Hegel's elevation of society is to relativize the importance of society, placing it beneath the individual's God relationship—at least for the person who has faith.[90] Implicit within *de silentio*'s articulation of faith is a theology of divine encounter in which a community does not wholly define who God is or what God can ask an individual to do.[91] (This is contrary, for example, to Hans Lassen Martensen's position, who in 1843, while arguing for the legitimacy of infant baptism, stated: "the *community* of the holy is the presupposition for the holy individuals."[92])

While *Either/Or, Part II* goads its readers beyond the ethical sphere by showing its inability to incorporate the aesthetic, *Fear and Trembling* shows how the belief that the ethical can fully incorporate the religious sphere is delusional and in fact rests upon a reduction of God's free ability to give an individual a divinely ordained task. The religious life is always potentially different from the ethical life, in that it involves an absolute relation to the absolute that relativizes the importance and applicability of socio-ethical (*Sittlichkeit*) norms. Temporal norms cannot bear the weight of the absolute, which at times escapes them, as the story of Abraham paradigmatically shows. The person who has a concern for her eternal happiness and thus wants to be religious cannot, then, simply be defined by her ethical life as a good member of society. She must be open to a potentially disruptive divine encounter. To think otherwise is to divinize society and thus temporality insofar as social life (*Sittlichkeit*) is a thoroughly temporal matter; but neither society nor temporality are God.[93] They are poor beggars in comparison to the wealth of the absolute and the eternal. The socio-temporal pretension to capture the absolute and the eternal within social norms is, therefore, delusional.

The critique prosecuted in *Either/Or, Part II* and *Fear and Trembling* has the Danish Golden Age squarely in its crosshairs. Insofar as the Golden Age was a self-affirmation of Danish society as a kind of ultimate good, Kierkegaard's position is a rigorous critique of Golden Age sensibilities. No, Kierkegaard is saying, our society is not an ultimate good: in fact, no society can be. No human society can sustain the infinite investment of a desiring human subject; it will always end up disappointing with its drab pleasures (which it asks us to consider as great and wonderful). And no human society can completely subsume the God-relationship into civic obligations, without thereby abrogating the freedom of God to make requests of human persons which do not fit the temporal goals of the nation. That is, no society can totally encompass all human duties to the divine without making God to be not God.

Concluding Unscientific Postscript, published some two and half years later, reinforces at length the message of *Fear and Trembling* by making clear that the absolute relation to the absolute is what constitutes the religious as a separate sphere of existence in comparison to the ethical. The religious person renounces all finite ends in order to fully embrace obedience to the divine (CUP 460–461, 483/SKS 7:418–419, 438). While giving readers a clear idea of what makes the religious sphere distinct from the ethical and aesthetic spheres, the depiction of the religious sphere remains abstract. In *Concluding Unscientific Postscript*, the religious is generally identifiable only in the negative as a renunciation of the other spheres (CUP 524–525, 532/SKS 7:476–477, 484). *Philosophical Fragments* and Part II, Chapter IV, Division Two, B of *Concluding Unscientific Postscript* clear the ground for a new, more content rich conception of the religious life by speaking of the eternal entering into time in the person of the God-man. It is, however, really the task of the second authorship to delve more fully into what the religious life in a specifically Christian sense looks like.

That life begins with confession. In *Upbuilding Discourses in Various Spirits* (1847), the first work of Kierkegaard's "second authorship" (given this label because Kierkegaard had planned to end his authorship with *Concluding Unscientific Postscript*), we see that *confession* is the essential prerequisite for having an encounter with God, an encounter that then defines the rest of the individual's life and actually makes the Christian life possible.

This prerequisite—confession—also has a prior condition: namely, purity of heart. The layers then continue to peel back, for purity of heart requires a purification of the heart, which for Kierkegaard refers to subjective motivations which are generated by temporality (UDVS 113–116/SKS 8:215–218). This reform of consciousness, what might be called an ascetic phenomenology (in that the intentions of the subject's consciousness are re-forged through an embrace of *askēsis*), occurs through a general renunciation of temporal goods in favor of eternity. Only once this renunciation is achieved can one consider the possibility of a true confession before God.

Continuing to seek after temporal goods prevents encountering God-as-God, for the human subject who is dominated by temporal concern will always attempt to wrap God into her projects.[94] Again, Kierkegaard speaks to the necessity of an absolute relation to the absolute, if an encounter with God is to occur: We must not seek a relation to God for our own worldly benefit, so that—receiving God's blessing—such blessing ensures for us a secure life of comfortable enjoyment. To relate to God in order to have benefit in the world is not to have purity of heart; it is to want two things, God and the world; it is to be what Kierkegaard labels "double-minded." The fracturing of the subject's intentionality occurs when securing the objects of the world becomes its own pursuit apart from a simple waiting upon God's providential economy.

Such double-mindedness reveals itself in the frustration the unpurified believer has when things do not go well for her in the world. On this theme, Kierkegaard says bluntly: "All double-mindedness with regard to sufferings has its basis and its mark in the unwillingness of the double-minded person to let go of temporality" (UDVS 115/SKS 8:217). We must choose whether we find our good in temporality or eternity, for "temporality and eternity cannot be reconciled in the same person (*Timeligheden og Evigheden ikke kan fordrages i det same Menneske*)" (UDVS 62/SKS 8:171).

If we are unwilling to let go of temporality and its concerns, we can encounter neither God nor eternity. Eternity is that realm in which God resides,[95] and stands for a concern that is set apart from the temporal life. It cannot be encountered through relating to others; it must be found through individual encounter. This encounter is possible for everyone, since everyone—qua their status as human beings—has access to the eternal: "This awareness of being a single individual is the basic consciousness in a human being because it is his eternal consciousness" (UDVS 134/SKS 8:233).[96] This sentence contains a key anthropological principle that animates the entirety of this discourse on confession. Eternity is a part of the human being;[97] the human task is therefore not to ecstatically enter some eternal realm but is instead to ascetically suppress the temporal aspects of one's person in order to let the eternity that resides in the person rise to the surface and become "transparent" as the deepest reality of the human person (UDVS 121/SKS 8:222). In the third discourse on the lilies and the birds in *Upbuilding Discourses in Various Spirits, Part II*, Kierkegaard summarizes these elements of human being as follows:

> If the visible does not deceive him, as the person is deceived who grasps the shadow instead of the form, if temporality does not deceive him, as the person is deceived who is continually waiting for tomorrow, if the temporary does not deceive him, as the person is deceived who procrastinates along the way—if this does not happen, then the world does not quiet his longing. Then it helps him only by means of repulsion to seek further, to seek the eternal, God's kingdom. (UDVS 209/SKS 8:304)

Human beings can get trapped in worldliness and derailed from the track of their ultimate calling.[98] But the human being who avoids temporal deception and truly realizes her nature achieves intimacy with God,[99] or realizes the gift of her connection to the divine, which is the natural orientation given to each human being. The "basic consciousness" of eternity is occluded through the life of temporality and comparison, yet it can be regained if worldly concerns are renounced.

What *Upbuilding Discourses in Various Spirits* is offering its readers is Kierkegaard's theological anthropology, which can be summarized as follows: at the base of the human self is the eternal, a reality which is occluded by the other, temporal element of the self, concerned above all with living a comfortable life in this world.[100] This anthropology is ascetic in that the fundamental disciplinary challenge for the human self is set up right within the anthropological definition of what constitutes the self: the human person must discipline the urges, desires,[101] and states of consciousness that are generated by the temporal element of its being. To be a human is to be called to *askēsis*, if, that is, the eternal that resides in the self is to come to fruition.

The emphasis on encountering God, existing as a single individual *coram deo*, occurs precisely within these ascetic anthropological coordinates. The bracketing of the temporal world whereby one becomes an individual before God requires *askēsis*. Temporal urges for material comfort and societal respectability are what drive the self to the faux divine relation of comparison; these urges must be disciplined if one is to transcend relating to the divine by comparison. And once such bracketing is performed, eternity is there to be found. It is at that moment that one's existence as an individual becomes actual: "eternity takes hold of each one separately with the strong arms of conscience, encircles him as the single individual, sets him apart with his conscience" (UDVS 133/SKS 8:232). Eternity sets one apart and asks: are you doing the good for the sake of the good alone? Is your heart pure? Or are you pretending to be religious in order to accrue the temporal benefits such a pretense secures?

In this way, Kierkegaard's discourse leads the reader to the confessional. By herself, set apart from all others, she must examine her own heart and see if its motivation is pure. 'Did I relate myself to God in order to attempt to avoid some worldly calamity, or am I willing to undergo any earthly suffering God calls me to undertake?' In this either/or is what Kierkegaard calls "the decision of the eternal (*det Eviges Afgjørelse*)" (UDVS 114/SKS 8:216) in which one declares one's absolute loyalty to God above all else, thereby severing "the nerve of temporality."[102] This must be a continual choice,[103] such that one continually resolves to "keep himself out" in the decision, choosing the eternal over the temporal and—precisely in that decision—relating absolutely to the absolute (UDVS 120/SKS 8:221).

Considering the various forms of life treated in Kierkegaard's first authorship (both aesthetic and ethical) that do not embody this absolute relation to the absolute, it is only appropriate that the encounter with God begin with confession: one states all the temporal diversions that have concerned one up to that point, confesses these as sin, and then one examines one's heart to see if one is now totally dedicated to the eternal apart from any other motivations.[104] This act of confession is the final step in the suppression of temporal motivations in favor of dedication to the eternal. The confession of impure intentions is simultaneously a victory over that impurity; bringing the double-minded heart out into the open in such a way defeats the division the sinner attempts to keep hidden. Confession of one's grasp of the relative in the face of the absolute annihilates that attempt to grasp the relative; the absolute is reestablished in its rights when one admits, via confession, its claim over the relative. Once one admits all that has kept one from truly seeking the divine, the path is cleared for the encounter with God.[105] One can now receive God's directives with a heart that is pure enough to really hear them.

So: God has been encountered and the Christian life begun. Where does one go from this point? Naturally, to love,[106] for "to love people is the only thing worth living for" (WL 375/SKS 9:368); love is the quintessence of the Christian life, a life lived in self-denying service of the other. Yet love is not always well-understood; therefore, Kierkegaard authored a series of "deliberations"[107] titled *Works of Love* (1847), which chronologically comes on the heels of *Upbuilding Discourses in Various Spirits*.

These deliberations build upon and presuppose *Upbuilding Discourses in Various Spirits*, for the God who has been encountered by the separated individual has—in that very encounter—commanded the individual to love the neighbor. Kierkegaard captures this twofold movement with a memorable image:

> There is indeed a big dispute going on in the world about what should be called the highest. But whatever it is called now, whatever variations there are, it is unbelievable how much prolixity is involved in taking hold of it. Christianity, however, immediately teaches a person the shortest way to find the highest: Shut your door and pray to God—because God is surely the highest. If someone goes out into the world to try to find the beloved or the friend, he can go a long way—and go in vain, can wander the world around—and in vain. But Christianity is never responsible for having a person go even a single step in vain, because when you open the door that you shut in order to pray to God and go out the very first person you meet is the neighbor, whom you *shall* love. (WL 51/SKS 9:58)

According to Kierkegaard, love (*Kjerlighed*) begins in the closet, where one prays to God as a single individual. Then, the God whom one meets in that encounter sends one out of one's closet to go into the world, where one has been commanded—while in that closet—to love one's neighbor. Once one leaves the closet, then, the first person one comes across—that one is one's neighbor, whom—as God has commanded—one *shall* love.

We can be more specific with respect to what love means, in a Kierkegaardian sense. To love the neighbor is to lead the neighbor to her own encounter with God, to play some role in opening the neighbor up to her own God-relationship. Yet we know from *Upbuilding Discourses in Various Spirits* that such an encounter with God is both born of self-denial and that it generates further self-denial in its aftermath. Christian love is an *askēsis*, a discipline, a duty, whereby one leads the neighbor to her own corresponding *askēsis*.

Each expression of Christian love has as its *telos* the neighbor's embrace of *askēsis*. If Kierkegaard's definition of what it means to be a Christian is fundamentally an ascetic one, and to love the neighbor is to assist her in becoming a Christian, such love necessarily entails leading the neighbor further into ascetic life, beliefs, and commitments. This is personally ascetic for oneself, in that it is a refusal to draw the neighbor into one's own project, a refusal to use the neighbor to augment the happiness one seeks in one's own life. Yet it is also always expressed through encouraging the neighbor to embrace her own discipline of self-denial.

This account of the meaning of love leads the Christian into an embattled space. For encouraging the kind of self-denial that helps the neighbor to love God is what generates the hatred of the world: "The Christian idea of self-denial is: give up your self-loving desires and cravings, give up your self-seeking plans and purposes so that you truly work unselfishly for the good—and then, for that very reason, put up with being abominated almost as a criminal, insulted and ridiculed"—even martyred (WL 194/SKS 9:194).[108] With this in mind, Kierkegaard issues the following memorable warning for those thinking about embracing Christian love: "But if your ultimate and highest goal is to have life made easy and sociable, then never become involved with Christianity, shun it, because it wants the very opposite; it wants to make your life difficult and to do this by making you alone before God" (WL 124/SKS 9:127). If we recall that the world and the human being are by nature opposed to the ascetic, then the consequences of the expression of *Kjerlighed* will not be surprising. If love of the neighbor is to lead the neighbor into a further embrace of her own asceticism, and that neighbor is a human being and part of the world, then of course the expression of Christian love will meet resistance.

The true lover is never welcome in human community, because "[i]n his company one cannot really feel comfortable; even less does he help one to adjust the cushions of comfort with temporal or even pleasantly pious exemptions" (WL 370/SKS 9:364). Imagine how awkward it must be to interact with such an enthusiast, who seems to keep maligning the ordinary human goods that are often so fragile and difficult to achieve. After all, "If eternity's requirement is properly pressed home, it looks as if such a person hated everything that most people live for" (WL 370–371/SKS 9:364).[109] Such conversation makes for a poor guest at the party; try, for example, to imagine one of the apostles[110] speaking at a cultivated 19th century Danish literary salon, such as the Heibergs[111]—nothing and no one could be more out of place, and the difference is not simply one of language. The one dedicated to eternity ostracizes herself because she refuses to play the game of softening the demand. No, if one wants to be loved in this world, one must commit "treason against the eternal" (WL 370/SKS 9:364).

Receiving hatred from those one sets out to love completes Kierkegaard's ascetic definition of love. Love is a discipline; it is not merely something one likes to do. It is born out of self-denial and encourages self-denial, while self-denial is the very gadfly that irritates the world's innate selfishness.

The consequence of expressing works of love, then, is persecution.[112] The form such persecution takes is not yet specified by Kierkegaard, but it can include everything from private ostracization to public mockery[113] to literal physical martyrdom. What is important to note here is that the expression of love will, inevitably, lead to the consequence of persecution of one kind or another. This connection between the expression of love and its persecution is so sure that, beginning in *Works of Love*, Kierkegaard incorporates it into his definition of Christianity itself, under a new concept called the "double danger": "the truly Christian struggle always involves a double danger (*Dobbelt-Farens*) because there is struggle in two places: first in the person's inner being, where he must struggle with himself, and then, when he makes progress in this struggle, outside the person with the world" (WL 192/SKS 9:191–192).[114] This is then a twofold template of asceticism: there is the discipline of encountering God and the burden of encountering the suffering that inevitably follows obedience to that God. Note the use of the word "always" in the above quote in reference to persecution: opposition to *Kjerlighed* is not accidental but essential.[115] In fact, if one is not receiving persecution as a response to one's works of love, it is a sure sign that one is *not* a Christian: "What Christianity calls self-denial specifically and essentially involves *a double danger*; otherwise the self-denial is not Christian self-denial" (WL 194/SKS 9:193).[116] There is a kind of self-denial that perhaps looks Christian, but really just wants the worldly benefits of appearing wise: "*The merely human idea of self-denial* is this: give up your self-loving desires, cravings, and plans—then you will be esteemed and honored and loved as righteous and wise. It is easy to see that this self-denial does not attain to God or the relationship with God; it remains worldly within the relationship among human beings" (WL 194/SKS 9:194). Don't be fooled, Kierkegaard is saying: anyone who really calls their neighbors to self-denial will be hated; and if he or she is not hated, one can be certain that some compromise has been made.[117] For the expression of Christian love *always* results in the consequence of persecution. To think otherwise is to have an over-realized eschatology, to think that this world has already become the next; to deny oneself and expect things to go well for oneself in the world is to treat the world "as if it were eternity" (WL 194/SKS 9:193). Furthermore, such persecution increases in exact proportion to the purity of one's expression of love: what is promised to the Christian is "the world's ingratitude, opposition, and derision, and continually to a higher degree the more earnest a Christian one becomes" (ibid.).

Two further works from Kierkegaard ground the picture of the Christian life from *Works of Love* in a more robust theological grammar: namely, *Practice in Christianity* (1850) and *For Self-Examination* (1851). *Practice in Christianity* supports the conclusions Kierkegaard reached in *Works of Love* by engaging in a long exposition of the life of Christ. The principle of the double danger is not some Kierkegaardian metaphysical innovation: rather, it flows directly from the life of Christ. There we see how true love of neighbor is met with the world's hatred. Christ is shunned from polite society: he is a marginal, persecuted, and poor figure. Furthermore, since Christ is the eternal in time, we can know that any period in the history of humanity—whether Christian or not—would have had exactly the same reaction to him. There is no progression in the human relation to Christ: it will always want to kill him, for Christ's self-denial threatens the self-assertion inherent in human nature. What was true of Christ is also true of any authentic follower of Christ, and that is how the principle of the double danger—flowing from what we see in the Gospels—applies directly to any and every truly Christian life.

For Self-Examination then explains how it happens that someone might actually become a follower of Christ. Human nature seems in all its inclinations to lead in exactly the opposite direction: namely, not to follow Christ but to actively eliminate his presence. Exactly right, says Kierkegaard: that is why every true follower of Christ has had his or her human nature put to death. Here is where Kierkegaard's ascetic pneumatology appears, for this death is a death that has been effectuated by the Holy Spirit.

The introduction of the Holy Spirit is a fitting end to Kierkegaard's second authorship, as it provides theological description for how all the previous ascetic themes are to be actually implemented by the human being, who, after all, was born and continues to live in selfishness (*Selviskhed*).[118] The human does not become an ascetic through subjective effort, but through the gracious presence of the Holy Spirit, who—if allowed to be effective—is continually putting the natural human to death.

For Kierkegaard, the most fundamental gesture of the Christian individual is that of self-denial, just as the most basic act of human nature is selfishness.[119] But how is the human supposed to overcome her nature and become something other than human, so to speak? Only by means of something outside the human. The Holy Spirit is the One who roots out selfishness, which is the death of the natural self: "The life-giving Spirit is the very one who slays you" (FSE 76/SKS 13:98).

Given the complexity and length of Kierkegaard's first and second authorships, we have had to sustain their summary over several pages. However, I hope the point of this summary has not been lost. In what follows, I will be arguing that Kierkegaard's attack upon Christendom is a public application of an ascetic theology. In the summary just offered, I argued that Kierkegaard's whole authorship can be seen as the development of an ascetic theology: worldly pleasures are rejected as unsatisfactory, societal ethics truncate the God-relationship and attempt to blunt irrepressibly infinite human desires, renunciation of the world enables a confession which initiates human existence *coram deo*, God gives us a mission to love the neighbor in such a way that they are led to see the value of *askēsis*, this mission causes us to be persecuted by human society and to thus take on the aspect of the suffering and abased Christ, and the Holy Spirit is the one who allows these new disciplines—which the natural human being detests—to take root and become actual in real human lives. Furthermore, this ascetic theology is critical of the Golden Age setting within which it was articulated, with its consumerism, its obsession with bourgeois respectability, and its self-assertive nationalism (an assertiveness that will not brook renunciation).

Considering this collected evidence, I affirm the conclusion the great Kierkegaard scholar Julia Watkin reached over 25 years ago: namely, the writings of the late Kierkegaard do not constitute a theological distortion of his earlier work, but are instead a coherent conclusion to an authorship that was—all along—dedicated to an ascetic interpretation of Christianity.[120] Even earlier, Walter Lowrie wrote that in this last year of his life, Kierkegaard "was never more sane, and the attack upon the Established Church was the logical and necessary outcome of all his thinking."[121] I would not go so far as to say "necessary," but Lowrie is correct that the attack was a "logical" conclusion to a fundamentally ascetic authorship.

I conclude this section with a qualification of the critique of Walsh just offered. It could be that the shift in Kierkegaard's theology she is referring to is a difference in his conception of the church, which she does seem to indicate near to the end of the passage quoted above. Kierkegaard's understanding of the church certainly does change during the attack. But it is difficult to see how such a shift would be theological in nature. Kierkegaard's conception of the church has chiefly to do with whether it can enable or only hinder the individual's relation to his ascetic interpretation of Christianity.[122] His understanding of the church is therefore not distinctly theological; it is considered only with respect to how it *relates to* theology. If this is in fact what Walsh means by speaking of a change in Kierkegaard's theology, such a claim is made on shaky grounds—grounds which, in order to be convincing, would need more development than what is provided.

Against Walsh, I argue that the change that is perceptible in the attack literature has little to do with the content of Kierkegaard's ascetic theology. Rather, it is a shift in the public role that theology is allowed to play.

Kierkegaard's decision to take his theology onto the public stage was made and sustained over the years between his publication of *For Self-Examination* (September 1851) and the first article of the attack (December 1854). This decision to 'go public,' was articulated in his journal entries. A selective look at these journal entries will therefore complete our preparation for reading the attack literature with its rich context in mind.

THE JOURNAL YEARS

By 1851, Kierkegaard had achieved his mature vision of Christian life. Kierkegaardian Christianity involved the renunciation of the world, the rejection of *Sittlichkeit*, the work of love as a missional act that leads the neighbor to God, and the embrace of suffering as the essence of Christian life. For the remainder of his life, these aspects of the Kierkegaardian vision will not change. So what leads Kierkegaard to apply this articulated vision in such a new way, writing in newspapers with little to no sense of decorum, attempting to drum up a sizable audience for his contentions and advocating large scale social change? The best way to answer this question is to look to his own writings, to see if we can discover reasons for this shift in strategy.

From September 21st of 1851 to December 17th of 1854, Kierkegaard wrote furiously in his journal, yet he did not publish anything in this time. In these 'journal years,' we increasingly find Kierkegaard taking his mature definition of Christianity and comparing it to the Christianity he finds around him, with the conclusion that the latter is wanting. Kierkegaard begins to ask questions such as: Is it really the case that only an inward reform is needed? Is it true that we need only to uproot the 'Christendom' in our hearts, as I, Kierkegaard, have earlier contended? Or must Christendom as a real worldly structure be demolished? Already by 1852, Kierkegaard recognizes the untenability of maintaining his position that all which is required is a confession:

> The official position that pretends that something which is not at all Xnty is Xnty and flatters God with trumpet blasts and by binding the Bible in velvet and gilding the apostles—this is now utterly intolerable.
>   The next thing is to say quite openly: ["]I am toning down Christianity.["]
>   But this cannot be sustained either, for how could a pers. go on day after day announcing to God: ["]I am toning down Xnty, forgive me.["] Indeed, it must end with God proving the stronger and having his will prevail.
>   But above all what is at stake is truly getting out of the lying and mendacity that is the established order. (KJN 9:101/SKS 25:103–104)

This entry in Kierkegaard's journal is a complex one; the work we have done thus far will help us unpack it in two steps. First, notice the language of "toning down Christianity." It is only possible to understand what this means if we bear Kierkegaard's ascetic definition of Christianity in mind. Christianity is the suffering truth, the renunciation of the world; it is honest existence before the face of God, and it results in works of love. Second, the entry also contains a logical continuation of an earlier form of what Kierkegaard was asking of Christendom. In the final sentence, the act of confession is once again affirmed: those who are a part of the church must admit they have toned down the difficult requirements of Christian life. But here Kierkegaard also recognizes that, if a true confession is made, such a word would lead inexorably to destructive action. A confession by Bishop Mynster or by any similar church official would not simply be a personal admission of inward contrition; it would be a public act. At this point, Kierkegaard understands that his position ultimately entails not simply an inward reform, but large scale social and political changes. This understanding is present as early as 1852; however, it is not articulated frequently nor at length. One must wait until the attack itself for a full presentation of the theme.

In addition to greater clarity with respect to the logical consequences of what he is asking, there is in these journals an increasing focus on and animosity toward Bishop Mynster. While in 1846, Kierkegaard writes of Mynster as "the noble paradigm from whom anyone can learn,"[123] in 1852 we find Kierkegaard using increasingly negative language concerning Mynster:

> Quite apart from the other things that are concealed in Mynster's preaching of Christianity: M. has also failed Xnty, dislocating Christianity or its point of view. Xnty is the unconditioned; it is being-in-and-for-itself, and M. has at most a finite teleology. (KJN 8:478/SKS 24:471)

These sorts of comments are combined with a continuing affirmation of Kierkegaard's personal affection for Mynster, as mentioned above, in what seems like genuine care for an elderly person, whom Kierkegaard does not want to upset in the last years of his life: "After having enjoyed life as he indeed has, it can certainly be bitter in his final years to have illuminated what sort of Xnty this actlly is" (KJN 8:510/SKS 24:501). As already noted, Kierkegaard's personal respect for Mynster was one of the crucial reasons for the attack's delay. However, Kierkegaard's increasing clarity with respect to his true opinion of Mynster—that he was "only a Sunday orator and, what is more, a worldly-wise eudaemonist" (KJN 10:253/SKS 26:249)—meant that, once Mynster's relative tranquility could no longer be disturbed, Kierkegaard was willing to publicly contend over how Mynster should be interpreted: which is precisely how the attack begins.

NOTES

1. This portion of the work is explicitly authored by Kierkegaard, otherwise listed as the editor of the work whose pseudonymous author is Anti-Climacus.
2. In his book *Om det borgerlige Ægteskab* (On Civil Marriage), Dr. Andreas Gottlob Rudelbach had recruited Kierkegaard into the cause of instituting a formal separation between church and state in Denmark (COR 51/SKS 14:111). To this, Kierkegaard issued a stern rebuke: "In proportion to the capacities granted to me and also with various self-sacrifices, I have diligently and honestly worked for the inward deepening of Christianity in myself and in others insofar as they are willing to be influenced. But simply because I have from the beginning understood Christianity to be inwardness and my task to be the inward deepening of Christianity, I have over-scrupulously seen to it that not a passage, not a sentence, not a line, not a word, not a letter has slipped in suggesting a proposal for external change or suggesting a belief that the problem is lodged in externalities, that external change is what is needed, that external change is what will help us" (COR 53/SKS 14:112).
3. See Garff, *Kierkegaard*, 10–11.
4. See JP 6:6842/*Pap.* X 6 B 232 n.d. 1853.
5. The critique of Mynster takes the form of a criticism of 'observational' sermons. See PC 233–257/SKS 12:227–249, and the title of one of Mynster's most famous books, *Betragtninger over de christelige Troeslærdomme* (Observations on the Christian Faith).
6. Kirmmse, *Kierkegaard in Golden Age Denmark*, 449; cf. KJN 8:508–510/ SKS 24:499–501. Though Kirmmse uses the language of "concession" here, the concession would be Mynster's admission that his life was not one lived according to the Christian ideal. Thus, a concession would be a confession.
7. In *Yderligere Bidrag til Forhandlingerne om de kirkelige Forhold i Danmark* (1851), Mynster had mentioned Kierkegaard and Goldschmidt, and described them both as talented writers. To this, which he interpreted as a virtual equation between him and Goldschmidt, Kierkegaard took offense: for it was Goldschmidt who was the principal architect of *The Corsair* affair. See COR, *passim*.

8. Cf. JP 6:6854/*Pap.* XI 3 B 15 (March 1854). It should be noted the KJN series preserves Kierkegaard's abbreviations in English, thus "Xnty" for "Christianity," for example.

9. See Garff, *Kierkegaard*, 729.

10. See Curtis Thompson, *Following the Cultured Public's Chosen One: Why Martensen Mattered to Kierkegaard* (Copenhagen: Museum Tusculanum Press, 2008), 91–143, for a comprehensive treatment of Kierkegaard's writing on Martensen.

11. See *TM* 623n.15.

12. Kirmmse, *Kierkegaard in Golden Age Denmark*, 450–451.

13. Kierkegaard's strategy in the attack is illuminated by an 1853 journal entry analyzing *Practice in Christianity*:

> In 1850 a book came out entitled *Practice in Christianity*. There the specific something I have to say is actually said.
> But, but. In the first place, it got to be a big book, and I know very well that few people read books, especially the bigger ones. In the second place, a pseudonym was used, which almost poetically distances what was said from actuality. In the third place, in a thrice-repeated preface I let the book recoil upon myself and thereby deflect the attack so that it does not really drive home to actuality. In the fourth place, when the book came out, I did manage to lead attention away from it—and those few I mention were, as I secretly wished, quite properly sagacious enough to keep completely calm—it turned out all right, everything went off very quietly. (JP 6:6842/*Pap.* X 6 B 232)

The attack departs from *Practice in Christianity* on all these points: the communications are brief, authored by Kierkegaard himself, demanding with respect to readers, and intended to draw as much attention and controversy as possible.

14. Kierkegaard often listed the 1854 date of composition at the beginning of the article; see TM 3, 28, 30, 33/SKS 14:123, 151, 155, 159.

15. See KJN 11: 555 (editors' note).

16. After a description of the audacity of Martensen's claim to the "truth-witness" label, Kierkegaard says: "Therefore an objection should be raised, and then as emphatically as possible the blood should be stirred, passion set in motion" (TM 12/SKS 14:131); cf. TM 68/SKS 14:210: "It was for religious reasons that I decided to use a widely circulated political paper: in order to make people aware."

17. TM 361–362.

18. See Stephen Backhouse, "State and Nation in the Theology of Hans Lassen Martensen," in *Hans Lassen Martensen: Theologian, Philosopher and Social Critic*, ed. Jon Stewart, 293–318.

19. *Encounters with Kierkegaard*, 102. Incidentally, it appears that Martensen followed the advice at the end of Ingemann's letter, as no further responses from Martensen's pen were forthcoming during the course of the attack—a silence that seems to have particularly irritated Kierkegaard (see TM 79–85/SKS 14:217–221).

20. See TM 364–366.

21. *Encounters with Kierkegaard*, 101.

22. *Encounters with Kierkegaard*, 103.

23. *Encounters with Kierkegaard*, 108.

24. Cf. PC 297–303/*Pap.* X 5 B 34, *Pap.* X 5 B 36, *Pap.* X 5 B 38–40.

25. The newspaper phase of the attack includes twenty-one articles. However, only twenty had been published before the first issue of *The Moment* was released. The first issue of *The Moment* was published May 24, 1855; the final article of the attack, "That Bishop Martensen's Silence Is (1) Christianly Indefensible; (2) Ludicrous; (3) Obtuse-Sagacious; (4) in More Than One Regard Contemptible," was published May 26, 1855. Garff states that Kierkegaard published "no fewer than twenty-two articles" in *Fædrelandet* (*Kierkegaard*, 752); however, he is perhaps mistakenly including *This Must Be Said; So Let It Be Said*, when it is in truth an independent pamphlet (see facsimile at TM 374).

26. On the significance of this title, see Christopher A. P. Nelson, "The Eye-Glance: On the Significance of Øieblikket as a Concept, a Title, and a Figurative Expression," *IKC* 23, 1–32.

27. "The acid-like rhetoric should not hide from us the fact that many of the literary skills we associate with the pseudonymous literature are still used in the instant writing: powerful analogies, conceptual analysis, maxims, humor, and irony" (Robert L. Perkins, "Introduction," *IKC* 23, xiv).

28. *Kierkegaard in Golden Age Denmark*, 3.

29. A phrase used by the popular Romantic poet Adam Oehlenschläger; see Kirmmse, *Kierkegaard in Golden Age Denmark*, 86–99.

30. See the narrative in Garff, *Kierkegaard*, 781–793.

31. *Encounters with Kierkegaard*, 135.

32. With respect to Kierkegaard's refusal of communion, see *Encounters with Kierkegaard*, 125–126.

33. See Kirmmse, *Kierkegaard in Golden Age Denmark*, 35–39.

34. Kirmmse, *Kierkegaard in Golden Age Denmark*, 100.

35. Kirmmse, *Kierkegaard in Golden Age Denmark*, 101.

36. See the account, with quotations from his autobiography, in Kirmmse, *Kierkegaard in Golden Age Denmark*, 101–102.

37. K. Olesen Larsen, *Søren Kierkegaard læst af K. Olesen Larsen*, Vol. I (Copenhagen: G.E.C. Gad, 1966), 117, cited and translated by Kirmmse, *Kierkegaard in Golden Age Denmark*, 103. Kirmmse ultimately agrees with this assessment: see *Kierkegaard in Golden Age Denmark*, 107.

38. For a recounting of Mynster's series of promotions, see Kirmmse, *Kierkegaard in Golden Age Denmark*, 117–118.

39. See Jon Stewart, *A History of Hegelianism in Golden Age Denmark. Tome I. The Heiberg Period:1824–1836* (Copenhagen: C.A. Reitzel, 2007).

40. "[W]hether as a pastor I have the best patronage depends artistically on what gifts of eloquence I have, depends on whether I have a good voice, how my clerical gown fits, how much of the most recent philosophy I have studied so that I can satisfy the demands of the times" (PC 216/SKS 12:212).

41. See Hans Lassen Martensen, *Christian Ethics: Special Part. Second Division: Social Ethics* (Edinburgh: T&T Clark, 1892), trans. Sophia Taylor, 39–50.

42. See Thomas J. Millay, "Kierkegaard, Hegel, and Augustine on Love," in *The Kierkegaardian Mind* (Abingdon: Routledge, 2019), eds. Adam Buben, Eleanor Helms, and Patrick Stokes, 450.
43. See Martensen, *Christian Ethics: Special Part. Second Division: Social Ethics*, 47–50.
44. For example: Oehlenschläger's famous *Poems* were published in 1802, while Wordsworth and Coleridge's *Lyrical Ballads* were published in 1798.
45. See, e.g., Kirmmse's analysis of Oehlenschläger's "The Golden Horns" in *Kierkegaard in Golden Age Denmark*, 87–90.
46. See further Dan Ch. Christensen, *Hans Christian Ørsted: Reading Nature's Mind* (Oxford: Oxford University Press, 2013).
47. On Danish painting, see Patricia G. Berman, *In Another Light: Danish Painting in the Nineteenth Century* (New York: Vendome, 2007). For Ditlevsen, see Tove Ditlevsen, *The Copenhagen Trilogy* (New York: Farar, Straus and Giroux, 2021).
48. *Kierkegaard in Golden Age Denmark*, 9–10.
49. Lars Jensen in *A Historical Companion to Postcolonial Literatures: Continental Europe and its Empires* (Edinburgh: Edinburgh University Press, 2008), np.
50. *A Historical Companion to Postcolonial Literatures*, np.
51. See Mikkel Venborg Pedersen, "Med verden I stuen," in *Danmark og kolonierne. Danmark: En kolonimagt* (Copenhagen: Gads Forlag, 2017), 278–333.
52. For my account of Denmark's 19th century economic crisis, I rely on Kirmmse, *Kierkegaard in Golden Age Denmark*, 23–26.
53. *Kierkegaard in Golden Age Denmark*, 1.
54. *Kierkegaard in Golden Age Denmark*, 77.
55. Ibid.
56. Ibid.
57. *Kierkegaard in Golden Age Denmark*, 78–79.
58. See Kirmmse, *Kierkegaard in Golden Age Denmark*, 86–99.
59. See Kirmmse, *Kierkegaard in Golden Age Denmark*, 100–135.
60. See for example Andersen's tale "The Bell," in *The Annotated Hans Christian Andersen* (New York: W. W. Norton & Company, 2008), ed. Maria Tatar, 370–377.
61. See J. L. Heiberg, *On the Significance of Philosophy for the Present Age*, in Jon Stewart, ed. and trans., *Heiberg: "On the Significance of Philosophy for the Present Age" and Other Texts* (Copenhagen: C. A. Reitzel, 2005), 107–118.
62. Most recent scholarship still focuses on the first, pseudonymous authorship. See Paul Cruysbergs, Johan Taels, and Karl Verstrynge, "Kierkegaard Literature from 2005 to 2013. A Descriptive Bibliography," in *KSYB* 2017, 441–553; cf. Sylvia Walsh, *Living Christianly*, 1: "Kierkegaard has been interpreted for the most part on the basis of his writings up to and through *Concluding Unscientific Postscript*[.]"
63. See, e.g., N. H. Søe, "Søren Kierkegaard og kirkekampen," in Gregor Malantschuk and N. H. Søe, eds. *Søren Kierkegaards Kamp mod Kirke* (Copenhagen: Munksgaards Forlag, 1956), 45–75.
64. Sylvia Walsh, *Kierkegaard: Thinking Christianly in an Existential Mode* (Oxford: Oxford University Press, 2008), 198–199.

65. She writes elsewhere: "Kierkegaard's critique of Christendom in all its aspects—philosophical, theological, ecclesiastical, cultural, and sociopolitical—began in his earliest writings and was sustained throughout his authorship, culminating in the attack literature of the last year of his life" (*Kierkegaard*, 173).

66. For a different exploration of the relation between *The Concept of Irony* and the attack which does, however, agree with the premise of continuity, see David R. Law, "Irony in the Moment and the Moment in Irony: The Coherence and Unity of Kierkegaard's Authorship with Reference to *The Concept of Irony* and the Attack Literature of 1854–1855," *IKC* 23, 61–89.

67. Other failures include the "highly doctrinaire character" of the novel (CI 290/SKS 1:324) and the "dramatic idiocy" of Lisette's final speech (CI 299/SKS 1:333—though Kierkegaard does admit that such idiocy is in keeping with her theatrical character).

68. See *Friedrich Schlegel's "Lucinde" and the Fragments* (Minneapolis, MN: University of Minnesota Press, 1971).

69. "[I]t is easy to see that [*Lucinde*] misses the highest enjoyment, the true bliss in which the subject is not dreaming but possesses himself in infinite clarity, is absolutely transparent to himself, which is possible only for the religious individual, who does not have his infinity outside himself but inside himself" (CI 298/*SKS* 1:331).

70. Sylvia Walsh, *Kierkegaard and Religion: Personality, Character, and Virtue* (Cambridge: Cambridge University Press, 2018), 61.

71. I do not offer a full explanation of Kierkegaard's use of pseudonyms in this chapter. Kierkegaard's employment of pseudonyms has been extensively treated in the scholarly literature. For a good introduction to the complexity of the issue, see Edward F. Mooney, "Pseudonyms and 'Style'," in the *Oxford Handbook of Kierkegaard* (Oxford: Oxford University Press, 2013), 191–210. For a comprehensive treatment, see Kaitlin Nun and Jon Stewart, eds., *Kierkegaard's Pseudonyms*, KRSRR Vol. 17. I do, however, generally respect Kierkegaard's wishes to use the name of the pseudonym when citing a passage from a pseudonymous work, rather than Kierkegaard's own name.

72. "It is very curious that boredom, which itself has such a calm and sedate nature, can have such a capacity to initiate motion" (EOI 285/SKS 2:275).

73. See, for example, EOI 25/SKS 2:33–34: "On the whole, I lack the patience to live. I cannot see the grass grow, and if I cannot do that, I do not care to look at it at all. My views are the superficial observations of a '*fahrender Scholastiker* [traveling scholastic]' who dashes through life in the greatest haste. It is said that our Lord satisfies the stomach before the eyes. That is not what I find. My eyes are surfeited and bored with everything, and yet I hunger."

74. "[T]o forget is an art that must be practiced in advance. To be able to forget always depends upon how one remembers, but how one remembers depends upon how one experiences actuality. The person who runs aground with the speed of hope will recollect in such a way that he will be unable to forget. Thus *nil admirari* [marvel at nothing] is the proper wisdom of life. . . . From the beginning, one curbs the enjoyment and does not hoist full sail for any decision; one indulges with a certain mistrust" (EOI 293/SKS 2:282).

75. Hughes, *Kierkegaard and the Staging of Desire*, 41.

76. Judge William "unabashedly conflates the universal—that is, ethical duty—with the absolute—the individual's relationship to God. . . . Judge William's tendency to absolutize first love and marriage leads him to nothing less than blasphemy. . . . Judge William's praise of marriage becomes so excessive that he comes to accord it the very attributes that Christian theology classically applies to Jesus" (Hughes, *Kierkegaard and the Staging of Desire*, 64–65).

77. SLW 82–86/SKS 6:81–84. Hughes labels this "the Judge's soporific parlor" (*Kierkegaard and the Staging of Desire*, 68).

78. Hughes, *Kierkegaard and the Staging of Desire*, 187.

79. Hughes, *Kierkegaard and the Staging of Desire*, 61.

80. See Hughes, *Kierkegaard and the Staging of Desire*, 67.

81. Hughes, *Kierkegaard and the Staging of Desire*, 47–49.

82. See G. W. F. Hegel, *Elements of the Philosophy of Right*, ed. Allen W. Wood, tr. H. B. Nisbet (Cambridge: Cambridge University Press, 1991), 142–360.

83. For more on the category of bourgeois—which includes psychological, political, social, and economic dimensions—see Franco Moretti, *The Bourgeois: Between History and Literature* (London: Verso, 2013); cf. Kirmmse, *Kierkegaard in Golden Age Denmark*, 365–371 (with reference to *The Sickness unto Death*), for specific application to Kierkegaard's Danish context.

84. "Therefore, Abraham is at no time a tragic hero but is something entirely different, either a murderer or a man of faith" (FT 57/SKS 4:150); "If faith cannot make it a holy act to be willing to murder his son, then let the same judgment be passed on Abraham as on everyone else. . . . The ethical expression for what Abraham did is that he meant to murder Isaac; the religious expression is that he meant to sacrifice Isaac—but precisely in this contradiction is the anxiety that can make a person sleepless, and yet without this anxiety Abraham is not who he is" (FT 30/SKS 4:126). Cf. Hebrews 11.8–12.

85. See Immanuel Kant, *Religion within the Bounds of Mere Reason and Other Writings* (Cambridge: Cambridge University Press, 1998), 100: "For as regards the theistic miracles, reason can at least have a negative criterion at its disposal, namely, if something is represented as commanded by God in a direct manifestation of him yet is directly in conflict with morality, it cannot be a divine miracle despite every appearance of being one (e.g., if a father were ordered to kill his son who, as far as he knows, is totally innocent)."

86. Mark C. Taylor gives a useful summary of Hegel's treatment of Abraham in his "Journeys to Moriah: Hegel vs. Kierkegaard," in *The Harvard Theological Review*, Vol. 70, No. 3/4 (Jul.–Oct. 1977), 305–326. Hegel considers Abraham explicitly in his *The Spirit of Christianity and its Fate*, found in *Early Theological Writings* (Chicago: University of Chicago Press, 1948), 182ff.

87. On this see further Thomas J. Millay, "Concrete *and* Otherworldly: Reading Kierkegaard's *Works of Love* alongside Hegel's *Philosophy of Right*," in *Modern Theology* 34:1 (January 2018), 27–41; Millay, "Kierkegaard, Hegel, and Augustine on Love," in *The Kierkegaardian Mind* (London: Routledge, 2019), 446–456; and Millay, "Against Flourishing: The Continuing Relevance of Kierkegaard's

Asceticism," in *Taking Kierkegaard Personally* (Macon, GA: Mercer University Press, 2020), 147–153.

88. Paul Martens, *Reading Kierkegaard I: Fear and Trembling* (Eugene, OR: Cascade, 2017) and Merold Westphal, *Kierkegaard's Critique of Reason and Society* (Macon, GA: Mercer University Press, 1987). Cf. esp. FT 54/SKS 4:148–149, where Hegel's *Philosophy of Right* is explicitly referenced, and FT 55/SKS 4:149 where Kierkegaard writes that he is speaking of "the ethical—that is, social morality (*det Ethiske [det vil sige] Sædelige*)."

89. See esp. "Problema II" in *Fear and Trembling*, subtitled "*Is there an Absolute Duty to God?*" FT 68–81/SKS 4:160–171.

90. When speaking of the individual's duty to God, Johannes *de silentio* writes: "if this duty is absolute, then the ethical is reduced to the relative" (FT 70/SKS 4:162).

91. On the solitude of the knight of faith, see esp. FT 80/SKS 4:171.

92. Hans Lassen Martensen, *Den christelige Daab betragtet med Hensyn paa det baptistike Spørgsmall* (Copenhagen: C. A. Reitzel, 1843), 8; tr. by Curtis L. Thompson in *Following the Cultured Public's Chosen One: Why Martensen Mattered to Kierkegaard* (Copenhagen: Museum Tusculanum Press, 2008), 39.

93. On society's self-divinization, see FT 68/SKS 4:160.

94. On Kierkegaard's spirituality as an antidote to a project-based consciousness, see Kangas, *Errant Affirmations*, *passim*.

95. "[E]ternity" is the "place where the Good has its home" (UDVS 47/SKS 8:158).

96. Cf. UDVS 103/SKS 8:207, on the availability of the eternal: "The eternal is much nearer to you than any foreign country is to the emigrant."

97. Eternity is not only a part, but an ineradicable part of the human: UDVS 129/SKS 8:228–229.

98. This is a frequent theme in Christian ascetic literature. Compare, e.g., Maximos the Confessor: "The devil is both God's enemy and God's avenger (cf. Ps 8:2). He is God's enemy when he appears, in his hatred for God, somehow to have acquired a love for us human beings that is destructive, persuading our power of free choice, through pleasure and modes of voluntary passions, to value what is transitory more than eternal good things. In this way, stealing the whole of the soul's appetite for God, he utterly separates us from divine love, making us willing enemies of the One Who created us" (*On Difficulties in Sacred Scripture: The Responses to Thalassios* [Washington, DC: The Catholic University of America Press, 2018], 172–173).

99. On the theme of intimacy or closeness, see UDVS 121/SKS 8:222.

100. The theological anthropology given in *Upbuilding Discourses in Various Spirits* is then further clarified in *The Sickness unto Death*.

101. "Immediate feeling is certainly the first, is the vital force; in it is life, just as it is indeed said that from the heart flows life. But then this feeling must 'be kept,' understood in the same way as when it is said, 'Keep your heart, for from it flows life.' It must be cleansed of selfishness, kept from selfishness; it must not be left to its own devices, but, on the contrary, that which is to be kept must be entrusted to the power of something higher that keeps it" (UDVS 71/SKS 8:179).

102. UDVS 116/SKS 8:218: "in the decision the nerve of temporality is severed."

103. On "choice," see UDVS 207–208/SKS 8:302–303: "God is present in the moment of choice, not in order to watch but in order to be chosen.... To have choice is the glorious perilousness of the condition."

104. Not only is confession about dedication to the eternal, it is also enabled by the eternal in a human being, for "repentance and regret belong to the eternal in a human being" (UDVS 15/SKS 8:130).

105. On the relation between confession and encounter, see Kierkegaard's exposition of the "eleventh hour," the moment just before the encounter occurs, which is precisely a moment of confession: "O eleventh hour, how changed everything is when you are present; how still everything is, as if it were the midnight hour; how earnest everything is, as if it were the hour of death; how solitary, as if it were among the tombstones; how solemn, as if it were in eternity! O strenuous hour of work (although the task is at rest) when the accounting is made and yet there is no accuser, when everything is mentioned by its proper name and yet there is no one who speaks, when every idle word must be repeated in the transformation of eternity!" (UDVS 15/SKS 8:130–131).

106. "What is this refreshment that Truth promises to those who are climbing and which he gives to those who reach the top? Perhaps it is love itself? To this, as the blessed Benedict says, the monk will quickly come when he has climbed all the steps of humility" (Bernard of Clairvaux, "On Humility and Pride," in *Selected Works*, 104).

107. "A deliberation [*Overveielse*] does not presuppose conceptual definitions as given and understood; therefore, it must not so much touch, relieve, [and] convince as *awaken* and prod ppl. and sharpen their thinking" (KJN 4:210/SKS 20:211).

108. See the mention of martyrdom on WL 195/SKS 9:194.

109. Cf. WL 107/SKS 9:111: to the world, the Christian's love looks like "lovelessness (*Ukjerlighed*)."

110. Kierkegaard raises the example of the apostles precisely in connection to the expression of love being hated by the world: "If the apostles had not maintained firmly that love is the fulfilling of the Law and therefore something different from the fulfillment of human agreements and participation in human alliances, if they had not held fast to loving people in this sense without wanting to become involved in adapting themselves to the world's idea of what it is to love—would they then have been persecuted?" (WL 121/SKS 9:124–125).

111. See Henning Fenger, *The Heibergs* (New York: Twayne Publishers, 1971), tr. Frederick J. Marker.

112. See Barnett, *Kierkegaard, Pietism and Holiness*, 107: "*In nuce*, Kierkegaard held that Christian piety presses one into the midst of society, not as a leader, but as a suffering servant."

113. For an equation of mockery and persecution, see KJN 4:52/SKS 20:53.

114. Cf. TM 332/SKS 13:396: "The Christianity of the New Testament is to love God in a relation of opposition to people."

115. The persecution of a love lived in imitation of Christ's love is a theme that goes back, if not to the New Testament, at least to Ignatius of Antioch (d. c. 108), for whom "imitation is oriented primarily to *suffering*, not to the cross specifically

but to suffering as the inevitable consequence of loving like God loves," Willard M. Swartley, "The 'Imitatio christi' in the Ignatian Letters," *Vigiliae Christianae* 27 (1973), 100.

116. Cf. esp. KJN 4:339/SKS 20:338: "Xnty doesn't take a trivial position with regard to what happens to a pers., for example, if it happens that everyone speaks well of him. For Xnty says: This must not happen to you, any more than stealing, whoring, etc. You must not defend yourself by saying that you didn't want it to happen, that it wasn't your fault—for you shall live as Xnty demands and if you do, it is *eo ipso* impossible. If it happens, it is *eo ipso* proof that you aren't living as Xnty demands."

117. See WL 195/SKS 9:194–195: "[T]he world continually sees to it that there is a sufficient number of forged notes of counterfeit self-denial in circulation . . . it takes a more expert eye to recognize the counterfeit note immediately. . . . Yet it is easy to recognize the forgery, because as soon as the double mark is missing the self-denial is not Christian self-denial"; cf. WL 196/SKS 9:195: "[A]ll self-denial that finds support in the world is not Christian self-denial."

118. Human nature did not always have such a narrow interpretation in Kierkegaard, but it does at this point in his authorship. The development of Kierkegaard's theological anthropology from a varied thematic complex to a narrow focus on human selfishness as constitutive of human nature is the subject of an excellent piece by Sylvia Walsh. According to Walsh, it is possible to isolate three different usages of "the human" in Kierkegaard's writings: "the natural human (immediacy), the universal human (the ethical-religious) and the new human (the Christian)" (Sylvia Walsh, "Dying to the World and Self-Denial in Kierkegaard's Religious Thought," *IKC* 21:179–181). In earlier writings such as *Concluding Unscientific Postscript* and *Upbuilding Discourses in Various Spirits*, "the human" can therefore have either a positive or negative valence, depending on which of the three senses in which it is used. In the late Kierkegaard, on the other hand, "the human" refers *only* to the natural human being who lives in immediacy and thus exclusive self-interest (see Thomas J. Millay, "The Late Kierkegaard on Human Nature," in *Acta Kierkegaardiana Vol. 6* [Toronto: Kierkegaard Circle, 2013], 137–151). In a late work such as *For Self-Examination*, being a Christian means putting human nature to death, and, subsequently, being put to death by those who embrace their selfish nature as human beings. Christianity is an attack on the human being; "love of God is hatred of the world." It cannot be otherwise, given the definition of what a human being is.

119. "But naturally there is nothing a human being hangs on to so firmly—indeed, with his whole self!—as to his selfishness (*Selviskhed*)" (FSE 77/SKS 13:99).

120. Julia Watkin, "The Logic of Søren Kierkegaard's Misogyny, 1854–1855," *Kierkegaardiana* 15 (1991), 76.

121. Walter Lowrie, *A Short Life of Kierkegaard* (Princeton, NJ: Princeton University Press, 1942), 242. Cp. Kirmmse: "Far from being the politics of an authoritarian conservative or demented irrationalist, Kierkegaard's politics should be seen as the healthy and enormously fertile and insightful self-criticism of bourgeois liberal society, posited from a radically otherworldly Christian point of view" (*Kierkegaard in Golden Age Denmark*, 4).

122. See e.g., KJN 4:197/SKS 20:199, for a positive evaluation of the potential of church. However, Kierkegaard's evaluation of church is, on the whole, resoundingly negative; it more often prevents than encourages a true encounter with Christianity. See J. Michael Tilley, "Church," KRSRR, Vol. 15, Tome I, 211–214.

123. JP 5880/Pap. VII 1 B 131.

Chapter Two

Concepts

The Truth-Witness, New Testament Christianity, and Denmark

THE ATTACK AS CONCEPTUAL CLARIFICATION

As Kierkegaard's attack develops, he eventually asks for concrete actions from his audience: he asks them to stop going to church, and he asks for a change in civic policy such that the state no longer financially supports the church. These requests, and the path that led to them, are the subject of the next chapter. Initially, the attack is all about conceptual clarification. In the second newspaper article of the attack, Kierkegaard writes that he knows he will be disparaged, but that it is worth it because what he is doing is "to the benefit of the clarification of Christian concepts" (TM 10n./SKS 14:129). He will suffer a "blow," but in the end, Kierkegaard believed, people will see that he was right about the definition of the concepts being discussed; thus, his personal suffering will be worthwhile (ibid.).

The attack begins, therefore, as a debate about "language usage."[1] Kierkegaard objected to Bishop Mynster being labeled a "truth-witness"; he objected to the confused notion of "Christianity" which supported such an outlandish label for the rather ordinary Bishop Mynster; he objected to the prevailing understanding of Denmark (viz., as a Christian nation). Furthermore, he had his own definition of each of these terms, and he wanted his contrary positions to be known.

Why are such definitions important? Is this all simply an academic matter of linguistic wrangling? Kierkegaard was convinced otherwise. To confuse the definition of something is not an abstract matter; it is instead related to a quite concrete attempt to make one's life easier. For Kierkegaard, obfuscation is the mother of ease. If there is no clear definition of Christianity, it gets one off the hook with respect to whether one is or is not a Christian.

Earlier in his authorship, Kierkegaard attacked "mediation" (the dialectical relating of two seemingly separate phenomena, such as the ethical and the religious) for just this reason: it collapsed what should be kept separate, it made the aesthetic life of pleasure equivalent to the ethical life of duty, and the life of social duty or *Sittlichkeit* equivalent to a religious existence. Within the reign of mediation, there is no either/or, no need to choose: one can enjoy all the pleasures of life, rejoice in one's life, family, and station, and be pleased to know one is going to heaven when one dies. The confusion of definitions which happens under the reign of mediation is thus not simply a matter of intellectual error. Rather, "Mediation wants to make existence easier for the existing person by omitting an absolute relation to an absolute *telos*. The practice of the absolute distinction makes life absolutely strenuous" (CUP 421–422/SKS 7:384). In its insistence on sharp distinctions, conceptual clarity preserves the difficulty of life. Conceptual confusion breeds the illusion that one can have it all; if there are no sharp distinctions to be made, neither are there choices to be made between this and that. With conceptual clarity, however, one knows that one must choose: either this world, or the next; either suffering or enjoyment; either a truth-witness, or a person of honor in the world; either a nationalist, or a Christian.[2]

If one is an average Christian in the Denmark of Kierkegaard's age, reading the attack literature makes one newly aware of such stark choices. In so doing, Kierkegaard prepares his readers for eternity's accounting, in the midst of a situation which attempts to occlude and to bracket the ideal by which one will be judged.[3] Thus, the importance of the attack literature *as* literature: this is conceptual material, yet it is anything but abstract. To get a handle on the definitions Kierkegaard lays out in these articles and pamphlets is to change one's life. After reading Kierkegaard, one can either: (a) confess one's inadequacy to the ideal before God, or (b) renounce one's society and commit oneself to its destruction—or some mixture of both. One cannot remain the same.

There are all kinds of incendiary rhetoric scattered throughout this literature, with plenty of *ad hominem* and the aforementioned accusations of cannibalism.[4] But the heart of the attack happens by way of conceptual clarification. What is a truth-witness? What is Christianity? What is Denmark, and what relation does it have to Christianity? When these questions are answered with conceptual precision, the illusions which support Christendom are punctured, and at that point the destruction has already commenced: "it is 'Christendom' that has been set afire" (TM 51/SKS 14:189).

THE TRUTH-WITNESS

The definition of the truth-witness is what sparks the beginning of Kierkegaard's attack. Bishop Martensen has called his predecessor, Bishop Mynster, a "truth-witness," and Kierkegaard cannot let this stand; he says, "To this I must raise an objection" (TM 3/SKS 14:123). Is Bishop Mynster, who occupied a position of "power," whose life was full of "goods, advantages" and the "abundant enjoyment of even the most select refinements" (TM 6/SKS 14:125)—is Bishop Mynster a truth-witness—is this the truth?

Of course, the implied answer is 'No.' So, if this is not the truth, what in fact is a truth-witness? Kierkegaard is not just a nay-sayer. He is happy to provide us a lengthy definition:

> A truth-witness is a person whose life from first to last is unfamiliar with everything called *enjoyment*—ah, whether much or little is granted you, you know how much good is done by what is called enjoyment—but his life from first to last was unfamiliar with everything that is called *enjoyment*; on the contrary, from first to last it was initiated into everything called *suffering*. . . .
> A truth-witness is a person who in poverty witnesses for the truth, in poverty, in lowliness and abasement, is so unappreciated, hated, detested, so mocked, insulted, laughed to scorn—so poor that he perhaps has not always had daily bread, but he received the daily bread of persecution in abundance every day. For him there was never advancement and promotion except in reverse, step by step downward. A truth-witness, one of the authentic truth-witnesses, is a person who is flogged, mistreated, dragged from one prison to another, then finally . . . is crucified or beheaded or burned or broiled on a grill, his lifeless body thrown away by the assistant executioner into a remote place, unburied. (TM 5–6/SKS 14:124–125)

The harsh rhetoric employed here helps to reinforce the stark difference between Bishop Mynster and Kierkegaard's authentic truth-witness. In the midst of this rhetorical display, one should not miss the key conceptual opposition of the definition, which is the distinction between suffering and enjoyment. To be a truth-witness in the world is to suffer. If one is to be a truth-witness, suffering must be the category under which everything in one's life can be placed.

The person whose life has some enjoyment in this world has departed from the truth and thus cannot be a witness to it. The world is implacably opposed to the true proclamation of Christianity, a proclamation which necessarily includes "what is too inconvenient for us human beings, what would make our lives too strenuous, prevent us from enjoying life—this about dying to the world, about voluntary renunciation, about hating oneself, about suffering for the doctrine, etc." (TM 4/SKS 14:123). Anyone who speaks such a word will receive the hatred of the world and their life will be made miserable as a result. This is why:

> The qualification *truth-witness* is a very imperious and extremely unsocial qualification and scrupulously allows itself to be joined only with: being nothing otherwise. *Truth-witness* relates to Christianity's heterogeneity with this world, from which it follows that *the witness* must always be distinguishable by heterogeneity with this world, by renunciation, by suffering, and from this it follows that to be this is so unsuitable to: being something else in addition. (TM 10–11/SKS 14:130)

That the entire life of the truth-witness is suffering might seem to be an exaggeration. Yet Kierkegaard means this literally, and there is a chain of logic at work here. The pieces of the chain are as follows: (1) the truth-witness voluntarily renounces the goods of this world (such as money, family, and official station), in imitation of Christ (see all four gospels, *passim*);[5] (2) the truth-witness proclaims this renunciation to be what God requires of the human being who wishes to survive eternity's accounting;[6] (3) the world is run by human beings who wish to keep their money, family, official stations, and other enjoyments beside; (4) such human beings will do anything to protect what they have, and thus make every effort to make life hell-on-earth for such a one who would threaten their goods by preaching a message of renunciation. Thus, it may truly be said, without exaggeration, that the life of the truth witness is suffering and nothing else besides.

Eventually, the attack moves on from a fairly exclusive focus on the definition of the truth-witness to the Christianity of the New Testament and to the source of all the confusion, namely, Denmark (or Christendom, or the "Christian" nation-state). But this definition of the truth-witness is never really left behind. It hangs over the attack, reminding us of Christianity's rigorous requirement for each individual: that their life be one of renunciation and suffering and pain. In other words, that their life be nothing like the lives of Bishops Mynster and Martensen.

Inevitably, the question arises: Why is Kierkegaard making such a big deal of Bishop Mynster and Bishop Martensen? Was Kierkegaard just bitter? Did he resent their success? I am sure some of these unconscious motivations are present. However, there is genuinely more than personal animosity at work here. In the definition of Bishop Mynster as a truth-witness, much more than Mynster's legacy is at stake. If such a label is able to be applied to Mynster, Kierkegaard claims, it loses all meaning:

> In other words, if Bishop Mynster is a truth-witness, then—even the blindest can see this—every pastor in the country is a truth-witness, because what was

esthetically remarkable and extraordinary in Bishop Mynster is not at all pertinent to the question of being or not being a truth-witness, a question that pertains to character, life, existence; and in this regard Bishop Mynster was altogether homogeneous with every other pastor in the country who does not sin against civic justice. Therefore, every pastor in the country is also a truth-witness. (TM 19/SKS 14:141)

In other words, Mynster was only extraordinary in a quantitative sense: he was slightly more eloquent, cultured, and refined than the pastors around him. By Christianity's criterion of suffering, qualitatively Mynster and the pastors under his leadership lived exactly the same type of comfortable lives. If the qualitative definition of truth-witness fits Mynster, then it fits all the pastors in Denmark. And if the concept is allowed to apply so broadly, it has been volatilized, dissolved into thin air; it has become meaningless. But, as we will see, to lose the concept "truth-witness" is not just to lose a part of Christian vocabulary; it is to lose Christianity itself.

NEW TESTAMENT CHRISTIANITY

As is clear from the first article of the attack, Kierkegaard's norm for conceptual definitions is found in the New Testament. This is the case for the matter of how to define a "truth-witness";[7] it is also the case for the definition of Christianity. Indeed, Kierkegaard writes, the Christianity of the New Testament is the only Christianity there is.[8] Contrary to Martensen's response to Kierkegaard, in which he speculates about the development of Christianity,[9] Kierkegaard insists that there is no change nor development when it comes to the matter of following Christ. What Christianity was in the New Testament is what Christianity still is today.

By virtue of its many repetitions, "the Christianity of the New Testament" is almost a slogan for the initial newspaper articles of the attack, and it remains a touchstone until the final issue of *The Moment*. Here is how Kierkegaard defines it: "the Christianity of the New Testament is to suffer" (TM 83/ SKS 14:219). A succinct definition, to be sure. We can clarify the meaning of suffering in this definition by looking to material that is a bit more expansive: "the Christianity of the New Testament is: in fear of God to suffer for the doctrine at the hands of people" (TM 137/SKS 13:180); it is "this about dying to the world, about voluntary renunciation, about hating oneself, about suffering for the doctrine, etc." (TM 4/SKS 14:123).[10] The Christianity of the New Testament thus completely overlaps with Kierkegaard's understanding of the truth-witness; one is the theory and the other is the practice. To be a Christian is to be a truth-witness; there is no Christianity of half-measures.

Therefore, to be a Christian is to suffer: to be poor, despised, rejected, mocked, persecuted, and killed. In other words, to be a Christian is to follow after or to imitate the life of Christ.

In a separate pamphlet titled "What Christ Judges of Official Christianity" published directly after the second issue of *The Moment* (June 16, 1855), Kierkegaard expresses the contrast between the Christianity of Christendom and the Christianity of following Christ, which is Christianity as it is found in the New Testament:

> It is so deceptive: are we not good people, true Christians, we who build the tombs of the prophets and adorn the graves of the righteous; are we not good people, and especially compared with the monsters who put them to death? Moreover, what are we supposed to do; after all, we cannot do more than to be willing to contribute money for building churches etc., not to scrimp on the pastor, and then to listen to him ourselves. The New Testament replies: What you are to do is this, you are to follow Christ and suffer, suffer for the doctrine. The worship service you want to hold is hypocrisy and equal to blood-guilt. (TM 134–135/SKS 13:178–179)

The Christianity of the New Testament is not to hear about suffering, but to practice it; it is not to admire Christ's suffering and honor it with pageantry, but to embrace the pain of renunciation within one's own life.

The contrast expressed in "What Christ Judges of Official Christianity" is no accident, for true Christianity always exists in a relation of contrast: "The Christianity of the New Testament is based on the thought that one is a Christian in a relation of contrast, that to be a Christian is to believe, to love God in a relation of contrast" (TM 168/SKS 13:216) thus "the concept 'Christian' is a polemical concept" (TM 143/SKS 13:187). Christianity is always set in a relation over against the world.

Why is this the case—why this 'always'? How can Kierkegaard know that this will always be the case? He believes he can know this because of his convictions concerning human nature. The relation of contrast has its origin in a more fundamental conflict: "What Christianity wants is: imitation. What the human being does not want is to suffer, least of all the kind of suffering that is authentically Christian, to suffer at the hands of people" (TM 135/SKS 13:179). Thus, the context for our original succinct definition of the Christianity of New Testament includes this relation of contrast:

> I am well aware that when someone as young as Bishop Martensen has been so fortunate (!)—indeed, when I think of the New Testament and the oath, it is quite satirical!—as to make such a brilliant (!) career (!), I am well aware that one can then wish for rest (but the Christianity of the New Testament is precisely restlessness) in order to enjoy (but the Christianity of the New Testament

is to suffer) these worldly things: the ample income, the high esteem in society, the pleasantness of having influence on the welfare of many people. (TM 83/ SKS 14:219)

Here Kierkegaard is speaking to Martensen's reaction to the attack, which after an initial newspaper article was an official silence. Kierkegaard's interprets this silence as a desire not to be bothered by controversy, but to settle into the worldly bounty that is rightly his, now that he is Bishop of all Sjælland. This is consistent with Martensen's "Christianity," in Kierkegaard's interpretation, for it is associated with all the good things in an individual's life, and with a successful nation-state in addition. But, Kierkegaard says— but (!)—Christianity is the opposite of all this. And not only *does* Christianity exist in such a way; it *will always be* the opposite of what the human being naturally wants; it will always exist in a situation of contrast. The contrast is definitional to the essence of this thing called Christianity.

The contrast between Christianity and the naturally human is not evident to everyone living in Denmark (to say the least). Because human beings do not want to suffer but to enjoy, they have reshaped Christianity in their image. This is why a recovery of the Christianity of the New Testament is necessary. Over the years, the definition of Christianity has been steadily humanized: "[I]n the course of time the human race has permitted itself to mitigate and mitigate Christianity, until we finally have managed to get it to be the very opposite of what it is in the New Testament."[11] To put it another way, "the truth *for* which one dies" has been made into "the truth *on* which one . . . lives with a family, steadily advancing" (TM 52/SKS 14:189; emphasis added). Or, to put it in yet another way, "all Christendom is the human race's striving . . . to be rid of Christianity" (TM 182/SKS 13:232). Kierkegaard's rejection of Hegel's philosophy of history is here on full display, for all of history is the muddying of the Idea, "which never is purer than at the beginning" (TM 219/SKS 13:273).[12]

The human opposition to suffering is Kierkegaard's etiology for why there are different meanings to "Christianity" than that provided by the New Testament. Rather predictably, Kierkegaard was challenged by such a human on precisely this matter: namely, if he could offer scholarly justification for his definition of Christianity. In the April 3, 1855, issue of *Fædrelandet*, an anonymous author asked Kierkegaard to give a kind of scholarly-systematic presentation of the content from the New Testament which supported his understanding of New Testament Christianity (echoing an earlier challenge from Pastor Paludan-Müller). In the April 4th issue, Kierkegaard responded:

To propose that I write an exposition of the New Testament's doctrine, perhaps a big book, a dogmatics, which in turn could perhaps best be written during a scholarly journey abroad, gives me (presumably also those who follow my articles in *Fædrelandet*) the impression either of fatuousness or of a trap set for me in order that I would be tricked out of *the moment*, would mistake my task, would enter into the prolix scholarly enterprise and possibly (which could well be the result) perish or lose myself in it. (TM 50/SKS 14:185)

Kierkegaard therefore interprets the anonymous request as a diabolical temptation, an invitation to get lost in inessential matters that he (Kierkegaard) must resist at all costs. Reflecting on Kierkegaard's response, it is interesting that for all the times the Christianity of the New Testament is mentioned, the New Testament itself is cited relatively rarely in the attack literature. There is a justifiable reason for this: Kierkegaard did not believe the problem in his audience's relation to New Testament Christianity was attributable to a lack of familiarity with the content of the New Testament. The problem is not a lack of knowledge, but a lack of willingness to apply that knowledge.

Kierkegaard's position is therefore as follows: We all know what the Christianity of the New Testament is. We simply don't *want* to know it, for we don't want to obey the summons to renunciation. A prolix debate about the precise nature of New Testament Christianity, replete with verses and the contextual labors of historical criticism, would be a distraction. For the real truth is: we are speaking and debating about these matters because we don't actually want to do what we already know the text says to do, namely, to give everything away to the poor and live in wretched abasement.

It is obvious what the Christianity of the New Testament is. It is suffering. It is renunciation. It is *contemptus mundi* and *contemptus sui*.[13] Everyone knows this. Just as surely, everyone wants to avoid knowing it. And what actant is of the greatest assistance to people as they seek to avoid knowing the truth of Christianity? The nation—that is to say, for Kierkegaard, Denmark.

DENMARK

Kierkegaard himself admits he is an unlikely critic of Danish nationalism. He is, after all, something of a royal sycophant:

> A royal certificate! Please do not misunderstand me; there are few people who—civically—have such an almost unconditional respect for a royal certificate as I have. It is something I have often had to hear from my acquaintances, that politically I was a pedant who bows seven times before everything that has a royal certificate. (TM 54/SKS 14:193)

The crucial difference for Kierkegaard arrives only in the consideration of Christian concepts. Yes, he wants to pay honor to the king and be a loyal and patriotic citizen of Denmark. But, Christianly, he finds he cannot:

But Christianly I understand the matter differently. By virtue of a royal certificate—a royal certificate is surely something that pertains to a kingdom of this world—to want to have any authority whatever with regard to what involves not only a kingdom of another world but a kingdom whose passion, a matter of life and death, is not to want to be a kingdom of this world.[14] (TM 55/SKS 14:193)

The sentence then ends with a complicated analogy to a character in a Heiberg play, but the basic meaning is this: to want to certify the religion of the other world by a certificate from this world is "ludicrous" (ibid.). Humanly, Kierkegaard wants to appeal to the crown; Christianly, he believes he must reject it.

The reason Kierkegaard believes he must reject the nation is because of the fundamentally different aims of the nation-state and Christianity. These differing aims are the subject of a scathing article in the second issue of *The Moment* titled "Comfort and—the Concern for an Eternal Happiness."[15] According to Kierkegaard, the basic aim of the nation-state is to provide comfort for its citizens. The nation-state gathers resources from its citizens and then attempts to make life easier for those citizens. Kierkegaard has no problem with this: "Far be it from me to speak disparagingly of comfort!" adding "For example, water. Water is something that can be obtained in the hard way by fetching it from the pump, but it also can be obtained in the convenient way by high pressure; naturally I prefer the convenient way" (TM 110/SKS 13:152). Kierkegaard's problem with the nation-state arises when, along with everything else, it attempts to absorb religion into its administrative capacities. When the nation-state observed religion, Kierkegaard hypothesizes, it must have understood it to be a scheme for the welfare of human persons just like everything else:

> It seems that the state's process of thinking must have been this. Among the many different things that people need in a cultured mode of life and that the state tries to provide for its citizens as cheaply and comfortably as possible, among these many different things, such as public security, water, lighting, roads, pavement, etc. etc., there is in addition—an eternal happiness in the life to come, a necessity that the state likewise ought to satisfy—how generous!—and in as inexpensive and comfortable a way as possible. (TM 109/SKS 13:151)

The only problem being that religion is not like everything else. Rather, "[t]he eternal is obtained in only one way," and that is through difficulty (TM 110/SKS 13:152). The aim of the nation-state is to make things easier for its citizens; the aim of Christianity is to make things more difficult for its adherents.

These competing aims are the reason why it is disastrous to allow the nation-state to have control over religion. If the nation-state is allowed this control, it will shape religion to suit its aims. It is therefore on account of allowing the nation-state control over Christianity that Denmark has ended up with something called "Christianity" that is in fact the diametric opposite of Christianity:

> But when in his Word he speaks about proclaiming the doctrine for nothing, we understand it in such a way that the proclamation naturally is the livelihood, the most secure way to bread and butter and with steadily advancing promotion. When in his Word he speaks about proclaiming the Word in poverty, we understand thereby a yearly salary in the thousands. When in his Word he speaks about proclaiming the Word in abasement, we understand it as a career, becoming His Excellency. And by heterogeneity to this world we understand becoming a royal officer, a person of rank. By disdain for the assistance and use of worldly power we understand being safeguarded by making use of worldly power. By suffering for the doctrine we understand using the police against others. By renunciation of everything we understand acquiring everything, the most select refinements, for which the pagan has in vain had itchy fingers—and in addition we are truth-witnesses. (TM 20–21/SKS 14:141–142)

Notice how the above paragraph not only tracks a series of reversals; in addition, each reversal is provided by the state: a livelihood, a position of social distinction, and a police force. These are the realities a worldly kingdom introduces, thereby corrupting the essence of that religion of the other world, Christianity.

The arrangement of comfortable positions in society for religious leaders is only a part of the problem, however. There is also the matter of how one becomes a Christian in Denmark. Because of the beneficent arrangement of the nation-state in providing religious leaders, Denmark is able to sustain a series of rituals. On account of these rituals (such as baptism), all one must do to become a Christian in Denmark is to be born. This is the way in which Denmark is a "Christian nation": all who are born in it automatically become Christians, thus it is a nation of Christians, thus a "Christian nation." Remember the husband who has doubts about his Christianity in *Concluding Unscientific Postscript*. To these doubts his wife replies:

> Hubby, darling, where did you ever pick up such a notion? How can you not be a Christian? You are Danish, aren't you? Doesn't the geography book say that the predominant religion in Denmark is Lutheran-Christian? You aren't a Jew, are you, or a Mohammedan? What else would you be, then? It is a thousand years since paganism was superseded; so I know you aren't a pagan. Don't you tend to your work in the office as a good civil servant; aren't you a good subject in a Christian nation, in a Lutheran-Christian state? So of course you are a Christian.[16] (CUP 50–51/SKS 7:55)

This is the ultimate abstraction from any conceptual precision with regard to Christianity: namely, that one can be a Christian simply because one is born in a certain place, without any reference to the qualitative character of one's life. "We are, as it is called, a Christian nation (*et christent Folk*)—but in such a way that not a single one of us is in the character of the Christianity of the New Testament" (TM 36/SKS 14:163).

The citizens of Denmark are living in an illusion (TM 107–108/SKS 13:149–150). It seems to them that they are Christian, but they are not. The illusion is produced by the nation-state and those whom it employs, who have a "pecuniary interest" in sustaining it (TM 151/SKS 13:195). If we ask the question: 'How did something as offensive as being asked to follow a crucified and abased man get turned around in such a way?' The answer is: 'We human beings allowed the kingdoms of this world to appropriate the kingdom of heaven and to shape that heavenly kingdom to the worldly kingdoms' own distinctive aims.'

For a contemporary reader, there is a potential misunderstanding which arises at this point which must be addressed. We who are reading Kierkegaard now are tempted to think: 'Oh, what he wants is the separation of church and state.' This is a reduction of the force of Kierkegaard's attack. What he is really taking aim at is any form of Christianity which says that you can have it all: that you can be happy in this life and the next, both here and in the hereafter (TM 42/SKS 14:173–174). This 'both/and' is the fundamental tendency which Kierkegaard rejects as incompatible with the essence of Christianity.[17] At the same time, the particular configuration of both/and Christianity which Kierkegaard faced was Christendom: a state-supported church. Given this situation, Kierkegaard takes the position that "the amalgamation or alliance of Church and state, must be brought to the most extreme decision. It cannot and must not go on as it did year after year under the old bishop" (TM 75/SKS 13:121). In other words, it is possible there are other configurations of both/and Christianity. Jason Mahn has argued at length that this is in fact the case.[18] If Kierkegaard had faced a different configuration, it is reasonable to hypothesize the attack would follow suit, making whatever adjustments were needed still to hit the target. Yet a state-supported church was the particular both/and configuration Kierkegaard faced; therefore, the attack is directed at this specific amalgamation.

Kierkegaard's attack may seem to be all about personal animosity. After all, Bishop Mynster is mentioned in the title of the first article of the attack literature, and Bishop Martensen repeatedly finds himself in Kierkegaard's crosshairs. An easy dismissal of the attack would write it off as the bitter ravings of a slighted old man. The attack is personal, to be sure; but it is also conceptual. The animosity which drives the attack is not limited to personal slights. Kierkegaard is angry because Christian definitions have become meaningless. The truth-witness, New Testament Christianity, and Denmark—in the society to which Kierkegaard is speaking, these terms mean whatever is humanly convenient for them to mean. No distinctions are made which would require any sacrifice from those who wield these words. The purpose of concepts in the Denmark of Kierkegaard's age was to support the regime of the comfortable. The ascetic voice of Kierkegaard invades this space and says: No! A decision must be made. If we face up to the definitions we have purposely repressed, we must admit: Here is an either/or. We must choose.

We will see in the next chapter exactly how Kierkegaard believed the decision between the Christianity of Denmark and the Christianity of the New Testament should play out, practically speaking. He arrives at different answers at different points of the attack. The next chapter is dedicated to tracking this development.

NOTES

1. TM 25/SKS 14:147: "It was the language usage, to call *witnesses, truth-witnesses* what we understand by pastors, deans, and bishops—it was the language usage I protested against because it is blasphemous, sacrilegious, but Bishop Martensen obstinately persists in it, as is evident in his ordination address, which he incessantly interlards with 'witnessing, being a witness, truth-witness,' etc."

2. On reading and the preservation of difficulty, see Thomas J. Millay, "Conceptual Clarity: Kierkegaard's Dialectical Method as a Response to the Religious Crisis of Golden Age Denmark," in *The Crisis of the Danish Golden Age and Its Modern Resonance*, 2020, ed. Jon Stewart and Nathaniel Kramer, 109–120. On the purpose of reading more generally for Kierkegaard, see Thomas J. Millay, *You Must Change Your Life: Søren Kierkegaard's Philosophy of Reading* (Eugene: Cascade Press, 2020).

3. See TM 58–59/SKS 14:198: "Finally, a word to you, you who for your own sake are reading with some genuine interest what I am writing. . . . What I point out is precisely that which is to the pastor's interest to conceal, suppress, tone down, omit. If you have no other knowledge of what Christianity is than at most what you receive by hearing the pastor, then you can be rather sure that you will go on living kept in complete ignorance of what is not convenient for official Christianity. This is the condition in which it is intended to hand you, dying, over to eternity's accounting, where it undoubtedly will serve you as an excuse that others bear most of the guilt, but where it still remains your responsibility whether you have not taken the matter too light-mindedly by too light-mindedly believing the pastor, perhaps even because he is royally authorized."

4. For an extended analysis of the rhetoric of the attack, see David R. Law, "The Contested Notion of 'Christianity' in Mid-Nineteenth-Century Denmark: Mynster, Martensen, and Kierkegaard's Antiecclesiastical, 'Christian' Invective in *The Moment and Late Writings*," *IKC* 23, 33–60.

5. As well as "renunciation" (*Forsagelse*) Kierkegaard also uses the language of "break" (*Brud*): "to have faith is to venture out as decisively as possible for a human being, breaking with everything, with what a human being naturally loves, breaking, in order to save his life, with that in which he naturally has his life" (TM 214/SKS 13:268); cf. TM 17/SKS 14:138. For more on renunciation in the New Testament, see Stuart T. Rochester, *Self-Denial: A New Testament View* (Eugene: Cascade, 2019).

6. On "God" in the attack literature, see esp. TM 177/SKS 13:227: "God is indeed a human being's most appalling enemy, your mortal enemy. Indeed, he wants you to die, to die to the world; he hates specifically that in which you naturally have your life, to which you cling with all your zest for life."

7. See TM 4/SKS 14:123. To be more precise, on this page the New Testament is the criterion which enables us to decide whether what the given person is witnessing to (both in word and deed) is the truth. In that way, it enables us to decide whether the given person is a truth-witness.

8. See TM 35/SKS 14:163: "The religious situation in the land is: Christianity (that is, the Christianity of the New Testament—*and everything else is indeed not Christianity, least of all by calling itself that*), Christianity does not exist at all, something almost everyone certainly must be able to see just as well as I do" (emphasis added); cf. TM 38/SKS 14:165: "Indeed, the New Testament decides what Christianity is and reserves eternity to judge us"; TM 124/SKS 13:166: "the New Testament is the completely unchanged handbook for Christians, for whom things will continually go in this world as it says in the New Testament."

9. See above, 18–19.

10. For the reference to the New Testament here, see the previous page (TM 3/SKS 14:123).

11. For more on Kierkegaard's philosophy of history and his rejection of "this insolent nonsense that Christianity is perfectible, that we are progressing," see TM 33–34/SKS 14:159.

12. TM 219/SKS 13:273. The full passage is a resounding rejection of Hegel's view of history: "Just as it is in the whole world of the spirit, so it is also in the religious sphere. History has often been compared to what the chemists call a process. The metaphor can be very appropriate if, note well, it is rightly understood. There is what is called a filtering process. Water is filtered, and in this process the impure components are removed. History is a process in an entirely opposite sense. The idea is applied—and now enters into the process of history. But this, unfortunately, does not consist in—ludicrous assumption!—the purifying of the idea, which never is purer than at the beginning. No, it consists, at a steadily increasing rate, in botching, babbling, and prattling the idea, in vitiating the idea, in—the opposite of filtering—putting in the impure components originally lacking, until eventually, by way of the enthusiastic and mutually approving collaboration of a series of generations, the point is reached where the idea is completely destroyed, the opposite of the idea has become

what is now called the idea and this, it is claimed, has been achieved by the historical process, in which the idea is purified and ennobled."

13. See, e.g., TM 47/SKS 14:179. What "Christianity requires for saving one's life eternally" is "hating one's own life in this world."

14. Cf. TM 150/SKS 13:194: "Christianity is the very antithesis of the kingdoms of this world, is heterogeneity."

15. In addition to this article, see TM 143/SKS 13:187: "state and Christianity are inversely related to or, indeed more correctly, away from each other."

16. On this kind of misogyny in Kierkegaard, see esp. Sylviane Agacinski, *Aparté: Conceptions and Deaths of Søren Kierkegaard* (Tallahassee: Florida State University Press, 1988). For more on geography, see TM 35/SKS 14:163: "A geographer, for example, if he was convinced of the existence of this staff [of bishops, deans, and pastors], would feel perfectly justified in entering in his geography: The Christian religion prevails in the land."

17. See Law, "The Contested Notion of 'Christianity,'" *IKC* 23, 59–60.

18. Jason Mahn, *Becoming a Christian in Christendom: Radical Discipleship and the Way of the Cross in America's 'Christian' Culture* (Minneapolis: Fortress, 2016).

Chapter Three

An Evolving Martyrdom

A MARTYR IN MODERNITY

"Without falsifying or sullying the concept, I may say that my life is a kind of martyrdom, though of a new model" (KJN 10:108/SKS 24:110). It is easy to dismiss Kierkegaard's claim in this 1854 journal entry, seeing it as the result of a budding persecution complex which was just about to burst forth in full glory. Kierkegaard was indeed sensitive when it comes to criticism, as his perceived slight at the hand of Mynster makes clear.[1] However, that does not mean there is no truth to his claim of martyrdom.

If we hew close to the original meaning of the Greek word *marturos*, it is clear that Kierkegaard did in fact end his life as a martyr. The attack should indeed be interpreted as a mode of witnessing wherein Kierkegaard takes a stand in a public venue for what he takes Christianity to be. Kierkegaard did consider himself to be risking what has become the typical contemporary association with the word "martyr"—that is, dying for one's beliefs. The thought that he might be put to death for his stand against Christendom did cross Kierkegaard's mind, and he reflects on martyrdom extensively beginning in 1847.[2] This did not happen; but that does not mean he failed to be a martyr. Kierkegaard did experience a kind of social death on account of his witness,[3] and this type of death does entail real suffering. The next lines in the journal entry with which this chapter begins capture that particular type of pain:

> What I am suffering as a public person can best be described as the slow death of being trampled to death by geese or as the excruciating method of killing a person bit by bit, which is in fact practiced in faraway lands, by being thrown to insects—to this end, the offender is first coated with honey in order to give the

insects a proper appetite—and thus my fame is of course the honey that gives the insects a proper appetite.

So you can just come, history, with your audit: everything is in order, nor have I neglected to expose myself to it *voluntarily*—it is not something that has simply happened to me. (KJN 10:108/SKS 24:110)

It is easy to paint Kierkegaard as possessing delusions of grandeur. Instead, we should take seriously his experience of social suffering. It is not as if Kierkegaard had to attack Christendom. He chose to do so, despite the social exile that was its consequence. It is therefore appropriate to conceive of Kierkegaard as a modern martyr (or a martyr to modernity), and in two senses: (1) he intentionally and publicly witnesses to the truth of Christianity; (2) he suffers for that witness.

If there is something new in Kierkegaard's attack, it should be located here. This is Kierkegaard's turn "from the phraseological to the real,"[4] as Bonhoeffer put it; the beginning of his attack was the becoming of his martyrdom. Furthermore, we might venture that part of being a modern martyr is that one is self-reflective about one's martyr-activity—and Kierkegaard himself did conceive of the attack as a martyrdom, as we have seen in the above cited journal entry. Kierkegaard was making his writings newly public, and these public writings were intended to be a witness and understood to bring suffering as a result. All this understanding was present from the beginning of the attack. However, when we look at what Kierkegaard wanted the attack to achieve, we see that his intentions and goals for the attack change and develop over time. The purpose of this chapter is to track the shifting *telos* of the attack, from confession to complete structural abolition.

The new form of Kierkegaard's writings, conceived as a public martyrdom, was calculated to produce new consequences. It is true that Kierkegaard is here addressing a broader reading public in a sustained way for the first time in his writing career. Yet he wanted not only to address the public, but to change the public: to lead it to conversion. The difference of the attack literature is not merely a matter of audience, but of consequence.

Earlier, Kierkegaard hoped that *Practice in Christianity* would lead Bishop Mynster to voluntarily confess—publicly—that neither he nor the Danish State Church met the ideal requirements of Christianity. Mynster's confession would in that case have been the result of an inward and considered relation to the ascetic Christian ideal as presented in Kierkegaard's writings, and in that way Kierkegaard's hopes for Bishop Mynster were the same as for his other readers: that they would confess inwardly their inadequacy before the ideal and begin to strive to actually embody the renunciatory truths of Christianity. The attack literature, on the other hand, is not calibrated to produce quiet inner reflection. It is an attempt to force the matter, to compel the members of the established order to admit, publicly, that they do not meet the ideal that can be read off the pages of the New Testament.

There is a certain amount achieved simply by putting such a challenge in the newspapers. Whether the clergy do or do not respond, the issue is now a matter of public debate; even silence would be a public silence. Previous to the attack, whether or not the issue of true Christianity became a public matter was dependent on potential and voluntary acts by Bishop Mynster. If he confessed, then the issue would be public. If not, it remained a personal challenge made by Kierkegaard to Mynster. Though there is certainly an obvious critique of Mynster in *Practice in Christianity*, the stakes of the criticism—namely, it being intended to provoke a confession—would not have been obvious to every reader of the text. With the attack, a debate about the apostasy of Danish Christianity is a public concern, whether Bishop Martensen likes it or not.

Kierkegaard wanted to speak in public so that it would be as clear as day that the professional clergy were avoiding making a response to him and to the charges he had made:

> And that they are not truth-witnesses has now through the impression of a current circumstance become plain to everyone who wants to see. If it is assumed that what I say is true—the clergy would not have kept silent but would have declared themselves for this truth if they had been truth-witnesses. If it is assumed that what I say is untrue—the clergy would not have kept silent but would have declared themselves against this untruth if they had been truth-witnesses. If they had been truth-witnesses, they would not have done the one thing that they have done, they would not have tried through silence to sneak away from something true—if it is assumed that what I say is true. Neither would they in silence have allowed something untrue to remain in force—if it is assumed that what I say is untrue. (TM 62/SKS 14:201)

With this method of public querying, Kierkegaard aims to put the clergy in a double bind. Presumably, one thing a truth-witness cannot fail to do is witness to the truth. *Either* the clergy (or at least some of its members) are truth-witnesses who—as a part of their activity of witnessing—will defend themselves against false accusations (and thus enter into the ludicrous situation of equating their comfortable lives with Kierkegaard's ascetic definition of the truth-witness), *or* the clergy will remain silent, which is tantamount to refusing to witness, thus invalidating any claim to the status of truth-witnesses.

The contradictory situation has become plain to everyone who wants to see, and that is Kierkegaard's goal. Everyone can see it—it is public—and everyone can see that the charges are not being answered.

The deeper truth that has been forced onto the public stage is not only that the clergy *have* not answered Kierkegaard's charges, but that they *cannot* answer.[5] To equate themselves with the daily existential danger of the apostles as found in the New Testament[6] would be too manifestly absurd, even for the clergy: thus, the pastors cannot say they are living New Testament Christianity. Neither, however, can they openly admit the fact that neither they nor their congregations are truly Christians, for then what would they be good for? Surely their livelihoods would dissolve.[7] All things considered, it is best for the clergy to remain publicly silent, which is by and large what they did, despite the fact that—in Kierkegaard's mind, at least—their silence was tacit admission that they were not truth-witnesses.

It is important to note that Kierkegaard is not simply poking fun at the selfish nature of the clergy[8] (though he is certainly doing that[9]); neither is he criticizing particular individuals for moral shortcomings. Rather, he is in a broader sense criticizing the structural role the clergy play in society.[10] In the interest of having satisfied citizens who are assured of their eternal salvation, the Danish state provides a certain number of officially sanctioned pastors with a livelihood. The object of Kierkegaard's critique is that the clergy are willing to fill this temporal role. That role, however, was not created by the clergy; they are not the origin of the problem. For that "[t]he responsibility actually lies with the state" (TM 53/SKS 14:190).[11] Still, the clergy have gladly become an arm of a nation whose aim is to provide a comfortable life for its citizens, which can be understood as a secure life both here and in eternity.[12] The clergy are but a part of a grand scheme of temporal welfare, a cog in the machine of bourgeois *joie de vivre*:

> When one sees what it means to be a Christian in Denmark, who would ever dream that it should be what Christ speaks about, a cross and agony and suffering, crucifying the flesh, hating oneself, suffering for the doctrine, being salt, being sacrificed, etc. No, in Protestantism, especially in Denmark, Christianity is sung to another tune, just as Jeppe sings, merrily, merrily, around, around, around—Christianity is the enjoyment of life, reassured as neither paganism nor Judaism was, reassured by having this matter of eternity settled, settled simply in order that we should really have the desire—to enjoy this life—as well as any pagan or Jew.[13] (TM 42/SKS 14:173–174)

The clergy play their part in this operation, and they play it well; Kierkegaard does not mock them on this score.[14] The only problem is that the part the clergy are playing has nothing to do with the suffering life of the true Christian. It has rather to do with the achievement of a comfortable temporal society, in this case known as Denmark.[15] The clergy have nothing to do with eternity; they are only functionaries of a project whose orientation is wholly

An Evolving Martyrdom 73

temporal, whose mention of eternity is only meant to secure a temporal happiness through the alleviation of anxiety. But the whole scheme—noble as it might seem in trying to make people happy—is a lie, a perpetuated illusion, insofar as it still claims the name of that religion of the other world, the religion of the next life—Christianity[16]—and assures citizens of the salvation of their souls.[17] Christendom is a sham. Now, what should be done about it? How should the public be converted? How should they turn themselves to God?

LEAVING CHURCH

Kierkegaard's initial goal in the first newspaper articles of the attack was only to register his objection against Bishop Mynster being declared a "truth-witness," and thus to make his protest known. It was essentially a matter of "language usage."[18] Eventually, however, Kierkegaard came to desire a certain effect from his writings, in fact the same effect he wanted *Practice in Christianity* to produce in Bishop Mynster,[19] only now vastly expanded. Namely, Kierkegaard wanted for there to be a confession or admission that the Christianity being lived in Denmark—both by the clergy and the laity—was not the Christianity of Jesus Christ or his followers. He wants everyone to "say forthrightly: We are incapable of being Christians in the New Testament sense" (TM 34/SKS 14:159).[20] Why?

> In order for it to be possible to say that the ordinary, the official Christianity here in the land even barely relates itself truly to the Christianity of the New Testament, it must first of all as honestly, candidly, and solemnly as possible be acknowledged at what distance it is from the Christianity of the New Testament and how incapable it is of being truly called a striving toward coming closer to the Christianity of the New Testament. (TM 39/SKS 14:169)

This kind of statement fits a pattern already in evidence in *Practice in Christianity*: Kierkegaard states the ideal, the reader is asked to confess that she has not met the ideal, subsequently this honesty is the context for the beginning of a new striving to meet the Christian ideal.[21]

At a certain point, Kierkegaard decides to break this pattern, calling not for a confession from the established church but for the consigning of the church to oblivion *via* its participants simply choosing to opt out: that is, to stop going. This break from the previous pattern does not happen all at once but evolves in three successive stages.

First, in the sixteenth newspaper article of the attack, Kierkegaard publicly admits that he has not been attending church. He makes this admission when responding to an ecclesiastical reprimand proposed by Dean Victor Bloch. The reprimand Dean Bloch recommends would include barring Kierkegaard from church. To this Kierkegaard responds with mock horror, "Horrible!" "What cruel punishment!" but also with the following important statement:

> Fortunately for me, however . . . the execution of the . . . punishment will not change at all a way of life I have chosen for Christian reasons and to which I have been accustomed for some time now. Thus, if the punishment is carried out, I will be able to go on living without noticing it any more than I here in Copenhagen notice that a man is beating me in Aarhus. (TM 56–57/SKS 14:197)

Essentially, the punishment proposed is to bar Kierkegaard from church, to which he responds: 'No need! I am not going anyway.' Thus, we see Kierkegaard's practical, personal commitment to his position: he, at any rate, is not going to attend this sham which calls itself church, even if that means he will not be receiving communion.[22]

The second stage of the call for abolition consists of Kierkegaard making a definitively negative judgment on the established order, one that seems no longer to hold out the previously extended possibility of confession:

> Now, however, I have completely made up my mind on two things: both that the established order is Christianly indefensible, that every day it lasts it is Christianly a crime; and that in this way one does not have the right to draw on grace. (TM 70/SKS 14:213)

Practice in Christianity, by contrast, was oriented by its relation to grace. In the thrice-repeated Preface, Kierkegaard states: "The requirement should be heard—and I understand what is said as spoken to me alone—so that I might learn not only to resort to *grace* but to resort to it in relation to the use of *grace*" (PC 7/SKS 12:15; emphasis original). Later, in "The Moral" to No. I, Kierkegaard again invokes grace: "'And what does all this mean?' It means that each individual in quiet inwardness before God is to humble himself under what it means in the strictest sense to be a Christian, is to confess honestly before God where he is so that he still might worthily accept the grace that is offered to every imperfect person—that is, to everyone" (PC 67/SKS 12:79). In the same newspaper article where Kierkegaard revokes the possibility of the recourse to grace, he says this about *Practice in Christianity*:

> If it were to come out now, now when both pious consideration for the late bishop has lapsed and I have convinced myself, also by having this book come out the first time, that Christianly the established order is indefensible, it would be altered as follows: it would not be by a pseudonym but by me, and the thrice-repeated preface would be dropped and, of course, the Moral to No. 1, where

the pseudonym turns the matter in a way I personally agreed to in the preface. (TM 69/SKS 14:213)

Notice, however, that there are two different considerations of confession which in this newspaper article are in danger of being collapsed: (1) there is the confession of the established order, which someone like Bishop Mynster could give as a representative of the established order; that is to say, if Bishop Mynster gave an individual confession, it would have importance not only for his own self, but for the entirety of the established ecclesial order, for Mynster is inseparable from (or symbolic of) the Danish Lutheran Church itself; (2) there is the confession of the individual qua single individual before God. Kierkegaard never revokes the possibility or importance of this second variety of confession, which a hasty reading of this newspaper article might lead one to believe.

The third stage of leaving church occurs when Kierkegaard publishes a small booklet titled *This Must Be Said; So Let It Be Said*. In this booklet, Kierkegaard takes the decisive[23] step of calling on others to join him in ceasing to participate in church:

This must be said; so let it be said:

> *Whoever you are, whatever your life is otherwise, my friend—by ceasing to participate (if you usually do participate) in the public divine service as it now is (professing to be the Christianity of the New Testament), you always have one and a great guilt less*[24]*—you are not participating in making a fool of God by calling something New Testament Christianity that is not New Testament Christianity.* (TM 73/SKS 13:115; emphasis original)

Rather than simply stating that he is personally not going to church, Kierkegaard is here asking others to join him in the refusal to participate: that is, the refusal to enter the church doors. This is quite a large change from the author who previously wrote: "I understand what is said as spoken to me alone" (PC 7/SKS 12:15) and "'And what does all this mean?' It means that each individual in quiet inwardness before God is to humble himself under what it means in the strictest sense to be a Christian, is to confess honestly before God where he is so that he still might worthily accept the grace that is offered to every imperfect person—that is, to everyone. And then nothing further" (PC 67/SKS 12:79). By contrast, Kierkegaard is now asking for a large-scale social protest: in essence, he is asking for a boycott of religion. There is nothing quiet, inward, or individual with respect to the actions Kierkegaard now requests of his audience.

The reason for this change seems to be connected to the previous step of development. Once Kierkegaard concluded that he could no longer extend the possibility of confession nor the related recourse to grace, he further concluded that not only was church not right for him, it was not right for anybody. Let's take a moment to further unpack Kierkegaard's reasoning here.

In *This Must Be Said; So Let It Be Said*, the reason for dismissing the possibility of the church making an admission or confession is further elaborated. Kierkegaard's analysis is now taking place at a structural level. The established church cannot simply admit its failure to meet the Christian ideal and, in the context of that failed striving, receive God's grace. No: the established church is itself a structure that rules out striving and the consideration of the ideal in the first place. Since there is no ideal and no striving in the established church, there can be no confession, either—for what is there to confess? Confession only takes place in relation to a recognized ideal. The established church actually therefore makes the reception of grace impossible,[25] in that—according to Kierkegaard—grace is only to be received within the context of striving.[26]

Therefore, Kierkegaard judges that Christendom makes the reception of grace impossible through its ability to completely obscure the requirement:

> If God by 'grace' nonetheless is to assume us to be Christians, one thing must still be required, that we, by being scrupulously aware of the requirement, have a true conception of how infinitely great is the grace that is shown us. 'Grace' cannot possibly stretch so far; one thing it must never be used for—it must never be used to suppress or to diminish the requirement. In that case 'grace' turns all Christianity upside down. (TM 47/SKS 14:179)

Grace is only relevant within the context of striving to meet the Christian ideal. It is a gift to the person who fails—but if there is nothing to fail at, there can be no gift. Ensnared in the illusion that all are Christians, ordinary people are not aware that there is a definition of "Christian" that they should be trying to meet (TM 157/SKS 13:205). Yet the very shape of the Christian life depends on getting this relation correct: ideal first, then grace (FSE 17/SKS 13:45–46).[27] If that relation is reversed, or if the first term of the relation is simply done away with, the result cannot be called Christianity. If there is no ideal for which one is striving, there is no imitation of Christ;[28] thus, there is no Christianity. This is the method by which Christendom has eliminated Christianity: it has muddied the concept of what a Christian is[29]—in other words, it has obscured the ideal—such that no one even knows she is failing to meet that concept, indeed no one has any impression of the truly Christian ideal whatsoever.[30] Thus, Christendom operates through conceptual obfuscation.

A confession of the ideal and the fact that it is not meeting it would seem to solve the crisis at which Christendom has arrived; such a confession, offered by the leading representatives of Christendom such as Bishops Mynster or Martensen, would restore the ideal to its proper place and enable honesty. Thus, it is clear why Kierkegaard would ask for a confession from the established order: he hoped for a confession because this would mean Christianity would be possible again without a wholesale destruction of the current order. So why did he change his mind? Why did Kierkegaard move from asking for a confession to giving up all hope with respect to the established church?

Though we cannot be certain, the shift in Kierkegaard's viewpoint is likely due in part to the fact that it seems the attack was not successful in generating a confession from either the clergy or the laity. That the attack *was not* successful means that the established order *was* successful in its efforts to obscure the ideal.[31] It has been and will continue to be—as long, it seems, as it exists—to successfully make Christianity impossible in Denmark.

The steps of the argument that depict the situation are as follows: (1) as is now clear, the established order will not confess that it fails to meet the ideal; (2) in order to maintain itself without confessing, it must obscure the ideal that it obviously is not meeting; (3) the resultant situation is a dishonesty that prevents striving because it will not openly admit what the ideal is. By the twentieth newspaper article of the attack, Kierkegaard is convinced that the situation he has described will not change. Though given an opportunity with *Practice in Christianity*, Bishop Mynster never confessed; neither will Bishop Martensen nor any of the rest of the established order. They have had their chance, and Kierkegaard has waited long enough. Now it is clear that the leaders and organizers of Christendom simply will not respond to Kierkegaard's accusations.[32]

Since a confession from the established order is no longer seen as possible, a different solution is necessary. Departure is that solution. The people must simply opt out of church. In short, Kierkegaard has given up a possibility he once held onto: defending the established order. Now, he is convinced that it must wither away if Christianity is to flourish once again (as in the age of the New Testament),[33] as Kierkegaard makes clear in the fifth issue of *The Moment*:

> According to Christ (who surely must be best informed about the way, since he is the Way) the gate is narrow and the way is hard—and few are they who find it. And perhaps the greatest cause of all for the smallness of the number, proportionately smaller with every century, is the enormous illusion that official Christianity has conjured up. Persecution, cruelty, bloodshed have certainly not done this kind of damage. No, they have been beneficial, incalculably beneficial, compared with the fundamental damage: official Christianity, calculated to serve human indolence, mediocrity, by leading people to think that indolence and mediocrity and pleasure are—Christianity. Do away with official Christianity, let persecution come—at the same moment Christianity exists again. (TM 200/SKS 13:251)

And so, Kierkegaard—writing in the moment—calls on the public to take action, or rather to take a specific kind of non-action. With *This Must Be Said; So Let It Be Said*, the attack ceases to exist in a purely theoretical mode of critique; Kierkegaard has moved into the realm of practical action, naming a specific act that he hopes people will perform.[34] This is asceticism in public,[35] and Kierkegaard is asking others to join in.

Still, the call is issued in a particularly Kierkegaardian way. Kierkegaard is careful to specify that he is not trying to become the *leader* of a public protest.[36] Rather, he wants each reader to make a decision for herself, having become consciously aware of the stakes of the decision through reading Kierkegaard's texts.[37] There is no departure from the Socratic here;[38] Kierkegaard is only a gadfly to the decision each individual must make.[39] This is a crucial insistence on Kierkegaard's part, for if the Danish people started following him they would make no progress at all past the very mindset that sustains the established order. That is, they would give in to a crowd mentality.[40] This is the mentality that prevents the necessary isolation before God which (according to *Upbuilding Discourses in Various Spirits*) stands at the beginning of Christian life. Following Kierkegaard instead of Martensen (for example) would simply result in a sectarianism which Kierkegaard detested just as much as the established order, inasmuch as sects offer an analogous life of comfort and ease.[41] There is honor and wealth in the sect, if on a lesser scale. Practicing asceticism in public must be each individual's choice, *coram deo*.

ABOLISH THE CLERGY

In 1851, Kierkegaard published an aforementioned newspaper article titled "An Open Letter," in which he disavows having ever advocated any external change. Kierkegaard insists that, on the contrary, he has only ever fought for "inward deepening," an internal change or renewal within single individuals; he has not argued for the disestablishment of the state church (COR 53/SKS 14:112). Obviously, by 1855 Kierkegaard has changed his mind on this issue. The change is for a particular reason, one that is not exactly a departure from his earlier position: namely, he is now convinced that the state church is capable—for the foreseeable future—of *preventing* internal change. Inwardness remains of paramount importance to Kierkegaard; it is only the conditions of inwardness that have changed. Now—at least for the majority of Denmark's citizens—those conditions include the absence of a state church.

Before turning away from the call to stop attending church, it is important to note again what has changed here. Nothing has changed with respect to Kierkegaard's theology, as Walsh alleges (and uses the allegation to dismiss these writings as being of lesser normativity); all the elements of Kierkegaard's theology tracked in chapter 1 remain essentially the same throughout the attack. Instead, what has changed is Kierkegaard's opinion with respect to how the established church of Denmark relates to that theology. To be more precise, Kierkegaard long thought there was a falsification in this relation; now, what has changed is that he is convinced that this falsification will remain as long as the established church remains. There is no longer a possibility of confession or admission.[42] This is not a theological judgment,[43] but a prudential judgment with respect to the possibility of a specific institution's ability to relate honestly to theological truth, and a conviction with respect to that institution's power to sustain a damaging illusion.

With this clarification noted, we must continue to follow the path of Kierkegaard's attack as it unfurls; there is in fact more to come. Kierkegaard's aim has moved from confession to abolition. We have in some sense already arrived at this point, since a mass movement of opting out of church would abolish the Danish People's Church, at least as it had existed up until that time. In that case, the people—the common man[44]—would let the establishment know that the game was up, that they now see through the illusion. At that point, Denmark could be called a "Christian nation" in only a very attenuated sense.

One might consider this a natural stopping point for Kierkegaard's evolving witness. He started with his own proclamation that he was no longer attending church. Now, he was asking others to join him in his witness. If successful in gaining mass adherents, the established church would cease to be established—at least, it would not be established in the same way, as the pillar of social morality, good order, and respect yoked to hierarchy.

However, this is not where Kierkegaard stops. He goes a step further. Kierkegaard had already exceeded his previous authorship by asking for an external change—namely, requesting that people cease attending church. Eventually, he goes yet further, asking not just for external change from individuals, but for a structural change in how Denmark and its church were organized. In other words, Kierkegaard began recommending a structural solution for what he had seen to be a structural problem.

That solution is a fairly simple one. Kierkegaard asks for the state to completely cease its financial support for the church; in short, he calls for the abolition of the clergy. This call initially occurs in *The Moment*, No. 2, where Kierkegaard describes the cessation of civically sanctioned and governmentally supported ecclesial positions as the second half of a twofold task:

> If Christianity is to be introduced here, then first and foremost the illusion must be removed. But since this illusion, this delusion, is that they are Christians, then

it of course seems as if the introduction of Christianity would deprive people of Christianity. Yet this is the first thing that must be done; the illusion must go.

This is the task; but this task has a double direction.

It is directed to what can be done to clear up people's concepts, to instruct them, to stir them by means of the ideals, through pathos to bring them into an impassioned state, to rouse them up with the gadfly sting of irony, scorn, sarcasm, etc., etc.

The task would not be something else if this illusion, that people imagine that they are Christians, if this illusion did not hang together with an enormously huge illusion that has a purely external aspect, the illusion that Christianity and the state have been fused together, that the state installs 1000 officeholders, whose interest, with the instinct of self-preservation, is that people do not find out what Christianity is and that they are not Christians. That is, the personal existence of these pastors is, Christianly, an untruth. Thoroughly secularized and in the service of the state (royal officeholders, personages of rank, career makers, etc.), they naturally are not in a position to tell the congregations what Christianity is, since to tell that would mean resigning one's state office.

Now, this illusion is different from that first one, which was related to people's conceptions, individual's entrapment in the delusion that they are Christians. With regard to this latter illusion, the work must be done in a different way; the state, after all, has the power to remove it. Thus the second aspect of the task is to work along the lines of getting the state to remove this illusion. (TM 107–108/SKS 13:149–150)

Here Kierkegaard, for the first time in print, begins to tease out two different issues. There are first of all the delusions and illusions that each person individually holds. Kierkegaard sees it as his own task to work to remove these; he is attempting to do so through the attack literature. Yet there is also a second issue. For even if Kierkegaard is successful in persuading some individuals that the established church is a harmful lie, that does not necessarily mean it will cease to exist. The state could continue to fund it regardless. Recognizing that this financial support will continue to operate in service of producing the delusions and illusions against which he is fighting, Kierkegaard therefore begins to take the step—even more unusual for him than asking his readers to take a specific external (in)action—of recommending governmental policy changes.

The solution reasonably presented in *The Moment*, No. 2 is then continued with more vehement rhetoric in following issues:

> This whole junk heap of a state Church, where from time immemorial there has been, in the spiritual sense, no airing out—the air confined in this old junk heap has become toxic.

. . .

> Let this junk heap tumble down, get rid of it: close all these boutiques and booths.
>
> . . .
>
> Yes, let it happen. What Christianity needs is not the suffocating protection of the state; no, it needs fresh air, persecution, and—God's protection. (TM 158/ SKS 13:206)

Going beyond asking for people to opt out of church attendance, Kierkegaard thus calls for a complete overhaul of the church's socio-ecclesial existence in Denmark. He does so because he believes the state's financial support has weakened Christian resolve, such that Christian dedication to eternity has been subsumed into the temporal interests of the state. Christianity thus needs to be set free of the seductive power of state support.

With this in mind, it is appropriate that Kierkegaard's attack began with criticism of Hans Lassen Martensen. Martensen's position on the matters just discussed was in fact diametrically opposed to Kierkegaard's:

> The Christian and specifically the Protestant State Churches rest on the presupposition that Christianity is a world religion and thus is able to be the center of the life of nations and states, the center for their moral and political, artistic and scholarly strivings and goals.[45]

According to Martensen, then, religion should "become the all-penetrating principle of the world in the large national masses."[46] Rather than the state enervating Christianity, luring it away from its true essence, Christianity instead depends on the nation for its existence; it is the nation that provides the surrounding context for Christianity to grow and infuse all aspects of human life. Martensen's thought is therefore a kind of ultimate endorsement of Christendom; he is saying that Christianity cannot really come into full existence until Christendom allows it to hold sway over every detail of human life. The Christian nation simply is Christianity, in the fullest sense of that word. Martensen's Christianity is inseparable from the life of Denmark as a nation.

In Kierkegaard's thought, by contrast, it is the nation that prevents Christianity's existence; for that reason, Kierkegaardian Christianity exists only in repudiation of the nation and the nation's goals. Kierkegaard asks the nation to release Christianity from its captivity; he asks for the dissolution of the state-church; he discards any possible positive role for the nation in determining the form of Christian life. The full significance of this point will become clear only later, in chapter 5, when discussing Kierkegaard's critique of Christian nationalism.

Asking for the state to cease its funding for the church completes the evolution of Kierkegaard's public martyrdom. This witness began with Kierkegaard's own refusal to go to church. He then asked others to join him in this protest. Finally, he pleaded for the nation to stop financially supporting the church. Each of these external actions was undertaken in newspapers and brief pamphlets, which were the most public venues of Kierkegaard's age. They were the form of mass media available to him. Just as Christ served as a public and irritating gadfly in the first century, so Kierkegaard analogously suffers in public as a witness against the world. Although the specific details of Christ and Kierkegaard's lives are quite different, the form of life—public martyrdom, serving as a witness to the truth in an environment which is hostile to it—is the same.

NOTES

1. See above, 44n7.
2. Helpfully collected and translated by Howard Hong in JP 3:2632–2668.
3. For example, in regard to the attack on Mynster, F. C. Sibbern (Professor of Philosophy at the University of Copenhagen) said "that S. Kierkegaard had here revealed himself to be a philistine" (*Encounters with Kierkegaard*, 201); see also the negative reactions of the elite recorded in chapter 1. This was not the beginning of Kierkegaard's social ostracization, however, which began in earnest after *The Corsair* affair: "After 1846 he was a dead man, socially speaking" (Garff, *Kierkegaard*, 418).
4. See Charles Marsh, *Strange Glory: A Life of Dietrich Bonhoeffer* (New York: Penguin Random House, 2014), 125.
5. See, e.g., TM 95/SKS 13:134: "to be obliged to proclaim what Christianity in truth is would of course be the same as opening people's eyes to the fact that the pastor's own existence is malpractice, that even if the teacher of Christianity receives something to live on, being a pastor cannot become a royal appointment, a career, and steady promotion."
6. See, e.g., Paul's litany of existential dangers in 2 Cor 11.23–33.
7. See TM 62–63/SKS 14:202: "[I]n a generation ruined by sagacity and lack of character, in which therefore also the pastors—how deplorable to earn money in this way—live off the delusion that all are Christians. On looking more closely, one might rather say that what they live off is this—the most deplorable way to earn money!—that the majority do not want the inconvenience or are unwilling to expose themselves to the civic troubles associated with acknowledging that they neither are nor imagine themselves to be Christians."
8. As Karl Marx, for example, does so effectively: "The Established Church, for instance, will more readily pardon an attack on thirty-eight of its thirty-nine articles than on one thirty-ninth of its income. Nowadays atheism itself is a *culpa levis*, as compared with the criticism of existing property relations" *Capital, Vol. 1* (London: Penguin Books, 1990), 92.

9. "If, however, it is assumed that making a living is what occupies the clergy, then the silence is quite in order" (TM 60/SKS 14:201), that is, "if one considers the clergy as a merchant class" (TM 61/SKS 14:201); from the context, it is clear Kierkegaard makes the referred to assumption and consideration.

10. This is why Kierkegaard can claim that *all* pastors are hypocrites: TM 253–258/SKS 13:309–314.

11. Cf. TM 164/SKS 13:212. Yet see also TM 112–114/SKS 13:154–156, where Kierkegaard tells a narrative of craven pastors duping the state in order to get its protection. Furthermore, even though the blame for the situation is placed on the state and pastors, there is also an element of *mundus vult decipi* with respect to the ordinary Danish citizen (TM 169–171/SKS 13:217–219).

12. See TM 185/SKS 13:235: "we are living paganism refined by means of eternity," and as applied especially to pastors see TM 198/SKS 13:249. By contrast, "Christianly the requirement is poverty" (TM 48/SKS 14:180). At every point, an ascetic interpretation of Christianity stands behind Kierkegaard's critical analysis.

13. Cf. TM 170–171/SKS 13:218–219.

14. See TM 53/SKS 14:190: "What I am writing certainly is not motivated by any hostility to the clergy. Indeed, why should I have such a hostility? To my mind, the clergy—if they are not supposed to be 'truth-witnesses'—are of course as competent, respectable, and worthy a class in society as any other. The theological graduate has entered *bona fide* into—well, it surely is something quite wrong he is entering into, but he has entered *bona fide*."

15. That Kierkegaard is thinking of modern and not medieval Denmark (and thus means something very specific by Christendom) is evident in TM 109–110/SKS 13:151–152.

16. See TM 312/SKS 13:374: "One certainly does not have religion for the sake of this life, in order to get through this life happy and well, but for the sake of the other life (*men for det andet Livs Skyld*); in this other world lies the earnestness of religion."

17. Kierkegaard brings up the matter of eternal judgment numerous times during the attack; see esp. TM 274/SKS 13:333, on "the accounting of eternity." It is clear that Kierkegaard wants to unsettle the assurance the state has provided its citizens regarding the status of their souls.

18. See TM 25/SKS 14:147: "It was the language usage (*Sprogbrug*), to call *witnesses, truth-witnesses* what we understand by pastors, deans, and bishops—it was the language usage I protested against because it is blasphemous, sacrilegious[.]"

19. See JP VI:6854/*Pap.* XI-3 B 15 (March 1854).

20. Cf. TM 113/SKS 13:155: the pastors of the present age are characterized by "faithlessness to the New Testament."

21. The one thing eternity's judgment cannot tolerate is dishonesty: TM 46/SKS 14:179.

22. See *Encounters with Kierkegaard*, 125–126. In this conversation with his good friend Emil Boesen (which took place on October 19, 1855), Kierkegaard says that he will take communion only from a layman, not a pastor, which—as Boesen indicates—was not really possible at the time. Kierkegaard's position is therefore effectively a refusal.

23. That Kierkegaard saw *This Must Be Said; So Let It Be Said* as a decisive turning point in the attack is confirmed by a piece in the first issue of *The Moment*, titled "*Addition to* This Must Be Said, *or How Is Something Decisive to Be Introduced?*" (TM 93–94/SKS 13:131); cf. TM 131/SKS 13:175, where Kierkegaard refers to the call to stop attending church as "these words that changed everything."

24. See TM 168/SKS 13:216: "Every hour that this order of things stands, the crime is continued; every Sunday divine worship service is conducted in this way, Christianity is made a game and a fool is made of God. Everyone who participates is participating in playing at Christianity and in making a fool of God, is involved in the Christian criminal case."

25. More precisely, Kierkegaard states that if it is possible to make Christianity impossible, Christendom has done so: "what the state has done and is doing amounts to making, if possible, Christianity impossible; and this can be explained very easily and very briefly, because the factual situation in the country is actually this, that Christianity, the Christianity of the New Testament, not only does not exist but, if possible, is made impossible" (TM 95/SKS 13:133). Whether it is possible or impossible to make being a Christian impossible, Christendom has at least succeeded in this: Christianity does not in fact exist. Furthermore, we can know for certain that the established order is invested in "hindering Christianity" (*ibid.*), and it has been successful in fact if not, perhaps, in the order of possibilities as well. For these reasons, the situation is intolerable for Kierkegaard no matter which side of the above equation (possible or impossible to make Christianity impossible) is actually the case.

26. In this way, the Christendom that the established order supports actively damages the everyday person, who is prevented from realizing the truth. On this matter of "damage," see TM 29/SKS 14:151: "But what use is it—and even if it were ever so pious and well-intentioned—what use is it to want (lovingly?) to strengthen you in the delusion that you are a Christian, or to want to change the conception of being a Christian, presumably so that you are able to enjoy this life all the more securely; what use is it, or more correctly, must this not simply damage you, since it will help you to allow temporality to be unused Christianly—until you stand in eternity, where you are not a Christian if you were not one[.]"

Hugh Pyper formulates this dynamic of confession in Kierkegaard quite beautifully: "What Kierkegaard constantly promotes for his readers is the message that only by admitting our despair can we hope to be caught up in a joy that is grounded in the eternal and changeless love of God" (*The Joy of Kierkegaard* [Sheffield: Equinox, 2011], xii). This admission of despair is precisely what the established order cannot do. As the promoters of earthly happiness, the members of the established order must themselves be (or appear to be) happy.

27. 'Ideal first, then grace' may seem like a straightforward application of Luther's law/gospel dialectic. Though it bears some formal similarities, this is not the case, as Lee Barrett points out: "[Kierkegaard] departs from Lutheran tradition by using the example of Christ to convict the individual of sin, rather than by using the Ten Commandments or natural law, as has been the case in the older theological heritage. . . . Kierkegaard feared that those less rigorous ethical norms discoverable by reason and enshrined in the Old Testament had been co-opted by Christendom to lower moral

standards to a level that most moderately decent citizens could attain, thereby fostering the self-flattering illusion of holiness" (*Eros and Self-Emptying*, 337).

28. For "imitation" in the attack literature, see TM 129/SKS 13:173: "[O]fficial Christianity is a falsification that solemnly assures that Christianity is something else entirely, solemnly declaims against atheism, and by means of this covers up that it is itself *making* Christianity into poetry and abolishing the imitation of Christ (*Christi Efterfølgelse*), so that one relates oneself to the prototype (*Forbillede*) only through the imagination but oneself lives in totally other categories"; cf. TM 133, 135, 321, 322–323/SKS 13:177, 178, 383, 385. According to TM 316–317/SKS 13:378–379, Christendom is what happens in order to replace the imitation of Christ.

29. Kierkegaard writes of his task: "It is directed to what can be done to clear up people's concepts, to instruct them, to stir them by means of the ideals" (TM 107/SKS 13:149). This is opposed to the pastors employed by Christendom: "the state installs 1000 officeholders, whose interest, with the instinct of self-preservation, is that people do not find out what Christianity is and that they are not Christians" (*ibid.*; cf. TM 133/SKS 13:177).

30. See, e.g., TM 143/SKS 13:187–188:

Christianity is related inversely to number—when all have become Christians, the concept 'Christian' has dropped out [. . .]

[S]tate and Christianity are inversely related to or, indeed more correctly, away from each other.

But this becomes difficult to understand in 'Christendom,' where one quite naturally has no intimation of what Christianity is, and where one could least of all hit upon the idea or, if it is stated, get it into one's head that Christianity has been *abolished* by *propagation*, by these millions of Christians in name only, the number of which presumably is supposed to cover up that there is no Christian, that Christianity does not exist at all.

31. See especially TM 257–258/SKS 13:313–314. Yet if Christendom was so successful, how then did Kierkegaard discover the deviation from the ideal in the first place? By means of his rare "detective talent" (TM 40/SKS 14:169).

32. Kierkegaard places the responsibility for the maintenance of the situation of Christendom squarely on the shoulder of elites (leaders and organizers generally, but especially Heiberg, Mynster, and Martensen [KJN 5:37–39/SKS 21:39–41])—an attribution he explicitly models on Christ (TM 136/SKS 13:180). In the twenty-first newspaper article, "On Bishop Martensen's Silence," for example, Kierkegaard exalts the "common man" while denigrating the "demoralized pastors" and "corrupted upper class" (TM 84/SKS 14:220); he then goes on to claim that "what keeps the establishment going is the 1000 royally authorized teachers, who maintain the established order in the capacity of stockholders" (TM 85/SKS 14:220). At one point, Kierkegaard also states that his aim is to save the people "from becoming guilty of a crime in which the state and the pastors have actually implicated them" (TM 97/SKS 13:135). Furthermore, he believes that it is still possible that the people or laity will make a confession, even after he has concluded that (for pecuniary reasons) the established order will never do so (*ibid.*). Cf. further TM 111, 245/SKS 13:153, 301.

33. This is also reflected in the fact that the terms of the confession change in *The Moment*, No. 2. Here, a true verbal confession would necessarily entail a simultaneous resignation from one's office (TM 107/SKS 13:150). Thus, a true confession by all the members of the People's Church of Denmark would immediately result in the non-existence of that church.

34. Kierkegaard later expresses disappointment with those who theoretically agree with his attack, but—practically speaking—continue going to church as is their custom. See TM 259–261/SKS 13:315–317.

35. The specific aspect of *askēsis* at work here is renunciation, which is especially apropos if one thinks of church attendance as procuring social benefit in Golden Age Denmark.

36. See TM 76/SKS 13:122: "But also do not misunderstand me as if I intended in any way, if from the side of the government such measures are taken against me, to counter-demonstrate if possible by means of a popular movement—certainly not. I am so far from this that I understand it as my task to avert such things as much as possible, I who have nothing at all to do with popular movements but, if possible, purer than the purest virgin in Denmark, am kept pure in the separateness of singleness"; cf. TM 197/SKS 13:248–249.

37. See TM 59/SKS 14:198: "What I point out is precisely that which is to the pastor's interest to conceal, suppress, tone down, omit. If you have no other knowledge of what Christianity is than at most what you receive by hearing the pastor, then you can be rather sure that you will go on living kept in complete ignorance of what is not convenient for official Christianity"; TM 73/SKS 13:115: "This must be said; I place no one under obligation to act accordingly—for that I do not have authority. But by having heard it you are made responsible and must now act on your own responsibility as you think you can justify it before God." Though he did not want to become a leader, it is clear Kierkegaard was convinced his texts could have an awakening effect on his readers: see especially TM 58/SKS 14:198, where Kierkegaard bids his readers to "read my articles often." Readers could get something from him that they could not get anywhere else (see TM 73/SKS 13:116), given the clergy's investment in suppressing the truth.

38. Contra J. Michael Tilley, "Christendom," KRSRR, Volume 15, Tome III, 210, who claims that at a certain point Kierkegaard gives up on the Socratic. In *The Moment*, No. 10—published posthumously, though Kierkegaard finished drafting the issue before his death—Kierkegaard writes, in an entry titled "My Task": "The only analogy I have before me is Socrates; my task is a Socratic task, to audit the definition of what it is to be a Christian—I do not call myself a Christian (keeping the ideal free), but I can make it manifest that the others are that even less" (TM 341/SKS 13:405). Tilley is only correct if one limits the Socratic task only to reintroducing Christianity into a still existing Christendom; clearly, however, Kierkegaard himself did not limit his task in such a way. The destruction of Christendom was still a Socratic task, in that it relies on individuals realizing that what is claimed to exist and represent the good on earth is in fact an illusion.

39. In this way, Kierkegaard never departs from his program of indirect communication, as developed in his authorial works and also the outline for his never-

completed "Lectures on Communication," where in 1847 he writes: "To help a person relate themselves to God is seriousness. But it must be done indirectly, for otherwise I become a hindrance to the one being helped" (JP 1:649 / *Pap.* VIII-2 B 81).

40. On the concept of "the crowd" in Kierkegaard, see Leo Stan, "Crowd/Public," in KRSRR, Vol. 15, Tome II, 107–114.

41. See FT 79–80/SKS 4:170–171.

42. Walsh does recognize this as the specific changed element in the attack literature: "What is different is the fact that he has now given up on the church as an institution, finding it completely indefensible and encouraging others to join him in ceasing to participate in it" (*Kierkegaard*, 198).

43. Perhaps it would be if there were a robust ecclesiology operative throughout Kierkegaard's earlier authorship, but such is not the case. This does not mean he has no theory of the church (on which see Walsh, *Kierkegaard*, 191–192), only that it is far from an essential element of his theology. The church community is always secondary to the encounter with God and is by no means necessary to Christian life.

44. On Kierkegaard and the "common man," see Jørgen Bukdahl, *Søren Kierkegaard and the Common Man* (Eugene, OR: Wipf and Stock, 2001 [1961]).

45. Hans Lassen Martensen, "The Present Religious Crisis," tr. Jon Stewart, in *KSYB* 2017, 430. "The Present Religious Crisis" is a concise apology for the Danish State Church, written against the influence of David Friedrich Strauss and the growing popularity of Anabaptist "sects" in Denmark. It was published in 1842.

46. Martensen, "The Present Religious Crisis," 433.

Chapter Four

Asceticism in the Streets

KIERKEGAARD: AN ASCETIC LIFE?

Kierkegaard attacked Christendom not only with his writings, but also with his life. We have seen Kierkegaard's ascetic definition of Christianity as developed in *Upbuilding Discourses in Various Spirits*, *Works of Love*, *Practice in Christianity*, and *For Self-Examination* (chapter 1), and how this definition was carried through and even enabled the attack literature (chapters 2 and 3). Now, I attempt to answer the question: how close did Kierkegaard himself come to embodying this ascetic ideal?

There is a danger here of collapsing into historical curiosity. After all, since Kierkegaard's ascetic ideal is an ideal, one should be able to compare this ideal to the life of any human person. So why should we look to Kierkegaard in particular? The justification here lies in the fact that Kierkegaard was attempting to appropriate the ideal he himself had articulated in his writings. Looking at his life can therefore give a more concrete articulation with respect to what the ascetic ideal looks like in modernity, even if we can still detect moments of incongruity between Kierkegaard's own life and the content of the ideal.

The question of how closely he himself hewed to the ideal is a topic that Kierkegaard himself reflected on in the attack literature. On the one hand, there is the Socratic refusal to equate his own life with the Christian ideal, which crops up even in the last (posthumously published) issue of *The Moment* (TM 340–347/SKS 13:404–411). On the other hand, even before the attack, Kierkegaard indicates that he believes he has—at least to some extent—appropriated the ideal he has written about so extensively.[1] What is it about his life at this point that supports such a belief? Because Kierkegaard provided little justification for this newly positive judgment, we cannot know for sure, but supplemental evidence from what we know of his own life can help us to see how he actively shaped his life toward the ascetic ideal found in his writings.

There are several dimensions of Kierkegaard's daily life which approach a traditional ascetic ideal. We can begin with how he used his wealth. In his meticulously researched book *Kierkegaards København*, Peter Tudvad documents how Kierkegaard gave a good deal of his money away to those impoverished members of Copenhagen who asked for it.[2] We can add further that Kierkegaard spent a good deal of his own money publishing his books;[3] and since he considered the writing and publication of these books part of a task given to him by God, this money should be seen as in some sense dedicated or sacrificed by Kierkegaard to God's action in the world.

Kierkegaard's life as a single man can be taken as further evidence of his ascetic commitment. He lived a single life of prayer, devout exercises, reading,[4] and self-examination. Although his original reason for breaking off his engagement to Regine Olsen may not have been (or not only have been) a strict adherence to Christian asceticism,[5] in the attack literature Kierkegaard openly and vehemently argues for the correctness of a Christian commitment to celibacy,[6] even sounding at times like Christianity's most vociferous opponent of marriage, John Chrysostom.[7] It is important to acknowledge that his life matched this argument, whatever the original reasons for his single life may have been.

A further word on this point: Kierkegaard's commitment to celibacy does not actually have much to do with abstaining from sex. It is rather tied up with his rejection of the typical bourgeois path to happiness, which in his age included marriage and family. It is Kierkegaard's rejection of this whole style of life—with its attendant commitments to sensible, salaried work as well as a broader acceptance of the comforts his society provided (comforts, it should be recalled, which relied upon extractive colonialism)—that is at stake in his commitment to singleness.

As we have seen in chapter 1, Kierkegaard's theology of divine encounter—found in *Upbuilding Discourses in Various Spirits* and *Works of Love*—entails an openness to God's call which gives its recipients a task. Those who remain true to this task obey God's will for their life, and inevitably suffer as a result of their faithfulness. A life of obedience is a suffering life, as one takes the ideality of one's task into the reality of this world. In the attack, we can see a mirroring of this theology of faithful, obedient Christian life in Kierkegaard's own existence.

How so? Throughout his life, what Kierkegaard enjoyed most was writing.[8] Kierkegaard luxuriated in the well-formed sentence and precisely chosen word, and he would dedicate whatever time was necessary in order to achieve these writerly perfections.[9] Yet in the attack, Kierkegaard renounced these enjoyments in order to write in a different way, and he did so because he believed God was calling him to do so. Writing "in the moment" was a discipline for Kierkegaard, a practice of *askēsis*, which he did not enjoy but considered his duty (TM 91/SKS 13:129–130). Kierkegaard conceived of the attack on Christendom as an act of obedience to a divine call.

Furthermore, just as Kierkegaard's ascetic theology would predict, the reaction to his following of the divine call was persecution. True, Kierkegaard was not martyred. But he was mocked and ostracized.[10] In this mockery, he suffered martyrdom as it takes shape within a reflective and passionless age.[11] In Kierkegaard's self-understanding, he was "fighting for eternity" and suffering the inevitable temporal consequences of such a battle (TM 313/SKS 13:375). In spite of this, Copenhagen's greatest peripatetic remained in his city to the end of his life.[12]

Taking these elements together and analyzing them, we can affirm that Kierkegaard to some extent lived the ascetic life he advocated. This is, furthermore, an ascetic life that bears affinity to earlier ascetic Christian lives. To those familiar with traditional monastic literature, the parallels I have drawn above to earlier articulations of Christian asceticism will already be clear: Kierkegaard's life follows a pattern of poverty, chastity, and obedience.

In addition to these broad historical-ascetic resonances, more distinctive elements of Christian asceticism are also on display: namely, Kierkegaard insists on practicing his asceticism in public, and he suffers for such practice. In this sense, there are parallels between Kierkegaard and a movement like the 14–16th century *devotio moderna*. The Modern Devout lived as monks-in-the-city. They practiced their asceticism before others, and it was precisely this that irritated their fellow late medieval urbanites. Kierkegaard understood the separated space of the medieval cloister to be a kind of cop-out, an effort to avoid the difficult suffering that practicing one's asceticism before the world entailed (CUP 405–419/SKS 7:368–381). There is no evidence members of the *devotio moderna* felt this way about the Benedictines and Cistercians of their age, but regardless, their form-of-life ends up in close parallel to Kierkegaard: without taking formal vows, both Kierkegaard and the Modern Devout lived lives of intense devotion within an urban context and considered this to be a witness to the surrounding public (a witness this public did not particularly appreciate).

It is not typical to consider Søren Kierkegaard an ascetic in this traditional sense. The work which comes closest to doing so is Noreen Khawaja's *The Religion of Existence: Asceticism in Philosophy from Kierkegaard to Sartre*.[13] However, Khawaja uses *askēsis* in a Foucauldian rather than a traditional sense. By using the label of 'asceticism,' Khawaja means to refer to how

Kierkegaard sees self-development as a task or discipline which one must choose to take up, a theme which is then inherited by the existentialists Jean-Paul Sartre and Martin Heidegger. I believe Khawaja is correct in her analysis; Kierkegaard is an ascetic in this sense, too. However, it is not this meaning of the word I am using here. I intend to say Kierkegaard is an ascetic in a way like unto earlier Christian ascetics; his life demonstrates poverty, chastity, obedience, and other ascetic virtues in addition.

KIERKEGAARD AND THE *DEVOTIO MODERNA*

As mentioned, it is not typical to understand Kierkegaard as an ascetic. He has been labeled an existentialist, a dialectical theologian, a philosopher of religion, a mystic, and a virtue ethicist; rarely has he been labeled an ascetic. Precisely because it is not typical to consider Kierkegaard in this fashion, it is necessary to argue for my contention at greater length. If successful, this label will have importance for the next chapter, when I place asceticism and nationalism in opposition to one another. In what remains of this chapter, I will attempt to establish my contention that Kierkegaard is an ascetic by delving deeper into one traditional ascetic movement—the aforementioned *devotio moderna*—excavating their ascetic practices to a greater extent, and then using this description to reinforce the parallel practices in the life of Kierkegaard which we have already noted. The argument will thus take this shape: if we agree that the members of the *devotio moderna* were ascetics, then we must also agree that Kierkegaard was an ascetic.

First, we must argue precisely for that initial point, namely that the *devotio moderna* was an ascetic movement in the traditional sense of the word. It is true that in critical scholarship the Modern-Day Devout are at times labeled 'mystics' instead of 'ascetics.'[14] There is a measure of accuracy in this label, in that some members of the *devotio moderna*—such as Gerard Zerbolt (1367–1398)—wrote mystical works,[15] and mystical tendencies were never formally proscribed among the Devout. At the same time, as the premier English historian of the *devotio moderna* John Van Engen has noted, the overall tendency of the life and writings of the *devotio moderna* is oriented toward asceticism, not mysticism.[16] Furthermore, the founder of the *devotio moderna*, Geert Grote (1340–1384),[17] writes as follows: "An ascetic life is an extraordinary good and one necessary for us and for all men,"[18] and Salome Sticken (1369–1449), a first generation Sister, admirably and self-consciously sums up this distinction: "Most beloved sisters, to sense and to taste the sweetness of the Lord God is highly delightful, but the foundation of all sanctity lies rather in complete self-denial, mortification of the evil affections in our corrupt natures, and the conversion of our will to the Lord[.]"[19] Rather than emphasizing rest, ecstasy, and divine union (as predecessors such as Meister Eckhart, Marguerite Porete, and Jan Ruusbroec had done), the Devout focused on action,[20] suffering, and discipline.

With this matter of classification dealt with, we can turn to the characteristics of the form of life lived by those participating in the *devotio moderna*. The Devout way of life is above all characterized by nine practices: refusal of vows, celibacy, poverty, renunciation, reading, exercises, self-examination, living an urban life, and undergoing persecution.

Refusal of Vows. Though they lived lives of indigence, celibacy, and humility, the members of the *devotio moderna* did not take formal monastic vows of poverty, chastity, and obedience; theirs was "a resolution to live religiously apart from the recognized religious orders."[21] The Devout's refusal to take vows was one of their most distinctive attributes, and it frequently occasioned opposition. For the Devout, living a disciplined life of service to God outside of vows was the most perfect form of life. In holding to this judgment, they challenged the authority of Thomas Aquinas, who taught that acts undertaken in obedience to vows were more meritorious than acts freely chosen, on account of the virtuous displacement of the self that occurs in obedience to external, formal vows.[22] For the Devout, on the other hand, acts freely chosen have more merit than deeds done in obedience to an external authority, and this for two reasons. The first has to do with a conformity to the divine nature that happens only in free acts; as John Pupper of Goch (d. 1475) states, "humans conform more closely to the divine will the more they act in freedom of will."[23] Second, lack of vows is intimately connected with the Devout's understanding of the nature of conversion, which is continual. According to the Devout, there is not one specific moment—as presumably there is in monastic life—in which one definitively leaves the world. Rather: "Life turned on a resolution and continuing conversion in an act of willing love[.]"[24] The 'founding father' of the Devout, Geert Grote, wrote "resolutions not vows,"[25] and he renewed these resolutions daily. The *devotio moderna* was a life of perpetual striving. The truly devout Christian, it was thought, would not escape into the surety of vows, but instead faced the difficult task of daily conversion.

Celibacy. Though they took no vows of celibacy, both the Brothers and Sisters of the Common Life lived single lives.[26] This further assimilated the members of the *devotio moderna* to monastic forms of life, though—as they still lived within the city—the refusal of sexual activity was not necessarily perceived as holiness by the wider public. Instead, at times it was seen as an attempt to benefit from civic life without making due contributions to it.[27] Celibacy is therefore connected to the animosity directed at the Devout.

Poverty. The Modern-Day Devout held all possessions in common. In fact, this is the explanation of another of their monikers, the 'Brothers and Sisters of the Common Life.' When an individual joined the Devout, she or he agreed to renounce all personal possessions, gifting them over to the specific house being entered. Furthermore, proceeds from the goods the Devout produced (mainly textiles from the women, hand-copied manuscripts from the men) went to the house, not to the individual laborer. The Devout did not beg, nor did they seek out large ecclesiastical benefices or donations. Instead, they labored and then shared the proceeds in common, with each house generally making enough for its survival, and little more. The life that resulted was not one of complete destitution, but a kind of self-sustaining poverty[28] at a communal level and complete lack of possession on an individual level.[29]

Renunciation. Devout lives followed two general patterns of renunciation, divided by gender. Men renounced successful clerical careers—the social climbing that was possible in the late medieval church, gaining multiple benefices and important political connections on the path to an altogether comfortable life (comparatively), free of the drudgery of *ponos*.[30] Women renounced successful marriages: a typical young woman entering the Sisters of the Common Life could have made a good marriage for herself, thereby entering the upper echelons of society, but chose not to do so. Also, many older women, oftentimes widows, renounced the management of their significant homesteads or estates in order to join the Devout.[31]

These patterns were not true of all the members of the *devotio moderna*. Yet they did happen, and they provide a kind of template for the ideal member of the Devout. She or he is there, in the house, by choice, and that choice involved the giving up or renunciation of other options that were meaningfully attractive to the average inhabitant of the late medieval world.

Reading. Though not all the Devout were literate, those who were (including both Brothers and Sisters) typically read every day for their own upbuilding.[32] They developed reading lists and libraries suitable to this task, typically focusing on the desert fathers, Augustine, Gregory the Great, and modern authors such as Bernard of Clairvaux (and others in his vein, like Henry of Suso and Jan Ruusbroec);[33] they generally eschewed scholasticism.[34]

Alongside this daily practice of reading, the Devout rejected any reading that took the activity as an end-in-itself. The purpose of reading, according to the Devout, was growing closer to God and further from the world and the self. Reading was conceived as simply a means, and reading that forgot its end was mistaken reading. Possibly the most well-read of the Devout, Gerard Zerbolt, puts this point with admirable clarity:

> The means [i.e., reading and meditation] we ought so to order in our hearts as will best serve to advance us toward the end of purity and love; when they

obstruct this end, they are to be abandoned. For we should not be so insistent upon reading and meditation that, should clarity be required, we leave them only with murmuring and sadness, thus incurring the impurity of sadness or some other evil which was supposed rather to be uprooted by sacred reading or meditation. We should never be so totally fixated upon such exercises as we are upon their end.[35]

Reading was for spiritual upbuilding; anything outside of this purpose was secondary, at best a byproduct of the practice. Such a rigorously exclusive definition of the end of reading puts reading for the purposes of knowledge under the ban. The pursuit of knowledge could easily become distracting and self-aggrandizing, according to the Devout.[36] Knowledge was beside the point; growth in love and purity was all.

Exercises. Every day, each member of the Devout set aside time to perform what they called "exercises." In a typical exercise, sisters and brothers brought the suffering Christ before their minds and attempted to affectively identify with his passion.[37] These exercises were key to the imitation of Christ as it was practiced in the *devotio moderna*. For now, it is enough to note that this practice was both crucial and basic to the Devout,[38] as it was in one's daily exercises that an individual connection with Christ was established.[39]

Self-examination. Alongside the exercises that enabled that connected the Devout to Christ, they practiced a rigorous self-examination meant to identify all the ways they were still refusing a connection with Christ. According to Van Engen, the way of the *devotio moderna* was characterized by "relentless self-examining and self-disciplining";[40] "self-examination and self-knowledge" were "the touchstone of their whole conversionary endeavor."[41]

We can see the truth of Van Engen's observations by looking at the representative example of Salome Sticken, who writes in her "Way of Life for Sisters":

> Each hour you should also look into yourself to examine your progress or decline, carefully reflecting on what gladdens or saddens you, what you love, what you hope in. Each evening as you sit before your bed, carefully scrutinize how you spent the preceding day, confessing to the Lord and humbly bemoaning your faults and failures and making a firm and strong resolution to make amends.[42]

Three attributes of the Devout practice of self-examination can be gleaned from Sticken's directions. First, the frequency of self-examination was indeed "relentless," as Van Engen puts it; Sticken bids her readers to practice it "each hour." Second, one is to examine the self not simply for obvious external misdeeds, such as breaking one of the Ten Commandments or neglecting liturgical observance. Instead, a kind of psychological analysis is recommended: a practice well-suited to the development of the inwardness so central to Devout life. In other words, during the time of self-examination one does not simply ask oneself if one has read the daily hours, one asks if one has read one's hours with attention, feeling the jubilation in words of praise and the contrition in words of confession.[43] Through constant self-scrutiny,[44] the Devout aimed to order their loves and achieve a true conversion inside and out.[45] Third, since this conversion was never fully achieved in this life,[46] self-examination was always to be oriented toward confession.[47]

Urban life. The Modern-Day Devout renounced marriage, property, and social advancement in order to devote themselves to quiet lives of reading and pious exercises, thereby in a significant way removing themselves from "the world." However, the Devout did not physically leave "the world" as traditional medieval monastics often did, the latter physically removing themselves from society, living a cloistered life at some distance from any inhabited city. Instead, the Devout practiced their disciplined lives of renunciation right in the middle of cities.[48] This was frequently construed as challenging the average lay person's piety, questioning the religious status of the every-day citizen of a medieval city. In a time where a comfortable spatial exclusion generally reigned between the estates of the perfect and the worldly (with Benedictine and Cistercian monks living secluded lives, protected from contamination by the city), the Devout upset spatial boundaries and—quite understandably—irritated other members of their society.

Persecution. The members of the *devotio moderna* practiced their renunciation before others, in the midst of the city. For some members of late medieval society, this was attractive: they joined the new movement, or sent their children to be educated by these earnest souls. For others, it was not. The Devout were persecuted. None were burned at the stake, as the aforementioned mystic Marguerite Porete (d. 1310) was. However, the very existence of several of the Devout communities was persistently under threat. Papal inquisitors threatened to use police force to shut down Devout houses.[49] Though ultimately unsuccessful, such attempts meant that Devout life was lived under the sign of precarity. Beyond overt hostility like the forced cessation of common life, persecution of the Devout often took the 'softer' form of mockery.[50] Sisters and Brothers of the Common Life were portrayed as holier-than-thou, as overly serious do-gooders whose ascetic practices took all the fun out of city life.[51] Yet whether the response was mockery or a more physical threat, one thing is clear: the asceticism of the Modern-Day Devout—practiced as a witness right before the eyes of late medieval city life—angered people, and the groups were often disliked.

AN IDEAL PARTIALLY REALIZED:
THE BODY AND SOCIETY IN THE MODERN AGE

A typical argument[52] against Kierkegaard being considered an ascetic is that he was not a monastic and indeed he explicitly critiqued medieval monasticism: "The error in the asceticism of the Middle Ages was that it dropped the suffering that is specifically Christian: suffering at the hands of hum. beings. The ascetic permitted peop. to venerate him as: the extraordinary" (KJN 11:399/SKS 27:690 [September 23, 1855]). The fact that the medieval monk cloistered himself away from the world aided this relation of admiration: the 'average Christian' admired the ideal as it was embodied someplace far away—a relation of distance which did not in fact require anything of the 'average Christian,' and even eased the requirement for the 'average Christian' insofar as they knew somewhere someone was embodying the ideal, thus they did not have to do so, since surely this way of life was not required of everyone. In this way, Kierkegaard is critical of cloistered medieval monasticism.

It is true that Kierkegaard did not live a cloistered life; nor did he take vows. He was not a medieval monastic, and he was in fact critical of medieval monasticism. However, our excavation of the form of life evident in the late medieval *devotio moderna* movement shows that Kierkegaard still fits within a pattern of traditional Christian asceticism, even though he did not take vows nor live in a cloister. Kierkegaard's poverty and celibacy are matched by a life devoted to the obedience of God even apart from vows. He renounced a life of advancement in the church, read spiritual works assiduously and for the purposes of self-reformation, and spent a great deal of time in self-examination if his relentlessly introspective journals are any indication. As far as urbanity goes, he never lived anywhere other than the city of Copenhagen, even when he became a bit of a laughingstock during *The Corsair* affair. Furthermore, as the attack preeminently demonstrates, Kierkegaard was clearly not afraid to make a public witness.

This is not to say Kierkegaard fits perfectly within a pattern of medieval asceticism. Take, for example, Vilhelm Birkedal's sighting of Kierkegaard during his last months:

> On another occasion I met him in a restaurant. He sat in front of no small portion of food fit for a king and a very large goblet of sparkling wine. At that point he had begun his stern polemic against "official Christianity," and I then saw for myself that he did not apply to himself this "dying away from the world" or this (at any rate bloodless) martyrdom, which he continually preached for us others and which he made the hallmark of the genuine Christian witness—because what he had prepared for himself here was a quite generous enjoyment of the world.[53]

It seems that Kierkegaard's life as an aesthete did not end with his (relatively) wild youth. Yet even in exceptions such as this, there is still continuity: he is, even at this moment of sensory delight, experiencing the scorn of the Copenhagen establishment precisely because of his attack on the church. Even while enjoying a lavish meal, at a different level Kierkegaard is still at this very moment practicing a renunciation which generates persecution. Furthermore, it is precisely this test which Kierkegaard himself considered most important when evaluating the success of one's renunciation: namely, whether it was causing hatred toward oneself. Beyond renunciation of respectability and of church office, the other traditional elements of poverty, chastity, and obedience—even if they are not perfectly embodied—are also playing a role here, specifically as witnesses to Kierkegaard's rejection of the Golden Age. Even if Kierkegaard enjoys the occasional lavish meal, there are many reasons he is hated; and these reasons have to do with his embrace of practices we have shown to be in line with traditional asceticism, specifically as it is manifested in the late medieval *devotio moderna*.

Considering the traditional elements of asceticism and Kierkegaard's own test of renunciatory witness, we can now offer a concluding assessment of Kierkegaard's asceticism. At the end of his life, Kierkegaard embodies the double danger he spoke of earlier in *Works of Love*. Yet he only does so to a certain extent. He is not martyred but dies of natural causes. Evaluating Kierkegaard according to his own categories, this means that there must have been some aspect of selfishness or self-preservation that kept Kierkegaard from being so offensive to his contemporaries that they would kill him. The very fact that he was not martyred speaks, in Kierkegaard's mind, to the fact that his embrace of Christian asceticism was not a full one. Thus, despite the growing affinity between Kierkegaard's life and what he sees as the Christianly ideal life, there is still a distance, and this distance explains why Kierkegaard continues to understand himself in a Socratic way, even in the last weeks of the attack. Essentially, he is confessing that he is only defining the ideal; he is not yet living it.

NOTES

1. See, e.g., KJN 6:127/SKS 22:130, where Kierkegaard positions himself "above" Johannes Climacus, but "below" Anti-Climacus.

2. Peter Tudvad, *Kierkegaards København* (Copenhagen: Politiken, 2004), 370–377.

3. See KJN 4:6/SKS 20:8: "whereas other authors do earn a bit of royalties with their books (even if it is always rather meager), I have actually had to spend money, so that my proofreader has literally earned more than I have"; though see Garff,

Kierkegaard, 514–519, for some doubts with respect to Kierkegaard spending much money in this way.

4. On Kierkegaard's reading habits, see Millay, *You Must Change Your Life*, 6–7, and Barnett, *Kierkegaard, Pietism and Holiness*, 63–109.

5. For analysis of the complicated causality surrounding Kierkegaard's broken engagement to Regine, see Kierkegaard's own reflections in *Notebook 15* (KJN 3/ SKS 19).

6. TM 186, 246–249/SKS 13:236, 302–303. I therefore agree with Daphne Hampson's supposition: "I find it not too far-fetched to think that Kierkegaard was one of those individuals who in effect had a love affair with God, making celibacy essential" (*Christian Contradictions: The Structures of Lutheran and Catholic Thought* [Cambridge: Cambridge University Press, 2001], 270).

7. See John Chrysostom, *On Virginity, Against Remarriage* (New York: Edwin Mellen Press, 1983), with an extensive introduction from Elizabeth A. Clark.

8. See Thomas J. Millay, "Writing," in KRSRR, Vol. 15, Tome VI, 275–276.

9. See, e.g., KJN 4:23–24/SKS 20:25.

10. *Encounters with Kierkegaard*, 90–92; Garff, *Kierkegaard*, 417–418; cf. KJN 4:122/SKS 20:122, where Kierkegaard records that the mockery he is experiencing as a result of *The Corsair* affair is like being slowly "trampled to death by geese[.]"

11. "If Christ were to come to the world now, he would perhaps not be put to death, but would be ridiculed. This is martyrdom in the age of reason. In the age of feeling and passion people were put to death" (KJN 5:178/SKS 21:171).

12. See the description of an English visitor to Denmark, Andrew Hamilton: "Kierkegaard's habits of life are singular enough to lend a (perhaps false) interpretation in his proceedings. He goes into no company, and sees nobody in his own house, which answers all the ends of an invisible dwelling; I could never learn that anyone had been inside of it. Yet his one great study is human nature; no one knows more people than he. The fact is *he walks about town all day*, and generally in some person's company; only in the evening does he write and read. When walking, he is very communicative, and at the same time manages to draw everything out of his companion that is likely to be profitable to himself" (*Encounters with Kierkegaard*, 96).

13. Noreen Khawaja, *The Religion of Existence: Asceticism in Philosophy from Kierkegaard to Sartre* (Chicago: University of Chicago Press, 2016).

14. They were so understood by some of their contemporaries: see Van Engen, *Sisters and Brothers*, 37–44. For a modern example, see Bernard McGinn, who in *The Varieties of Vernacular Mysticism (1350–1550)* (New York: The Crossroad, 2012) includes the *devotio moderna* in his survey, though he does qualify his assessment: he speaks of mystical "aspects" of the Devout (96–124), and writes: "The adherents of the movement were intent upon apostolic renewal in an age of moral and spiritual laxity; they were not directly concerned with fostering mystical contact with God. Insofar as a sincere attempt to live a more authentic Christian life aims at a deeper sense of the reality of God's presence, however, the Devout never excluded the possibility of mystical states, even of union with God, though they tended to say less about these than they did about ascetical and moral practice" (96).

15. See his "The Spiritual Ascents," *Devotio Moderna*, 243–315; see further Van Engen, *Sisters and Brothers*, 239.

16. See especially Van Engen, *Sisters and Brothers*, 79: "Where mystics threw themselves finally into the spiritual abyss and onto the favor of God, their nothingness sinking into God's all, the Devout called upon urban neighbors to take charge of their souls, to remake their inner powers and affections, like an expert craftsman. For them the energy was to go into recrafting rather than escaping or transcending the self; hence, making the turn, taking up the resolve, doing the exercises, checking on one's progress"; "The Modern-Day Devout were consistently wary of the perfect life conceived as a free and limitless emptying into God, transcending penance and discipline" (28); cf. *Sisters and Brothers*, 303.

17. Henricus Pomerius, writing ca. 1420, calls Grote the "fons et origo modernae devotionis in Bassa Almania inter canonicos regulares" *Vita B. Joannis Rusbrochii*, Cap. VIII, *Analecta Bollandiana* 4 [1885], 288—a claim that has not since been disputed, so far as I am aware.

18. *Devotio Moderna*, 97.

19. *Devotio Moderna*, 184.

20. See Grote's comment, *Devotio Moderna*, 99: "Yet exercise of the mind is pointless, devoid of all honor and purpose, if it does not lead and compel us to labor in the things of Christ and to bring them to completion with confession of the mouth and imitation in deed." For the Devout, meditation was always oriented toward action.

21. *Devotio Moderna*, 15.

22. Thomas Aquinas, *Summa theologica*, II-II q. 88 a. 6. The Devout's resistance to Aquinas was explicit: see Van Engen, *Sisters and Brothers*, 252.

23. John Pupper, *De quatouor erroribus circa legem evangelicam exortis et de votis et religionibus factciis dialogus*, ed. Christian W. F. Walch in *Monumenta Medii Aevi* 1.4 (Göttingen, 1760), 121; cited and trans. Van Engen, *Sisters and Brothers*, 252; cf. 265.

24. Van Engen, *Sisters and Brothers*, 260; cf. 311, "For the Devout, however, life turned on intention and interiority, personal resolves continuously sustained over time as a form of life," and also 314: "Apart from vows they worked all the harder to set up a self-instituted communal poverty based on New Testament Jerusalem and to discipline themselves into chastity and to humble themselves in loving obedience to one another. . . . Zerbolt first, John Pupper too, insisted that higher merit accrued to religious life only by way of interiority, acting in freedom."

25. Van Engen, *Sisters and Brothers*, 12.

26. Van Engen, *Sisters and Brothers*, 1–2.

27. Van Engen, *Sisters and Brothers*, 214.

28. The anonymous "A Customary for Brothers" (written in Zwolle, ca. 1415–1424) recommends giving away all excess income, such that the continual labor that characterized Devout life would always be required (*Devotio Moderna*, 171).

29. On all this see Van Engen, *Sisters and Brothers*, chapter 5, "Inventing a Communal Household: Goods, Customs, Labor, and 'Republican' Harmony," 162–199.

30. On *ponos* (drudgery, manual labor), see Peter Brown, *Treasure in Heaven: The Holy Poor in Early Christianity* (Charlottesville: University of Virginia Press, 2016).

31. See the example of Lady Zwedara: Van Engen, *Sisters and Brothers*, 58.

32. See Van Engen, *Devotio Moderna*, 24: "A certain portion of the day was set aside for edifying reading and self-examination in private."

33. See Grote's list, *Devotio Moderna*, 70; cf. Van Engen, *Sisters and Brothers*, 7–8, 241; *Devotio Moderna*, 25, 47.

34. See, for example, the following resolution of Grote: "Avoid and abhor every public disputation held simply to score a triumph or to make a good appearance, such as all those disputations of the theologians and artists in Paris" (*Devotio Moderna*, 68).

35. *Devotio Moderna*, 256.

36. See the remarks of Gerard Zerbolt, *Devotio Moderna*, 288: "Note, fourth, to what end you read. Certainly your principle intention, as in all your exercises, ought to be purity of heart, not vanity or the pursuit of knowledge alone. The point is not so much that you learn something but rather that it profit you and others through you"; cf. Van Engen, *Devotio Moderna*, 26; and see further Van Engen, *Sisters and Brothers*, 276.

37. The anonymous author of "On the Life and Passion of Our Lord Jesus Christ, and Other Devotional Exercises" (ca. 1391) recommends meditation on a different aspect of Christ's passion on every day of the week except Sunday (the latter is reserved for meditation on the resurrection) (*Devotio Moderna*, 190–196).

38. See Van Engen, *Devotio Moderna*, 29.

39. See especially *Devotio Moderna*, 188–190; here it is emphasized that she or he who does not 'exercise' is inwardly dead, bearing no connection to the source of life, Christ.

40. Van Engen, *Sisters and Brothers*, 6.

41. Van Engen, *Sisters and Brothers*, 294.

42. *Devotio Moderna*, 178–179; cf. Van Engen, *Sisters and Brothers*, 295–296: "Self-examination thus served as a kind of *basso continuo* that underlay and sustained nearly all other spiritual and communal exercises among the Modern-Day Devout."

43. See *Devotio Moderna*, 23–24, 71–72, 176.

44. Recommended as well by Thomas à Kempis: "Have always an eye to thyself" (*The Imitation of Christ* [New York: Harper and Brothers, 1943], tr. Richard Whitford [c. 1530], 39).

45. On the ordering of loves, see also Grote, *Devotio Moderna*, 65: "I intend to order my life," putting "no temporal good of body, position, fortune, or learning ahead of my soul's salvation."

46. See Van Engen, *Sisters and Brothers*, 260; *Devotio Moderna*, 28.

47. See Van Engen, *Sisters and Brothers*, 290–296.

48. According to Van Engen, the Devout lived "a lifestyle consciously set apart, yet lived out in the midst of urban society and parish routines" (*Sisters and Brothers*, 2).

49. See Van Engen, *Sisters and Brothers*, 200–237.

50. See, for example, *Devotio Moderna*, 44.

51. See the experience of Young Egbert: Van Engen, *Sisters and Brothers*, 2; cf. 173, 207.

52. The claim that Kierkegaard is critical of (rep: asceticism is made, for example, by David Coe) in KRSRR Vol. 15, Tome I, "Asceticism," 105–108. He does not, however, use the label "ascetic" in the same fashion as I will; Coe's particular referent is medieval monasticism.

53. *Encounters*, 107.

Chapter Five

Kierkegaard's Critique of Nationalism Reconsidered

THE ATTACK TODAY

Up to this point, *Kierkegaard and the New Nationalism* has been dedicated to historical investigation, attempting to answer questions like: What is the socio-political context for Kierkegaard's attack upon Christendom? How does the attack work, conceptually speaking? Through what specific steps does the attack unfold, in terms of what Kierkegaard asks his audience to do? Finally, might Kierkegaard's life also be understood as a kind of attack upon Christendom?

Answering such questions is an important task if we are to gain a more complete understanding of the attack on its own terms. However, even an exhaustive response to each of the above questions would not solve the problem mentioned in the Preface: namely, the relative neglect of the attack in current Kierkegaard scholarship. That neglect has its source in a laudable concern, as Kierkegaard scholars wish to give attention to those aspects of Kierkegaard's writings which can still be of use for us today. Because we are considering a thinker who put a major emphasis on existential appropriation,[1] such a concern seems legitimate and even internally necessary if we are to do justice to our topic. Yet it is precisely this concern which has caused the attack to be neglected. The general understanding is that these late writings in which Kierkegaard rejects church and embraces pessimism cannot possibly be of use for us anymore. The Kierkegaard who is a Christian thinker for our time is the Kierkegaard of *Fear and Trembling*, *Concluding Unscientific Postscript*, and *Works of Love*—not the Kierkegaard of "'Take an emetic!'"

Therefore, it is not necessarily a lack of historical knowledge about the attack which has caused its neglect in Kierkegaard scholarship. It is instead the conviction—whether explicitly stated, as in Walsh, or implicitly endorsed via neglect—that the attack is too extreme or bizarre to be helpful to the contemporary task of appropriating Christian truth amidst our own configuration of Christendom.

The remainder of this book is dedicated to undermining the assumption that the attack is irrelevant. Instead, I will argue that the attack is the most relevant portion of Kierkegaard's entire authorship for us, and it is so because of our current situation. That situation is one of resurgent nationalisms.

For example: Christian nationalism is resurgent in Bolivia. This is evident in the recent saga of Jeanine Áñez, interim president of Bolivia from November 2019 to January 2020. The United States should not consider itself special in having a president who weaponizes the bible. Áñez's ascension to the presidency suggests otherwise. After holding an enormous bible during her November 2019 speech declaring herself Bolivia's president, Áñez proceeded to the balcony of the Casa Grande del Pueblo in La Paz, where she brandished a smaller, pink-covered bible while declaring: "Power is God" (*El poder es Dios*).[2] Áñez's earlier career as a senator was marked by an anti-indigenous sentiment which had a religious element to it, in that she characterized some indigenous rituals as "satanic."[3] This anti-indigenous sentiment would characterize her brief presidential reign as well. The message of Áñez and her supporters was clear: God had granted them victory, and the wicked who stood up for the rights of non-Christian persons and thus allowed non-Christian influence in Bolivia—such as former president Evo Morales—were now being overcome by the righteous. In other words, Áñez's reign was a sign that the Christian God was becoming victorious, specifically over and against other gods. Although Áñez is no longer president (Áñez was arrested in March of 2021, and as of June 2021 her future has yet to be decided), her ascendancy speaks to the forceful currents of Christian nationalism in Bolivia, which transcend Áñez's own particular political career.

Hindu nationalism is resurgent in India. Christians should not believe they are unique; nationalism is not confined to Christianity. It seems the urge toward self-assertive dominance can weave its way into virtually any cultural system. Led by Prime Minister Narendra Modi and first coming to rule in 2014, the Hindu nationalist Bharatiya Janata Party is described by Angana P. Chatterji, Thomas Blom Hansen, and Christophe Jaffrelot as pushing a platform which "combines cultural nationalism and political strategies aiming at flagrant social dominance by the upper castes, rapid economic development, cultural conservatism, intensified misogyny, and a firm grip on the instruments of state power."[4] This political platform of self-assertion is based in Hindutva ideology, which the authors summarize as follows: "this ideology looks at Hindus not primarily as practitioners of a diverse faith tradition, but as a people descending from ancestral sons of the soil, the 'Vedic fathers.' In the ideological repertoire of Hindutva, the people are not defined only as the victims of the elite but in cultural terms as the true autochthons and owners of the land."[5] Thus identification with the label "Hindu" is shifted from a complex, content-rich association of devotional practices to blunt authoritarian claims regarding ownership of land and the right to rule.[6] These claims are intricately connected to the BJP's suppression of minority subjects, such as Adivasis and Dalits.[7] Modi and the BJP also rely on stoking fear with respect to Pakistan in order to solidify their grasp of power. In fact, the general tenor of the BJP is anti-Muslim in character: this is the greatly feared Other that brings the different factions of Hindu nationalists together, thereby achieving a successful, violently imposed hegemony.[8]

Bald assertion and celebration of power, alongside suppression of minority groups, are elements we have already seen in Bolivian Christian nationalism. In India's resurgent nationalism, power and suppression is married together with a gutting of the content of a traditional religion, replacing it with a kind of identity token which has little if anything to do with the scriptures or worship practices of the religion in question. Unfortunately, this whole complex of degradation is being repeated element-by-element in the United States of America.

White Christian nationalism is resurgent in the United States of America. As Andrew L. Whitehead and Samuel L. Perry argue in a crucially important sociological study, white Christian nationalism in the United States replicates all the characteristics we have seen as typical of nationalism thus far, while also possessing its own particular spin.[9] Utilizing data collected in the Baylor Religion Survey, Whitehead and Perry argue the following three points.

(1) Christian nationalism is all about power.[10] For whites in the U.S., this has the specific valence of hanging on to a position of control that is felt to be newly threatened.[11] This threat is not only domestic, but also international. The election of the forty-fifth president was seen as an opportunity "to fortify America's supremacy among other nations, which they believed to be rooted in fidelity to Christian principles and values."[12]

(2) This seizure of power entails the suppression of minority groups, especially Black, Hispanic, and Muslim peoples. For example, survey data shows that "the probability of agreeing that refugees from the Middle East pose a terrorism threat increases in lockstep with Christian nationalism";[13] hence, the policy goal of reducing or even eliminating refugee resettlement in the U.S. It is particularly in this suppressive activity that the whiteness of U.S. Christian nationalists manifests itself. Rather than explicit invocation of 'white power,' connections are made between minority groups and criminality: "Christian nationalists associate out-groups with character deficiencies and seek severe penalties on them so as to maintain order."[14] Furthermore, who is 'in' and

who is 'out' of the group is coded according to race, even when skin-color is not explicitly mentioned. Historically, the prevalent belief in the U.S. has been "that *real* Americans are native-born white Protestants. This ideology has been wholly preserved in contemporary Christian nationalism."[15] White self-assertion is crucial to Christian nationalism as it is found in the U.S.

(3) The religion of white Christian nationalists has little to do with the traditional content associated with Christianity. White Christian nationalism has to do with allegiance; it does not have to do with moral values sourced from Scripture. Indeed, "Christian nationalism is rarely concerned with instituting explicitly 'Christ-like' policies, or even policies reflecting New Testament ethics at all."[16] And what do Whitehead and Perry mean by this? "Christian nationalism . . . is unrelated to taking care of the sick and needy and consuming fewer goods. In fact, Americans who embrace Christian nationalism are *less* likely to believe actively seeking social and economic justice is important to being a good person."[17] In one of their study's most fascinating insights, Whitehead and Perry find that—when it comes to most issues—the less often you attend church, the more likely you are to align with Christian nationalism.[18] Although, perhaps this should not be surprising, given the content of the New Testament.

Whitehead and Perry's study thus provides detailed support for concluding that the pattern seen in other nationalisms is present in the U.S. as well. Nationalism is all about the self-assertive embrace of power, which exercises itself via suppression of minority groups, in abstraction from the actual content of the religion whose name it has commandeered.

Nationalism is resurgent across the globe. My specific context is the United States of America, and in this chapter I will be speaking primarily to this context. Whitehead and Perry's book is thus essential background for what follows, especially with respect to how exactly white self-assertion expresses itself in the United States. However, as one can see from the brief examples given above, it is certainly the case that similarities hold across contexts; analogies can be drawn from one nationalism to another, and therefore my hope is that this material can serve as a provocation for resisting nationalisms in a variety of contexts. In my understanding, if there are philosophical or religious resources a culture can muster which promote self-denial and undermine self-assertion, such resources can be used to engage in a struggle similar to the one found in Kierkegaard and promoted in this book.

KIERKEGAARD'S CRITIQUE OF CHRISTIAN NATIONALISM

In the situation of resurgent nationalisms described above, we also find critical philosophers, theologians, historians, sociologists, and others doing what they can to inspire resistance, from Jill Lepore's attempt to return Americans to democratic civic ideals in her book *This America* to a stream of articles by Achin Vanaik documenting the dangerous crisis that is Modi's politics,[19] to mention only two examples from a wealth of material. Scholarship on the Danish philosopher-theologian Søren Kierkegaard actually arrived early to this movement of resistance writing, thanks to Stephen Backhouse's pathbreaking 2011 book *Kierkegaard's Critique of Christian Nationalism*.[20] If Backhouse is correct and Kierkegaard is a critic of nationalism, perhaps he can say something of use to our current predicament. I do believe Backhouse is correct: Kierkegaard was a critic of Christian nationalism, and there is plenty of evidence to corroborate this contention. I also believe Kierkegaard has a specific and relatively unique message for us as we attempt to resist nationalism in the present moment. The goal of this chapter is to ground these beliefs in argument.

As an entry point for such an argument, I begin with how Backhouse has attempted to establish Kierkegaard as a critic of nationalism. After engaging with Backhouse's illuminating text, I will then suggest that our interpretation of Kierkegaard's critique of nationalism may need to shift or develop, given how the phenomenon of nationalism has further revealed its nature in the time elapsed since the 2011 publication of Backhouse's book.

So, let's turn to Stephen Backhouse and his effort to establish Kierkegaard as an opponent of nationalism. *Kierkegaard's Critique of Christian Nationalism* follows a clear tripartite structure. First, Backhouse defines nationalism. Then, he provides examples of nationalists contemporaneous to Kierkegaard. Finally, he shows how several major themes in Kierkegaard's authorship—such as the moment, the leap, contemporaneity, and Kierkegaard's philosophies of history and identity—undermine the nationalism of his contemporaries.

Given its fundamental importance for my contentions in this book, it will now be useful to walk through the three parts of Backhouse's book a bit more closely. It is a text eminently worthy of attention—even if, ultimately, I argue that we have to expand our consideration of nationalism beyond Backhouse's.

(1) First, Backhouse's definition of nationalism. When defining nationalism, Backhouse limits his object of inquiry to Christian nationalism in particular. He sets out a definition early in the text, stating: "By Christian nationalism, I mean the family or set of ideas and assumptions by which one's belief in the development and uniqueness of one's national group (usually accompanied by claims of superiority) is combined with, or underwritten by, Christian theology and practice."[21] This is a fairly straightforward and uncontroversial definition, combining elements of historical development, uniqueness, and nationality superiority, all supported by a kind of Christianity. In short, Christian nationalism is what happens when Christianity is tied to the

greatness of a specific nation, such that the greatness of the nation and its Christianity are seen to go in tandem with one another. This is a helpful and accurate definition; it is also fairly vague. Backhouse's treatment of particular Christian nationalists' contemporary to Kierkegaard helps to further explain what exactly such a nationalism would look like.

(2) Thus, we can ask: if nationalism is such a problem for Kierkegaard, as Backhouse is claiming, then what are some contemporaneous examples of thinkers he is reacting against? Here Backhouse gives us two excellent chapters, one on Hans Lassen Martensen and the other on N. F. S. Grundtvig. These are among the most eye-opening chapters of the book. If you know something of Kierkegaard's thought going into these chapters on his contemporaries, it all of a sudden becomes clear how Kierkegaard's whole project undermines exactly these types of thinking that support a nationalistic modernity. Let's walk through these illuminating chapters in turn.

Hans Lassen Martensen's nationalism is predicated upon a Hegelian philosophy of history, where the progression of history is equated to the unfolding of a divine logic. For Martensen, history is not one damn thing after another, nor is it cyclical; instead, it has a teleology: history is headed toward the creation of "unity" or "right relations" "between Creator and created."[22] The world doesn't just start out this way, with this unity or right relationship with God; rather, it evolves into it. As Backhouse summarizes, "Man was not created with the full capacity to enjoy union with God, and it is only in the development of history, with the growth of culture, religions and ethics, that mankind has come to the place where true relationship with God is possible."[23]

Crucial to this evolutionary development that has made union with God possible is the existence of nations. For Martensen, one cannot relate to God as a single individual without at the same time being embedded in a society that supports that individual relationship. Christianity is nothing without culture. Its existence in the world is dependent upon its influence on laws, education, and national missions. There can be no Christianity without society; society is the key point of mediation between God and the individual human being.[24] Since in modernity societies appear as nations, the nation is necessary to the existence of Christianity. Without the nation, there is no way for Christianity to realize itself in the world; unless Christianity makes itself actual in the concrete life forms of a nation, it does not make itself actual at all. Correlatively, the nation cannot reach its true purpose without Christianity: for the nation's true purpose is to instantiate in every concrete form of life a unity with God's will, and the God whose will this is has been revealed in Jesus Christ.[25] God's hand upon history is revealed in the existence of Christian nations who make actual God's will in the world.[26] Consequently, to act against a Christian nation is to act against the force of God realizing itself within history. In this sense, to act against Denmark is to act against God. The progression of history has made Christian life possible through the existence of the nation. Denmark, and being Danish within Denmark, is therefore what salvation looks like. Just the same, being German within Germany is what salvation looks like for Germans, and likewise for the English; the point is not Denmark in particular, but the fact that Christian life is only possible within Christian nations, who are the hope of the world, or the hope for the world: that is, they strive toward the full realization of unity with God upon this earth, presaged in the scriptures in a place like Revelation 21:1–6. In sum, God's will for humanity and the flourishing of Christian nations is one and the same.

N. F. S. Grundtvig (1783–1872), on the other hand, was not so sanguine about multiple nations being vehicles for God's will on earth. Instead, he proposes that Denmark has a special mission, a unique appointment from God. This moment in history is the moment for the "North" (by which Grundtvig means Denmark). It is the moment for the North to seize its destiny, so that it can show other nations what it means to embody the will of God in the world.[27] And it is precisely Denmark's emphasis on its own vernacular-popular language and culture as the means by which a people connects to God that is its gift to the rest of the world. As it becomes more and more popular, Grundtvig's program of "Menneske først og Kristen så," or human first and then Christian,[28] will teach the whole world that one becomes a Christian not through denying one's nationality or abstracting from one's place on earth, but through a full-blooded embrace and life-giving affirmation of one's language and culture as unique openings for God's action upon earth.[29] In short, if being Christian requires being human first, then being Christian requires a nation, because there is no human without the nation; the nation is what gives the human humanity, through language, through land, through dances, through mythology—through the whole complex of things summarized by the word "culture"—in Danish, "Dannelse."

Though Martensen and Grundtvig have their differences, Backhouse rightly emphasizes their broad similarities. The two key concepts Kierkegaard will contradict are held by both Martensen and Grundtvig: first, that history progresses and as it progresses it reveals a reason or logic given to it through the plan of God, and second, that God acts in the world through the mediation of the nation, rather than directly with individuals.

(3) As already hinted, Kierkegaard vigorously combats Martensen and Grundtvig's brands of nationalist theology. He does not often do so through an explicit naming and rejection of nationalism, as Backhouse readily admits. Yet he undermines every theological and philosophical tenant that supports

the nationalism of Martensen and Grundtvig. Crucial to Kierkegaard's antinationalist thought is his philosophical and theological category of "the moment," which receives a detailed exegesis from Backhouse.

Kierkegaard's understanding of "the moment," developed especially in *The Concept of Anxiety*, can be briefly summarized.[30] The moment is Kierkegaard's theory of how eternity enters into time: namely, it happens in a succession of discrete instants,[31] where eternity intersects and "touches" time. So far, this might not sound too promising as a ground for resistance to nationalism. But this is precisely why the context building in chapters 2 and 3 of *Kierkegaard's Critique of Christian Nationalism* (where Backhouse engages Martensen and Grundtvig) are so crucial: they help us to see just how far-reaching the implications are of Kierkegaard's theory of "the moment." For if eternity enters into time in a series of discrete moments, touching but not becoming an immanent part of temporality, that means the whole historical scheme of both Martensen and Grundtvig is bankrupt. It means that God is not revealed through the progression of historical movements; there is no ultimate significance, Christianly speaking, to the modern development of the nation.[32] When you add to this rejection of historical progression Kierkegaard's stipulation that the moment can only happen in an individual who has placed herself before God, we can see the totality of Kierkegaard's refusal, for if it is only individuals who connect to God through the moment, then membership in a specific culture plays no special role in forging unity with God. Thus, achieving unity with God may indeed be the purpose of life on earth, as Martensen avers, but such unity does not happen as he thinks it happens. It does not happen through the mediation of the nation and that nation's cultural and societal institutions; it happens in immediate encounter with the Divine.

According to Kierkegaard, we meet God in the moment, as individuals.[33] And the God we meet is the same God who has appeared in the Incarnation in the person of Jesus Christ. The moment is not an empty category, nor is it purely negative in its effects. There is a certain content generated when eternity touches time, and the perfect translation of that content into a holistic human life is Jesus Christ. He is what it looks like when eternity touches time. Thus, as a temporal being through whom the eternal is manifest, the person of Christ is crucial to sparking the encounter the rest of us temporal beings have with the eternal God.

This spark of encounter happens when we make ourselves contemporaneous with the person of Christ.[34] Here again, context is crucial to grasping why such an understanding of Christ and our relation to Christ resists nationalism. For Martensen and Grundtvig, Christ's Lordship is manifested through Christianity's successful achievement of world-dominance in the course of the development of history. For Kierkegaard, Christ's lordship has nothing to do with this world-historical perspective; Christ's lordship is only available in the moment of encounter which happens when we make ourselves contemporaneous to the eternal manifested in Jesus' life. We are not united with God as a result of being part of a culture that mediates God's truth to earth through its laws, civic institutions, and educational programs, but only through encounter with *this* person who was manifest on earth at *this* time in *this* way.[35] Eventually there is yet more content added to this stipulation of encounter with Christ in the moment; we will return to that content later. For now, I would like to highlight what I think Backhouse believes Kierkegaard's Christology achieves, which is to interrupt the modes of identity formation evident in Martensen and Grundtvig with a radically other method of identity construction, wherein one's nation has nothing to do with the realization of unity with God.

Having arrived at this point of identity formation, it is useful to pause, step back, and comment on the general method of Backhouse's book as a critique of Christian nationalism, asking the question: How does Backhouse's Kierkegaard go about critiquing nationalism? I propose that Kierkegaard critiques nationalism in two distinct ways, one that is made primary in Backhouse's account, and another that remains secondary. Here I focus on Kierkegaard's primary mode of critiquing nationalism in Backhouse's book; later, I will introduce the secondary method.

For Backhouse's Kierkegaard, the primary mode of critique is a critique of identity construction. Thus, Backhouse's Kierkegaard refuses the methods of nationalistic identity construction popular at the time and evident in Martensen and Grundtvig. And not only does he refuse these nationalistic identity constructions as invalid, he also substitutes his own method of identity construction *via* the moment, which can replace those false methods of identity construction. Another way to put this is to say that when we reflect rigorously on the founding documents of Christianity, we find that nationalistic identity constructions—which rely on conceptions of Christianity that identify it with triumphant nations embodying the will of God in the world—are essentially false myths which cannot withstand an investigation that questions their basic premises, that queries whether the Christ the nations endorse is the same Christ revealed in the Gospels.

Insofar as it endorses Kierkegaard's approach, Backhouse's book is primarily an attempt to undermine nationalism through the method of identity critique. This places his book within a category established by earlier critics of nationalism, such as Ernest Gellner and Eric Hobsbawm, and most paradigmatically Benedict Anderson.[36] Anderson's now classic text *Imagined Communities* is a thorough historical investigation of how national identities were constructed. In short, Anderson shows that nationalisms always rely on fictive constructions of ethnic pasts which are inevitably untenable when one takes the time to actually investigate their claims. By demonstrating that what various nationalisms claim to be natural and ancient is actually fictive and modern, Anderson deconstructs the basic position of a whole host of nationalisms. What we find in Anderson is therefore criticism of nationalism *via* identity critique. I propose that Backhouse's book exists in the same category as Anderson's: in looking closely at how Christian nationalisms have been constructed through a betrayal of actual Christianity (an actual Christianity recovered by Kierkegaard), Backhouse shows how Christian nationalisms rely on a false mythology that cannot be harmonized with Christianity as it actually is.

If this is a correct reading of his text, then what Backhouse accomplishes in *Kierkegaard's Critique of Christian Nationalism* is simultaneously brilliant and problematic. It is brilliant in its creative application of Kierkegaard and critical theological discourse within an approach to the critique of nationalism that (in Gellner, Hobsbawm, and Anderson, for example) has generally not seen theology as a possible resource for critique. It is problematic in that it is not clear that the method of identity critique as a way to criticize nationalism actually works anymore, given how nationalism has revealed itself since the publication of Backhouse's book.

THE "NEW" NATIONALISM

Backhouse's text was published in 2011. If one is attentive to the continuing manifestations of nationalism, I believe new aspects of the phenomenon have become apparent since that time. These new aspects problematize the standard mode of the theoretical critique of nationalism (viz., via a critical examination of identity construction). How so?

To answer that query, we must begin with the question: How has our understanding of nationalism developed since 2011? As a window into how nationalism has freshly revealed its nature since the publication of Backhouse's book, I will turn to two instances of the phenomenon: first to the media production of Richard Spencer and second to white evangelical Christianity as analyzed by Kristin Kobes du Mez. Obviously, these two sketches will result in a limited treatment of the new nationalism. A full exposition would require (at least) an entire book. I have also chosen to focus on my North American context, even though—as noted—resurgent nationalism is a worldwide phenomenon. Despite these limitations, an initial consideration of the new nationalism remains worthwhile, both because of its (sadly) burgeoning popularity and because of the way it newly inflects modes of resistance.

Richard B. Spencer (b. 1978) is famous for popularizing the term "alt-right." I begin by registering some hesitation about choosing to include Spencer in this account. I do not wish to give him too much credit, as if he were some kind of genius übermensch creating new values (which he certainly is not) or pretend that he is as popular now as he once was (which is also not true[37]). With these qualifications in mind, Spencer is still a useful figure if one wishes to come to an understanding of the new nationalism.

What makes Spencer worthy of a modicum of attention is his particular approach to nationalist identity construction. In part, Spencer is a traditional ideologue: you find him writing grandiose narratives of the "facts" that support nationalism, such as in his piece "Race: Stalking the Wild Taboo," published in 2017;[38] those facts being that there is such a thing as a purely white European racial heritage and that it produced a glorious history that we need to recover (etc., etc.). On the other hand, Spencer is occasionally not a traditional nationalist ideologue dispensing supposed facts. For example, when it is pointed out to Spencer that nationality and ethnicity are fictive constructed realities—when you, for example, note that the idea of a racially homogenous Roman empire or medieval Europe is complete garbage—Spencer will respond not by disputing your facts, but will say something like, 'Well, we all need a mythology to empower us.'[39] This kind of double-speak—of saying one thing and then winking at it whilst simultaneously affirming it on a practical level as useful (even if it is a 'fiction')—all this is typical of what makes the so-called "alt-right" a more 'intellectual' version of nationalism.

I bring up Spencer and the alt-right not because they are popular. Christian nationalism is indeed quite popular in America, as Andrew Whitehead and Samuel Perry have recently shown.[40] But the alt-right is different than typical Christian nationalism and has a negligible allegiance in comparison; we will turn to this more typical variety in a moment. I bring up Spencer and the alt-right not because they are popular, but because they are revelatory. In Spencer's dismissal of all challenges made on historical grounds, white nationalism is revealed for what it is: namely, naked self-assertion that can cloak itself in a number of guises, whether simplistic claims of 'facts' or more sophisticated postmodern philosophical maneuvers. Nationalism is all about self-assertion, and Richard Spencer has (perhaps unwittingly) revealed it to be so. Self-assertion as a basic motivation then bleeds into the language typical of nationalism, such as greatness and dominance. Nationalism is about the accruing of power; any constructions that support it (such as fictive historical narratives) are incidental to the essence of the phenomenon. Thus, criticisms of nationalism which only take aim at what is constructed upon this core of self-assertion do little to challenge what is motivating the whole discourse operation of nationalist ideologies.

The alt-right is a revelatory movement, but it is limited. It is not nearly as popular as Christian nationalism itself. The difficulty with studying more popular branches of Christian nationalism is that they do not always self-identify as nationalist, and they are rarely as explicit about their self-assertive goals as Richard Spencer. It takes critical scholarship to establish such descriptions (nationalist and self-assertive) as accurate.

One recent and exemplary critical work which undertakes just such a task is Kristin Kobes Du Mez's book *Jesus and John Wayne*. In this book, Du Mez describes how white evangelicals—a much more populous group than the alt-right—came to vociferously endorse Donald Trump, who might seem an unlikely candidate for religious voters (given his crude use of language, multiple divorces, affairs, etc.). On the one hand, *Jesus and John Wayne* fits the Benedict Anderson paradigm: through an examination of celebrity evangelicals and the networks that supported the dissemination of their message, it shows how Christian nationalism was constructed in America. On the other hand, throughout the book Du Mez consistently names white evangelical trends as nationalistic (establishing what might not be evident on the surface of, say, Focus on the Family), and furthermore she consistently interprets U.S. white evangelical nationalism as a project of self-assertion. Du Mez lays out the thesis behind these interpretive trends in the Introduction to her book:

> But evangelical support for Trump was no aberration, nor was it merely a pragmatic choice. It was, rather, the culmination of evangelicals' embrace of militant masculinity, an ideology that enshrines patriarchal authority and condones the callous display of power, at home and abroad. By the time Trump arrived proclaiming himself their savior, conservative white evangelicals had already traded a faith that privileges humility and elevates 'the least of these' for one that derides gentleness as the province of wusses. Rather than turning the other cheek, they'd resolved to defend their faith and their nation, secure in the knowledge that the ends justify the means. Having replaced the Jesus of the Gospels with a warrior Christ, it's no wonder many came to think of Trump in the same way. In 2016, many observers were stunned at evangelicals' apparent betrayal of their own values. In reality, evangelicals did not cast their vote despite their beliefs, but because of them.[41]

. . .

Christian nationalism—the belief that America is God's chosen nation and must be defended as such—serves as a powerful predictor of intolerance toward immigrants, racial minorities, and non-Christians. It is linked to opposition to gay rights and gun control, to support for harsher punishments for criminals, to justifications for the use of excessive force against black Americans in law enforcement situations, and to traditionalist gender ideology. White evangelicals have pieced together this patchwork of issues, and a nostalgic commitment to rugged, aggressive, militant white masculinity serves as the thread binding them together into a coherent whole.[42]

Du Mez goes on to weave together Teddy Roosevelt, Billy Sunday, Billy Graham, John Wayne, Cold War anti-communism, Christian high schools, James Dobson, Tim LaHaye, Jerry Falwell Sr. and Jr., the Southern Baptist Convention's inerrancy debates, Lt. Col. Oliver North, *Wild at Heart*, Mark Driscoll, Colorado Springs, Eric Metaxas, and *Duck Dynasty*; through all these historical epiphenomena, "rugged, aggressive, militant white masculinity" remains the binding thread.[43] In other words, Du Mez argues that self-assertion is at the core of white evangelical Christian nationalism. If the message of the bible seems to contradict a self-assertive embrace of power-as-dominion, so much the worse for the bible.

In both Richard Spencer as an individual and white American evangelical Christians as a group, it is evident that there is a willful disregard for the accuracy of the constructed narrative upon which their nationalism relies. Deconstruction seems a rather outmoded tool in such a situation. Rather, we should recognize that the only thing that can really reach the self-assertive core of nationalism and up-root it is the embrace of self-denial. If that is the case, it should cause us to reconsider how nationalism is critiqued.

KIERKEGAARD'S CRITIQUE OF NATIONALISM RECONSIDERED

This reconsideration brings us back to Kierkegaard. And not only to Kierkegaard, but to Backhouse's book on Kierkegaard. For although identity critique is the primary method by which nationalism is criticized in *Kierkegaard's Critique of Christian Nationalism*, there is in fact a secondary method: namely, the acceptance or even active embrace of suffering. Criticizing methods of identity construction is not the only way to go about resisting nationalism. Embracing suffering can also do important work. How so?

The answer is clear once one notes that the nation is devoted to success. The nation wants to achieve victory: to dominate all potential challengers and to provide good lives for its citizens. These good lives are lives of comfort, security, and general material blessing. Kierkegaard's Christian, by contrast, rejects the desire for precisely these worldly goods as a false lure, as things that—if achieved in this life, in this world, such as it is—always come at the expense of faithfulness to God. There is no willing of two things, then, according to Kierkegaard: one either wills worldly success, or one wills the Good.

It is precisely in this way that, in the sixth chapter of his book, Backhouse provides us with a remarkable reading of the first of Kierkegaard's *Upbuilding Discourses in Various Spirits*. Backhouse restores political meaning to a text that on its surface appears only to be about the individual soul before God.[44] In short, Backhouse reads Kierkegaard's "Purity of Heart" discourse as saying that to will the Good as an individual soul before God is politically offensive, because to will the Good is to reject those things the nation seeks.[45] It is a refusal of the happiness, blessed security, and comfort that the nation pursues as the good life. The nation thus rightly sees the Kierkegaardian Christian as a traitor to its cause. For the Kierkegaardian Christian renounces the self-assertion that is attempting to procure those worldly goods that the nation accords as valuable. Individual renunciation thus has political meaning; as Backhouse puts it, "Suffering is an indication than an individual person has looked beyond the self-referential material connections of the social-web for his identity."[46]

Here, resistance to nationalism looks less like exposing the fictionality or untenability of a grand historical narrative which gives unique destiny to oneself as a part of one's nation. Instead, it looks like renunciation and self-denial; it looks like *askēsis*. If one embraces such a renunciative discipline, one simply no longer wants what the nation is trying to give, and thus one has no reason to go looking for a fabricated identity construction that will justify one's otherwise naked self-assertion. The narrative of nationalism is no longer persuasive, but this is not because one has glimpsed its "imagined" character. Instead, it is no longer persuasive because one has uprooted the basic passions which make nationalistic narratives desirable in the first place. Through renunciation and the embrace of suffering, the basic motor which drives the desire for nations has ceased to operate.

Advocacy for this method of rejecting nationalism is a secondary operation in Backhouse's book. It shows up in only a few pages in the sixth and seventh chapters of *Kierkegaard's Critique of Christian Nationalism*.[47] What I am proposing is to make this secondary method primary. Given how nationalism has revealed itself in the time since Backhouse's book, identity critique should no longer be seen as a particularly effective method for resisting nationalism. Instead, we need to recognize that the core of nationalism is self-assertion, and that the only way to truly defeat nationalism is to embrace self-denial in pursuit of the Good.

This is precisely what we see Kierkegaard proposing throughout the attack upon Christendom. Kierkegaard does not object to the fact that the Danishness referenced by someone like Grundtivg is constructed. Instead, he argues that the whole project of accumulating goods, maintaining proper ethical order, and assuring souls of their comfortable resting place in heaven is antithetical to the true nature of Christianity. This is not simply an identity critique, for if one agrees with Kierkegaard about the essence of New Testament Christianity, then intellectual dissent from the project of nationalism is only a first step in a holistic ascetic project. One traverses a course from reading an issue of *The Moment* to ceasing to attend church to calling for the dismantling of the whole church-state apparatus; from that point, one does not stop until one has embraced poverty, chastity, and obedience in one's own life. In fact—though this speculation does go beyond Kierkegaard—I would like to suggest that ascetic course just proposed can be a two-way street; embracing poverty, chastity, and obedience can be a step on the way toward a criticism of nationalism. In other words, it is the practice of poverty, chastity, and obedience that can make us ready to renounce the lure of self-assertive nationalistic narratives. To put it another way, one is less likely to be a nationalist if one is consistently engaged in the self-mortification of fasting. Of course, it is possible to practice poverty, chastity, and obedience and endorse the dominance of the Christian nation state; I am only stating that, insofar as *askēsis* is able to work upon the self-assertive core of a human being, it makes such an endorsement less likely. This is why the element of identity critique retains its importance; the practical may be primary, but still it must be yoked to the theoretical if a critique of Christian nationalism is to achieve a kind of totality. At any rate, what is crucial to Kierkegaard is that a holistic rejection of the good life is also a rejection of the nation.

Furthermore, Kierkegaard's firm beliefs concerning the persecution of the true Christian within Christendom (the "double danger" of Christian life) may be more realistic than previously admitted. It is when our daily renunciations meet up with a moment of public refusal to get on board with the nation's demands that Kierkegaard's indelible watermark of the Christian life, persecution, becomes an incursive reality for the ascetic. The life of a Kierkegaardian Christian such as Dietrich Bonhoeffer demonstrates that the nation does not do a good job of tolerating those who see the bounty they could hold, and respectfully return their ticket.[48]

So, what does Kierkegaard have to say to this moment of nationalistic resurgence, especially to those who would resist it? Even though identity critique still prevails in the field of critical studies of nationalism,[49] the way nationalism will be defeated is not through painstaking deconstruction of how national identities have been imaginatively created. Rather, the way nationalism will be defeated is through embracing *askēsis.* It will be defeated through a disciplined renunciation of the desire for nations, at both a theoretical and a practical level. In this world, the self-assertion of those who have power always comes at the expense of others, and Christians—or those whose morality similarly forbids oppression of the "alien" and the "outsider"[50]—cannot remain faithful to their faith without a daily refusal of the *libido dominandi*, or the desire to dominate. Rather than the critique of nationalist identity construction as falsely fabricated leading to a sudden new desire for truth (which, given the preceding reflections on the nature of nationalism, I find unlikely), asceticism makes possible the desire for another identity to be constructed, the desire to be led out of the false nationalistic narratives that distort what we say we care about. When it comes to the critique of nationalism, therefore, it is the disciplining of desire that must come first.

As the invocation of Richard Spencer and white evangelical Christianity have already intimated, the focus of this chapter has been the renunciation of a particular perspective: that of the ruling class in America.[51] Just as Kierkegaard did, I have been speaking to those who have something to renounce. What Kierkegaard proposes is not a universal discourse, but an ascetic program for those who have access to power. He writes to the audience of which he was a part. But what if we were considering the criticism of nationalism from a different angle—from the perspective of the oppressed? Would things look differently? Would *askēsis* still be the answer? In the next chapter, I think with the contemporary theologian James H. Cone about how to answer these difficult questions.

NOTES

1. Existential appropriation is a major theme throughout *Concluding Unscientific Postscript*, but a good brief introduction to the theme in Kierkegaard can be found in *For Self-Examination*.

2. See footage at https://www.youtube.com/watch?v=TTVTUTcd6cU (accessed June 29, 2021).

3. See Matthew Casey-Pariseault, "Old Religious Tensions Resurge in Bolivia after Ouster of Longtime Indigenous President," *The Conversation* (November 19, 2019), https://theconversation.com/old-religious-tensions-resurge-in-bolivia-after-ouster-of-longtime-indigenous-president-127000 (accessed June 29, 2021).

4. Chatterji, Hanson, and Jaffrelot, "Introduction," in *Majoritarian State: How Hindu Nationalism is Changing India*, 1–2.

5. Chatterji, Hanson, and Jaffrelot, "Introduction," in *Majoritarian State*, 3.

6. As Romila Thapar has put it, "'Hinduism is a religion, Hindutva is an ideology for political mobilization'," as cited in Angana P. Chatterji, "Remaking the Hindu/Nation: Terror and Impunity in Uttar Pradesh," in *Majoritarian State*, 403.

7. See Chatterji, "Remaking the Hindu/Nation," in *Majoritarian State*, 402 and *passim* in what follows.

8. On hegemony, see Suhas Palshikar, "Toward Hegemony: The BJP Beyond Electoral Dominance," in *Majoritarian State*, 101–116, and James Manor, "Can Modi

and the BJP Achieve and Sustain Hegemony?" in *Majoritarian State*, 117–130. On violence, which is often particularly directed against women, see the extensive catalogue in Chatterji, "Remaking the Hindu/Nation," in *Majoritarian State*, 403–418.

9. Andrew L. Whitehead and Samuel L. Perry, *Taking America Back for God: Christian Nationalism in the United States* (Oxford: Oxford University Press, 2020).

10. See Whitehead and Perry, *Taking America Back for God*: "Christian nationalist ideology is fundamentally focused on gaining and maintaining access to power" (161); "In short, Christian nationalism is all about power" (86).

11. See Whitehead and Perry, *Taking America Back for God*: "the degree to which Americans seek to impose Christianity on the public sphere often operates as a powerful indicator of their commitment to a specific social order—with boundaries and hierarchies among natives and foreigners, whites and nonwhites, men and women, heterosexuals and others—an order they recognize is also being threatened" (5); in the U.S., Christian nationalism is an attempt to defend 'order' by those who have benefited from it (151).

12. Whitehead and Perry, *Taking America Back for God*, 65.

13. Whitehead and Perry, *Taking America Back for God*, 71.

14. Whitehead and Perry, *Taking America Back for God*, 105.

15. Whitehead and Perry, *Taking America Back for God*, 91; cf. 16: "Christian nationalism expresses a particular racialized understanding of national identity. It allows those who embrace it to express a racialized identity *without resorting to racialized terms*." For more on the history of American nativism and whiteness, see Daniel Denvir, *All-American Nativism: How the Bipartisan War on Immigrants Explains Politics as We Know it* (London: Verso, 2020).

16. Whitehead and Perry, *Taking America Back for God*, 11.

17. Whitehead and Perry, *Taking America Back for God*, 14–15.

18. Whitehead and Perry, *Taking America Back for God*: "as people more frequently attend church, pray, or read their sacred scriptures, they become *more* likely to recognize racial discrimination in policing" (21); "As Americans show greater agreement with Christian nationalism, they are more likely to view Muslim refugees as terrorist threats, agree that citizens should be made to show respect for America's traditions, and oppose stricter gun control laws. But as Americans become more religious in terms of attendance, prayer, and Scripture reading, they move in the opposite direction on these issues" (84). Interestingly, this correlation does not hold when it comes to conservative 'family' politics (143).

19. See Jill Lepore, *This America: The Case for the Nation* (New York: Liveright, 2019); Achin Vanaik's articles can be found at jacobinmag.com, and see also his *The Rise of Hindu Authoritarianism: Secular Claims, Communal Realities* (London: Verso, 2017).

20. Stephen Backhouse, *Kierkegaard's Critique of Christian Nationalism* (Oxford: Oxford University Press, 2011).

21. Backhouse, *Kierkegaard's Critique of Christian Nationalism*, xii

22. Backhouse, *Kierkegaard's Critique of Christian Nationalism*, 47.

23. Backhouse, *Kierkegaard's Critique of Christian Nationalism*, 42.

24. "The ethical choices that the will must make in accordance with the Good are presented to the individual in terms of civic morality through the structures of society" (Backhouse, *Kierkegaard's Critique of Christian Nationalism*, 50).

25. "It is only by means of Christianity that nationalities can attain the development to which they are really appointed" (Hans Lassen Martensen, *Christian Ethics: Special Part. Second Division; Social Ethics*, trans. Sophia Taylor [Edinburgh: T&T Clark, 1882], 94); "[A] nation's highest development only occurs in the event that it is a Christian state, as it is only then that it is able to know and attain the full potential allotted to it in the divine scheme of history" (Backhouse, *Kierkegaard's Critique of Christian Nationalism*, 51).

26. This includes a kind of Christian socialism as reflecting God's care for the poor, though it is decidedly a national, not an international, socialism (Backhouse, *Kierkegaard's Critique of Christian Nationalism*, 59).

27. Grundtvig "self-consciously sought to locate the unique Scandinavian cultural heritage at the centre of the Divine will as revealed in world history" (Backhouse, *Kierkegaard's Critique of Christian Nationalism*, 68).

28. Backhouse, *Kierkegaard's Critique of Christian Nationalism*, 75ff.

29. Adolf von Harnack held much the same understanding of Germany and German culture. See Rowan Williams, "The Deadly Simplicities of Adolf von Harnack: Liberal Theology in Germany on the Eve of the Great War," unpublished remarks available at https://lif.blob.core.windows.net/lif/docs/default-source/default-library/rowan-williams---the-deadly-simplicities-of-adolf-von-harnack---january-2014---lecture-transcript-pdf.pdf?sfvrsn=0 (accessed April 30, 2021).

30. See Backhouse, *Kierkegaard's Critique of Christian Nationalism*, 93ff.

31. On the discrete character of the moment, see especially David J. Kangas, *Kierkegaard's Instant: On Beginnings* (Bloomington: Indiana University Press, 2007).

32. "In the hands of theologians such as Grundtvig and Martensen, the category of 'the historical' is expected to provide proof for the truth of Christian doctrines, to point inexorably to the historical and logical necessity of the incarnation, and act as a vehicle for God's unfolding revelation in the world. This is a weight that 'the historical' cannot bear" (Backhouse, *Kierkegaard's Critique of Christian Nationalism*, 110).

33. See the summary of *Upbuilding Discourses in Various Spirits* in chapter 1.

34. Contemporaneity with Christ is laid out most fully in *Practice in Christianity* No. I. See PC 3–68/SKS 12:11–80.

35. See Backhouse, *Kierkegaard's Critique of Christian Nationalism*, 115–117.

36. See Ernest Gellner, *Nations and Nationalism* (Oxford: Blackwell, 1983); Eric Hobsbawm, *Nations and Nationalism since 1780: Programme, Myth, Reality* (Cambridge: Cambridge University Press, 1990); Benedict Anderson, *Imagined Communities: Reflections on the Origin and Spread of Nationalism* (London: Verso, 1983).

37. See the helpfully broad history of the alt-right developed in Alexandra Minna Stern, *Proud Boys and the White Ethnostate: How the Alt-Right is Warping the American Imagination* (Boston: Beacon Press, 2019).

38. The article can be found at https://altright.com/2016/07/06/race-stalking-the-wild-taboo/ (accessed April 30, 2021).

39. This is a paraphrase of frequent refrains from Spencer. See, for example, video of a question-and-answer session at Auburn University recorded in August of 2017, where Spencer says: "There is no fact you can throw that will destroy identity or make it irrelevant," and "Facts are lame. I want to talk about stuff that really matters" (https://www.youtube.com/watch?v=g1JJA6UiEio&t=1202s) (accessed April 30, 2021). Cf. Greg Johnson, *New Right versus Old Right*, "mere historical facts—no matter what they are—should never deter us," quoted in Minna Stern, *Proud Boys*, 48.

40. Whitehead and Perry, *Taking America Back for God*, 47–49 (although declining, Christian nationalism is still popular).

41. Kristin Kobes Du Mez, *Jesus and John Wayne: How White Evangelicals Corrupted a Faith and Fractured a Nation* (New York: W. W. Norton, 2020), 3.

42. Du Mez, *Jesus and John Wayne*, 4.

43. See for example Du Mez, *Jesus and John Wayne*, 88: "Beyond the home, the power of the patriarch ensured the security of the nation. In the aftermath of Vietnam, this required a renewed commitment to militarism. Family values politics, then, involved the enforcement of women's sexual and social subordination in the domestic realm and the promotion of American militarism on the national stage"; cf. 156, 185, 246, 271, 276, 296–298.

44. See Backhouse, *Kierkegaard's Critique of Christian Nationalism*, 179–186.

45. "The individual does not oppose 'the great' as something evil so much as he is indifferent towards it in relation to the good. As a result, the single individual suffers, for in his break with common sense and his abandoning of prudential sagacity, he is unable to attain the success of this world. The suffering individual thus stands as a visible wound in his surrounding culture, his public and visible lack of success posing a challenge to the rest of the group" (Backhouse, *Kierkegaard's Critique of Christian Nationalism*, 184).

46. Backhouse, *Kierkegaard's Critique of Christian Nationalism*, 186.

47. See Backhouse, *Kierkegaard's Critique of Christian Nationalism*, 179–186, 210–211.

48. On Bonhoeffer and Kierkegaard, see Matthew D. Kirkpatrick, *Attacks on Christendom in a World Come of Age: Kierkegaard, Bonhoeffer, and the Question of "Religionless Christianity"* (Eugene: Pickwick, 2011).

49. As a perusal of the helpful H-net forum on the topic demonstrates (https://networks.h-net.org/h-nationalism).

50. Here I suggest a point of contact between Kierkegaard's critique of Christian nationalism and other religious or non-religious critiques of nationalism. It seems to me Kierkegaard shares common ground with any tradition which rejects dominative self-assertion. For more on Kierkegaard and inter-religious dialogue, see George B. Connell, *Kierkegaard and the Paradox of Religious Diversity* (Grand Rapids: Eerdmans, 2016).

51. See Isabel Wilkerson, *Caste: The Origins of Our Discontents* (New York: Random House, 2020).

Chapter Six

Some Perspectives on Destruction
Kierkegaard, Cone, and Third World Theology

PERSPECTIVE

So far, everything in this book has been written from the perspective of someone in power to an audience of those who are also in power. Though Kierkegaard may be attempting to renounce his power—and, as we have seen in chapter 4, he was to some degree successful—he did have power to renounce. That is, in part, why Kierkegaard is significant. He was given all the gifts of the Golden Age, and still he said: No. Though occasionally he intentionally makes a broader appeal, in the main he is asking people like him to join him in his negation.

This is an important perspective. If the aim of the attack is the destruction of Christendom, it certainly makes sense to appeal to the rulers of Christendom. The attack is just such an appeal, saying: if you wish to save your soul, you will renounce what you have been given.

This is an important perspective. But it is certainly not the only perspective. In this chapter, I highlight a theologian who shares the same aim as Kierkegaard—the destruction of Christendom[1]—but who works for this aim from a completely different perspective. He writes from the perspective of the oppressed to an audience of those who are oppressed. The theologian in question is James Hal Cone (1938–2018).

Speaking from such a different perspective, Cone has a significantly different opinion of the culture from which and to which he writes. Though he endorses the destruction of American society, this is because American society is white: which is to say, it is dominated by white people (or, in Ta-Nehisi Coates's words, "those Americans who believe they are white"[2]). On the one hand, Cone has the same attitude toward white society as Kierkegaard does to Denmark: he desires its downfall. On the other hand, Cone embraces, endorses, and praises black culture within America.³

Perhaps this attitude to white and black culture seems contradictory. They are both human cultures. Does not all human culture stand under God's judgement, as Karl Barth taught us in his *Römerbrief*?⁴ Cone insists that his attitude is not a contradictory one. The attitude is not contradictory precisely because God is partial to black culture. In this way, Cone is not contradicting himself, but simply following God's leading. Cone makes this a matter of explicit theorization in his *God of the Oppressed*:

> [I]f the biblical Christ is the Liberator of the oppressed from the sociopolitical bondage inflicted by the oppressors, then can it be said that Jesus Christ relates to both cultural expressions in the same way? Of course not! . . . When the scriptural witness to divine revelation is examined, it cannot be said that Christ has the *same* attitude toward all cultural expressions. Indeed the message of the Exodus, prophets, and Jesus' life and death is the proclamation of God's decisive partiality toward the struggles of the unfree. Therefore, if we are to understand Christ's relation to culture, we had better be clear about whose human strivings we speak of, the oppressed or the oppressors.⁵

This differentiation of perspective is precisely why we are turning to Cone's work in this chapter. After spending so much time with Kierkegaard, we need to stretch our minds to imagine what the destruction of Christendom looks like from another perspective. This will enable us to develop an understanding of how resistance to nationalism can look like renunciation or like affirmation, depending on whose perspective we take. At the same time, Kierkegaard's emphasis on renunciation remains crucial, and not just for a white audience. As we follow the development of Cone's work, we will track his theory of black self-affirmation; but we will also see how Cone finds he requires the resources of the renunciatory tradition as well. Thus, our reading of Kierkegaard can inflect the story of how Cone's theological career is told, endorsing an interpretation of Cone which has recently been proposed. All told, putting Cone together with Kierkegaard will give us a much better sense of how resistance to nationalism can be conceived in a variety of ways, with that variety depending on the subject position of those who join Kierkegaard and Cone in the task of destruction.

JAMES H. CONE AND BLACK SELF-AFFIRMATION

During the late 1960s and into the mid-1970s—and in the midst of a society structured by white supremacy—James H. Cone wrote a quartet of theological works intended to support and actively cultivate black self-determination. These works are framed in terms of offering theological support for the Black Power movement. They take their starting point from the National Committee of Negro Churchman (later the National Conference of Black Churchmen)'s endorsement of Black Power in 1966 and develop that original affirmation in a rigorous and systematic fashion, resulting in a theology that—rather than being universal—is explicitly black in its sources and goals.[6]

Already we have a series of loaded terms—theology, black self-determination, and Black Power—and it is necessary to define them, which we will do with an eye toward the destruction of society. As Cone writes in his first book, *Black Theology and Black Power*, "Black Power means black freedom, black self-determination, wherein black people no longer view themselves as without human dignity but as men, human beings with the ability to carve out their own destiny."[7] Black Power translates into fields like education, employment, housing, and art; Black Power is "full participation in the decision making process affecting the lives of black people";[8] thus, Black Power means the ability to put black self-determination into practice.[9]

So then, what role does theology have in the Black Power movement? What is "the task of theology in the current disintegration of the world?"[10] Cone answers this question most extensively in his second book, *A Black Theology of Liberation* (1970): "The task of theology, then, is to explicate the meaning of God's liberating activity so that those who labor under enslaving powers will see that the forces of liberation are the very activity of God."[11] Furthermore, this means something specific in the United States of America, because here what liberation looks like is the free self-determination of the black community.[12] We cannot simply say 'liberation'; to use such a word without qualification is to ignore the history and present reality of U.S. oppression. Thus, we must say 'black liberation.'

In the context of white oppression, any theology which hopes to be true to God's historical revelation as liberator must speak about black liberation; that is the specific meaning of God's immutable nature for our time. Black theology therefore speaks openly about the black and white structure of our society, and it says that the denial of black being is the denial of God.[13] Black theology says to black men and women that their aspiration to self-determination is not only their own desire, but the desire of God.[14] And, thus, it will come about, because God is powerful: "the horse and its rider hath He thrown into the sea" (Exodus 15:1).

What Cone means by self-determination is different from what Kierkegaard means by self-assertion. For Kierkegaard, self-assertion refers to the base human desire for accrual of goods and worldly pleasures, unchecked by any moral consideration of the soul or spirit and very much willing to dominate others for its own purposes, if the need should arise.[15] For Cone, self-determination decidedly does not include domination as a constituent feature: "it is not the intention of the black man to repudiate his master's human dignity, but only his status as master."[16] Rather than domination, black people want "the grip of white power removed";[17] indeed, for the sake of their dignity as human beings created in the image of God, "Blacks must demand that whites get off their backs."[18]

This program of self-determination does involve assertion, but it is always an assertion of resistance, an assertion that is resisting a counter-assertion.[19] This is what Kierkegaard, from his subject position of the dominant class, could not envision: an assertion that does not entail domination, but the recovery of dignity for those whom the world is against. In fact, black assertion and black self-determination do not lead to the subjugation of whites, but rather their freedom. When black self-determination is able to make its way in the world, whites too are liberated: they are freed from enslavement to their own dominative egos, which is a form of unfreedom that has led to their own unhappiness and their own deformation from what a human being is supposed to be.[20] For both whites and blacks, black self-determination leads to the recovery of what they, as human persons, are created to be.

Black self-determination also leads to the destruction of U.S. society. Cone addresses this theme when speaking of the cost, for white people, of entering God's kingdom:

> For white people, God's reconciliation in Jesus Christ means that God has made black people a beautiful people; and if they are going to be in relationship with God, they must enter by means of their black brothers, who are a manifestation of God's presence on earth. The assumption that one can know God without knowing blackness is the basic heresy of the white churches. They want God without blackness, Christ without obedience, love without death. . . .
>
> When we look at what whiteness has done to the minds of men in this country, we can see clearly what the New Testament meant when it spoke of the principalities and powers.[21] To speak of Satan and his powers becomes not just a way of speaking but a fact of reality. When we can see a people who are being controlled by an ideology of whiteness, then we know what reconciliation must mean. The coming of Christ means a denial of what we thought we were. It means destroying the white devil in us. Reconciliation to God means that white people are prepared to deny themselves (whiteness), take up the cross (blackness), and follow Christ (black ghetto).
>
> To be sure, this is not easy. But whoever said the gospel of Christ was easy? Obedience always means going where we otherwise would not go; being what we would not be; doing what we would not do. Reconciliation means that Christ has freed us for this. In a white racist society, Christian obedience can only mean being obedient to blackness, its glorification and exaltation.[22]

A society that glorified and exalted blackness would precisely be not our society; it would mean that our society had been destroyed.[23] For Cone as well as Kierkegaard, true Christianity involves the destruction of our society as it now exists.

This theme of destruction may seem harsh to white Americans. Indeed, Cone does say things like: "First, let me say that reconciliation on white racist terms is impossible, since it would crush the dignity of black people. Under these conditions blacks must treasure their hostility[.]"[24] Furthermore, the destruction of white determined society may cause white people suffering and pain. It will also inevitably cause black people suffering and pain, inasmuch as they are resisting the forces of this world.[25] However, the initiation of suffering involved in the destruction of white society does not mean such action fails to fit the description of a work of love, according to Kierkegaard's definition, as we will see at greater length in the next chapter. Insofar as the destruction of white society liberates whites from the evils currently gripping their souls and keeping them from God, such destruction in fact perfectly fits the Kierkegaardian definition of a work of love.[26]

JAMES H. CONE AND BLACK SELF-DENIAL

Cone's reputation as a major black theologian depends in large part upon his initial quartet of books (*Black Theology & Black Power*, *A Black Theology of Liberation*, *The Spirituals and the Blues*, *God of the Oppressed*). However, Cone did not stop writing books in 1975, and his development from that point is instructive for us, especially given our reading of Kierkegaard's attack. As is documented in Matthew M. Harris and Tyler B. Davis's important article "'In the Hope That They Can Make Their Own Future': James H. Cone and the Third World,"[27] in the 1970s Cone began to regularly attend international and ecumenical dialogues where he met theologians interested in liberation from a multitude of contexts.[28] When he places himself in dialogue with these thinkers, a new theme eventually begins to emerge in his work: renunciation.

We see the results of this dialogue take shape in book form in *For My People: Black Theology and the Black Church* (1984). When Cone considers the relation of the black church in the U.S. to what were called at the time "Third World" churches, the first and most prominent theme is solidarity:

> As white Americans, Europeans, South Africans, and other oppressors band together in order to continue their rule over us, oppressed peoples throughout the world, across continents and nations, must band together for the liberation of all. . . .

> My concern in this chapter is to urge us to interact, in spite of our differences, with other oppressed groups in the Third World so that we can begin to build bridges of communication and cooperation in a common struggle for freedom and self-determination.[29]

This commitment to solidarity then takes the form of new political endorsements. Resistance to capitalism becomes explicit,[30] and socialism becomes a predominant concern as a way to resist the depredations of capitalism,[31] depredations which—given the racial character of capital[32]—were commonly experienced to some degree by all participants in the dialogue.[33] When speaking about his vision for a liberated social order, Cone is explicit, specifically in his endorsement of democratic socialism, while also connecting the democratic aspect of that socialism to antiracist struggle:

> The new social order should be democratic and socialist, including a Marxist critique of monopoly capitalism. It must also be a socialism that is critical of the authoritarian state socialism in Soviet Russia. Just as we should not reject Christianity because churches carry its name but do the opposite of what the faith stands for, likewise we should not reject socialism just because Soviet Russia adopted the name but does the opposite.
>   The new social order must view the necessities of life—food, shelter, work, play—as rights inalienably linked with membership in society. No one, absolutely no one, should control the wealth of a nation or community through the private ownership of property.
>   The socialist vision must be democratic, protective of individual liberties, and involving all persons in the community in its creation. That is why the team should include a wide representation of interests in the black community.[34]

While endorsing this positive vision, Cone simultaneously draws a strong disjunction between himself and "those blacks in the U.S.A. who define freedom in terms of their equal share in the American capitalist pie with no thought whatsoever of changing the economic system so that the true causes of poverty could be eliminated not only in the U.S.A. but throughout the world";[35] this disjunction between Cone and capitalistic black Americans allows for a solidarity with the Third World which translates into building international support for socialism. Via this separation and solidarity, Cone thereby situates the black liberation movement in the U.S. alongside Third World or anticolonial movements across the globe.

Alongside solidarity, another theme arises as its necessary accompaniment, and that is renunciation. Cone recognizes that black churches in the U.S., though oppressed in our society, stand in a hierarchical structural relation to the churches of the Third World. Because of that structural relation, renunciation becomes necessary.³⁶ This renunciation is of two types: (1) control, and (2) money.

(1) When it comes to the relation of black Americans to the rest of the globe, Cone recognizes that a certain whiteness has infected their subject position. This is especially the case when it comes to missions:

> African-American churches have been in "mission" work in Africa and the Caribbean for more than a century, but our behavior has been less than exemplary, often sharing a missionary outlook similar to that of white colonizers and seldom linking black churches with progressive political and theological ideas in those areas.
>
> It is sad that African-American churches still treat Africans and West Indians somewhat as whites treat us, at best as children and at worst as pagans in need of Christianity and the values of Western civilization. Instead of creating church structures that would develop quality indigenous leadership, African-American churches still send uninformed black Americans to those areas to help with charitable projects and then to decide how the charity can best be used.³⁷

Here Cone critiques black American churches for replicating the same posture of control which whites have exercised toward them back in their home country. Essentially, Cone charges that African-American churches are saying: 'Yes, we will share our resources with you—but only if you obey the following stipulations,' thus imitating the same condescending attitude of control which whites display toward blacks in America—an attitude which is destructive of dignity and self-determination. This posture of control must be renounced, Cone avers, if black Americans are not to become the very thing they hate.³⁸

(2) Black churches must also renounce their wealth. This involves a straightforward recognition that—although they may not be considered rich within the bounds of the U.S.—black churches have wealth when placed in relation to other churches around the globe. Such renunciation of wealth would take the direct form of funding dialogue between black theologians and Third World theologians:

> Black churches should assume the major economic responsibility for such meetings because of our advantaged financial status when compared with Third World Christians. We have rich churches in comparison with the churches among the poor of Africa, Asia, and Latin America. Because we have more, more is to be expected of us.³⁹

Giving of their wealth to fund dialogue, black theologians then collaborate with the oppressed from all over the globe to work for liberation.⁴⁰

This gift of wealth in order to fund a world-wide liberation movement presumes a preceding renunciation. It operates on the assumption that the goal of black churches is not the achievement of parity in America, especially considering that such equality would almost certainly continue to rely on the exploitation of the oppressed from other countries. If they are to join in solidarity with the world, black Americans must renounce the American dream. When in dialogue with the wretched of the whole earth, Cone sees the lure of bourgeois black American aspiration, and rejects this temptation in favor of a true joining with the co-victims of the structure that dominates us all.

So then, according to Cone, when black theologians from the U.S. open themselves to a global dialogue with the oppressed of the world, they see that a certain *askēsis* is required of them. Due to their location in the global configuration of capitalism, renunciation must be a component of black ecclesial life. Some African-Americans have the chance to wield control and the opportunity to retain wealth; Cone is urging them to reject that chance and refuse that opportunity, seeing both as parts of the demonic force which continues to subjugate them within the boundaries of "this cultured hell" called the United States of America.[41]

This leads us back to the subject of this book and the question of audience. To whom does the Kierkegaard of the attack speak? Primarily, he speaks to those who to some extent share his subject position, which in the U.S. is white citizens who have access to power. But Kierkegaard may also be of use to black theologians in the U.S. who recognize that in order to destroy whiteness at a global level, some renunciations will also be required of them. In this way, Kierkegaard continues to be helpful as a guide to destruction.

I submit this as a hypothesis generated by placing Kierkegaard and Cone in dialogue. In order for it to be confirmed, it would have to be tested on the battlefields where global solidarity is forged.

POSTSCRIPT: ON LISTENING TO ONE'S CRITICS

Once there was a man of God. He was sent on a journey to the north and told to go and speak to the king in the north and immediately return, without stopping, without eating or drinking. At first he followed these orders to the letter. The king tried to get the man of God to stay and eat with him, but he refused. Instead, he started on his way home. On the way home, he happened to be met by an old prophet. The prophet tried to get the man of God to come and stay and eat with him. The man of God refused. But the prophet insisted, saying that God had spoken to him as well, and told him to bring the man of God back to his house to eat food and to drink water with him. This persuaded the man of God. He went to the old prophet's house. He ate and drank. The next day, a lion met the man of God on the road and ate him.

Listening to critics is a complicated matter. When is engaging a critical response helpful? When is it a distraction from the word one has been given to speak? Our two theologians offer important instruction on this issue; I offer this postscript to the central questions of this chapter as an example of a further dialogue that could be staged between Kierkegaard and Cone. Certainly, much more than what I offer is possible; my hope is that this postscript will serve as an indication of that fact.

Søren Kierkegaard did not listen to his critics. James Cone did—but only to some of them. Here I will argue that both were correct to proceed as they did, with Kierkegaard closing both ears while Cone opened just one.

Kierkegaard did not listen to his critics. We have seen several examples of his practice exemplified during the attack period. When Martensen responded to him in *Berlingske Tidende*, Kierkegaard did not take that occasion to nuance his definition of the truth-witness. Instead, he continued to insist—when it comes to the matter of a Christian definition of terms—on the overriding importance of the New Testament. When Pastor Paludan-Müller requested that he write a kind of Theology of the New Testament (*Theologie des Neuen Testaments*), Kierkegaard refused. To undertake a dogmatics would be a distraction, both for himself and his readers. After all, everyone already knew that what he was saying about the Christianity of the New Testament was true, whether they wanted to admit it or not. Writing a dogmatic treatise would not change the willingness of his audience to admit *askēsis* into the heart of their definitions of Christianity, which was the issue at stake in this debate.

Thus, Kierkegaard did not listen to his critics. And it is good that he did not. If he had listened to Pastor Paludan-Müller (and a later anonymous critic who made a similar proposal), the attack would have dissolved into a rather ordinary display of academic gamesmanship. If he had listened to Martensen, Kierkegaard would have adopted a progressive-dialectical view of the church/world dynamic, such that the New Testament definition of the truth-witness would no longer hold, and a nation instantiating Christian truth would no longer be a contradiction in terms. Listening to either critic would have led Kierkegaard to be re-absorbed into the usual discursive operations of his age, thereby losing his distinctiveness as well as any continuing relevance. It is good, then, that Kierkegaard refused to listen to his critics.

James Cone did listen to his critics—but only some of them. He does not listen to Paul Holmer when the latter complains that Cone has "made everything about race" (alas, even the study of Kierkegaard);[42] nor does he listen to American Barthians who complain that, in his identification of the gospel and blackness, he has forgotten the "infinite qualitative distinction" between God and humanity.[43] He does, however, listen to Gayraud Wilmore and Charles Long when they point out that the sources of his black theology are consistently white theologians. He does listen to theologians from Latin America when they critique his lack of solidarity in anti-capitalist/pro-socialist struggle. And he does listen to Womanist and feminist theologians who expose the masculine presumptions of his God-talk and the potentially harmful effects of his atonement theology. So, Cone does listen to critics—just not to every one of them.

Cone himself reflected on this practice of listening to some critics while ignoring others. Eschewing the goal of listening to everyone, Cone writes: "I received all kinds of criticism, some worthless and others a blessing. I had to decide what was important and what wasn't."[44] So what is the standard he applied to decide which critics were important to his project? "Any critic who mattered would have to understand what set me on fire."[45] Only critics who had a basic sympathy to Cone's project—who understood something of its source and thus its aims—could assist him in the refining of that project. He had no intention of abandoning the word God had given him in order to switch to a different project, just because his initial effort had received criticism—a bevy of readers insisting they had received a different word from God. So, what was the initial source of Cone's theology? "It was the same things that set Martin and Malcolm on fire: black suffering. It was black fires burning in urban centers and at the foot of Southern lynching trees that created black theology."[46] Any critic who did not write out of, or at least understand, this fire was not worth Cone's time. This is why Cone can rather bluntly say: "White critics soon ceased to matter to me at all. Black critics, at least, were in my world, and I could learn from them."[47] He expands on this distinction in his fourth book, *God of the Oppressed*, which was itself the result of listening to black critics of his project:

> Thus if we black theologians are going to interpret correctly the meaning of the black people's struggle, we cannot be concerned with what white theologians are going to say about our theological perspective. Black theologians are not called to interpret the gospel in a form acceptable to white oppressors. Our calling is derived from the people who have been through the trials and tribulations of this world. Our task is to interpret their struggle in the light of God's presence with them, liberating and thus reconciling the oppressed to themselves and to God.[48]

Unlike Kierkegaard, Cone listened to critics. Yet, like Kierkegaard, he resolutely excluded any critical voice which was encouraging him to abandon the word he had been given. Thankfully, Cone was blessed in a way Kierkegaard was not fortunate enough to experience, such that he can say: "Nothing helps a writer or scholar to improve his or her craft more than worthy critics, and I was blessed in this regard."[49]

Listening to critics led Cone to change in four principle ways: (1) shifting the sources of his theology; (2) becoming an advocate of international solidarity and socialism; (3) eliminating masculine-centered language; and (4) thinking deeply about the meaning of the cross. We can only cover these four changes briefly here, but doing so will enable us to see, once again, how Cone differs from Kierkegaard while still retaining a significant overlap with him. Cone shows us a positive possibility not present in Kierkegaard, while Kierkegaard reminds us that this positive possibility is only possible because of Cone's negative refusal (viz., of his white critics). The goal of the following summary of change is to show how, through genuine criticism, authentic theological development can happen.

(1) The first critics to whom Cone listened were other black male theologians and scholars of religion. Their chief criticism was in regard to the sources Cone used to construct his "black theology." Although his first two books attempt to articulate a specifically black theology of liberation, the sources Cone utilizes in *Black Theology and Black Power* and *A Black Theology of Liberation* are chiefly white Europeans; especially frequent reference is made to Paul Tillich and Karl Barth. Cone summarizes his black male critics' objection as follows:

> Lee, Long, Wilmore, and Cecil Cone agreed that my theological perspective was too dependent on white theology. They claimed that both *Black Theology and Black Power* and *A Black Theology of Liberation* used conceptual categories that came from Europe and not Africa. This meant that I had not been fully liberated from the rational structure of Western thought forms. If theology is black, they asked, must not the sources for its articulation also be black? Where are the black sources in James Cone?[50]

This critique had a demonstrable effect on Cone's authorship. The first work to follow *Black Theology and Black Power* and *A Black Theology of Liberation* was *The Spirituals and the Blues*, a work whose express purpose was the theological interpretation of black sources. Then, in *God of the Oppressed*—Cone's fourth book—he re-articulates a kind of systematic theology of black liberation, only this time using predominantly black sources. This shift would continue to characterize the major works that followed, including *For My People*, *Martin and Malcolm in America*, and *The Cross and the Lynching Tree*. Intentionally delving into these sources deepens Cone's own appreciation for the theme of liberation already present in black arts of all kinds, as well as clarifying that what Cone is offering is a theological articulation of the black voice, rather than an intellectual construct hopelessly tinged by the white episteme.

(2) The second group of critics we have already encountered: Cone's dialogue partners from the Third World. One of the crucial results of this dialogue, as we have seen, is Cone's increasing interest in (and endorsement of) socialism. Along with this goes a reconsideration of Karl Marx.

In Cone's American context, Marx had mainly been used to elevate class analysis at the expense of reckoning with race. When Cone joined hands with Third World theologians, he finds himself led toward a different use of Marx, one that connects him to other marginalized groups in a common struggle against the devastations wrought by capital.

In other words, Cone is instructed by his new global relationships on how Marxian social analysis can be something other than a power-play by so-called radicals in America who seek to downplay the significance of race (and gender) in social analysis. Instead, it can help to support the liberation of black people in America and people of color across the globe. Through these interactions, Cone finds that "Third World theologians almost universally endorse democratic socialism and condemn monopoly capitalism."[51] One of the reasons Third World theologians take these positions is out of a commonly held acknowledgment of the significance of Marx's analysis of capitalism (though there is certainly not an absolute allegiance to his teachings). Cone finds that he arrives at exactly the same position as his Third World interlocutors, and he urges others to do the same: "I have been convinced that the black church cannot remain silent regarding socialism, because such silence will be interpreted by our Third World brothers and sisters as support for the capitalistic system, which exploits the poor all over this earth."[52] Once again, Cone has listened to a significant group of critics and developed his theology accordingly: a theology that supports liberation from oppression now embodies that liberation in the push to achieve democratic socialism.[53] Through this critical dialogue, Cone's theology becomes more positive and concrete in its political orientation.

(3) James Cone taught at Union Theological Seminary in New York City. This teaching position not only afforded him the chance to dialogue with black male and Third World theologians; it also gave him the chance to teach, and he ended up teaching some of the most brilliant black female theologians of the 20th century, including Kelly Brown Douglas and Delores S. Williams. Cone learned much by listening to these students.[54] In his first autobiography (or "testimony"), Cone openly admits: "When I began writing about black theology, the problem of sexism was not a part of my theological consciousness."[55] This is reflected in the masculinist language in his first books, referring to "man" and his problems.[56] Learning from his students,

Cone is able to recognize that: "Masculine language in religion and theology serves as theological justification for the subordination of women in church and society."[57] He thus changes his language-usage in subsequent books. Yet his dialogue with his black female students would also lead to more substantive developments.

(4) As mentioned, one of Cone's students was Delores S. Williams. Williams is the author of *Sisters in the Wilderness*, one of the most searching critiques of the use of the cross in Christian theology ever to be written.[58] In the pages of this book, Williams interprets traditional theologies of the cross as advocating surrogacy: the suffering of one person on behalf of another. Given black women's historical confinement to surrogate roles, the cross becomes a problematic symbol for them, insofar as it can be used to reinforce the goodness of surrogacy and thus the rightness of black women remaining where they have been placed. In other words, traditional theologies of the cross can buttress the subordinate position of black women, rather than serving their liberation. By way of contrast, Williams interprets the cross not as a good example of vicarious suffering, but as a symbol of evil. The cross is evil; only in the resurrection is it overcome. According to Williams, it is the resurrection that is good, not the cross.[59]

Although he does not have an extensively developed theology of the cross in his early works, Cone tends to hold to something like what Williams describes as a traditional theology of the cross, insofar as the goodness of the cross as a symbol is not questioned. Cone's response to Williams's critique is complex. On the one hand, he agrees with Williams that the cross is evil. On the other hand, the cross states as plainly as could possibly be desired that God is on the side of the oppressed.[60] This declaration of allegiance not only sanctifies the struggle of the oppressed; it also grants them assurance of victory, thus transforming symbols of torture into signs of victory: "As long as black people fight back, our resistance redeems the lynching tree."[61] The cross thereby does crucial liberation work when it comes to something like the interpretation of lynching. White supremacists saw lynching as a righteous act, re-instating the God-given order which they perceived to be under threat. The cross speaks a different truth. It says that God is on the side of the suffering one, that the one who causes suffering will receive judgment, and that the one who suffers will in the end be taken by the hand and moved from last to first. This revaluation of values—the stripping of interpretive efficacy from the dominant class—is where the liberatory potential of the cross can be found.[62]

It is not the goal of this chapter to evaluate whether this is a sufficient response to Williams. Here I only mean to highlight how Cone welcomed her as a critic, valued her voice, and became a better, more thoughtful theologian in the process. There were other theological critics he could have listened and responded to; Cone employed discernment and opened his ear to Williams instead. In the process, his understanding of the cross became both more nuanced, with respect to its evil and its redemptive elements,[63] and it became more visceral, by finding its counterpart in the lynching tree.

Kierkegaard and Cone are both engaged in the task of destroying their respective societies. In their engagement with their critics, they show different paths of faithfulness to one's mission in the midst of opposition. In short, one must be very careful in choosing partners for the destructive task. At best, one finds oneself in a situation like James Cone, who benefited from critics who—like him—wrote out of the fire created by black suffering. Yet it must be acknowledged that one can also find oneself in a situation like Kierkegaard's, where one must close one's ears to all critics, insofar as they are attempting to coax one back into conformity. As 1 Kings 13 illustrates, this is an important matter: one's very life may depend on it.

NOTES

1. Near the beginning of his first major work, *Black Theology and Black Power* (Maryknoll: Orbis, 2018 [1969]), Cone quotes LeRoi Jones (later known as Amiri Baraka) saying that the "task . . . for the black artist in America" is "'To aid in the destruction of America as he knows it.'" Kierkegaard shared this destructive sentiment for his own society completely; as we have seen, for the late Kierkegaard it was the explicit goal of his work. For more on destruction in Cone, see *God of the Oppressed* (Maryknoll: Orbis, 1997 [1975]), 202, 217.

2. Ta-Nehisi Coates, *Between the World and Me* (New York: Spiegel & Grau, 2015), 6, and *passim*.

3. There are now multiple competing conventions for the capitalization (or lack thereof) of 'black' and 'white.' In this chapter, because it deals extensively with the work of James Cone, I have adopted Cone's own usage.

4. See James H. Cone, *Said I Wasn't Gonna Tell Nobody* (Maryknoll: Orbis, 2018), 79–80, for explicit consideration of precisely this issue.

5. James H. Cone, *God of the Oppressed*, 82–83.

6. See the history recounted in James H. Cone, *For My People: Black Theology and the Black Church* (Maryknoll: Orbis, 1984), 5–30.

7. Cone, *Black Theology and Black Power*, 6; cf. *God of the Oppressed*, 179: "black liberation means a radical break with the existing political and social structures and a redefinition of black life along the lines of black power and self-determination[.]"

8. Stokely Carmichael as quoted by Cone in *Black Theology and Black Power*, 19.

9. On the overlap of Black Power and black self-determination, see James H. Cone, *A Black Theology of Liberation* (Maryknoll: Orbis, 2020 [1970]), 10.

10. Cone, *Black Theology and Black Power*, 94.

11. Cone, *A Black Theology of Liberation*, 3; cf. 4: "Whatever theology says about God and the world must arise out of its sole reason for existence as a discipline: to assist the oppressed in their liberation."

12. See Cone, *A Black Theology of Liberation*, 5–6: "The Jesus-event in twentieth-century America is a black-event—that is, an event of liberation taking place in the black community in which blacks recognize that it is incumbent upon them to throw off the chains of white oppression by whatever means they regard as suitable. This is what God's revelation means to black and white America, and why black theology is an indispensable theology for our time."

13. Particularly God as creator. See Cone, *Black Theology and Black Power*, 60: "In a world that has taught blacks to hate themselves, the new black man does not transcend blackness, but accepts it, loves it as a gift of the Creator"; cf. 156: "When man denies his freedom and the freedom of others, he denies God. To be for God by responding creatively to the *imago Dei* means that man cannot allow others to make him an It"; cf. 168.

14. See Cone, *Black Theology and Black Power*, 44: "Black rebellion is a manifestation of God himself actively involved in the present-day affairs of men for the purpose of liberating a people."

15. See esp. the self-assertion of the seducer in EOI 301–446/SKS 2:291–432.

16. Cone, *Black Theology and Black Power*, 16.

17. Cone, *Black Theology and Black Power*, 45.

18. Cone, *Black Theology and Black Power*, 26; cf. *For My People*, 86.

19. See Cone, *Black Theology and Black Power*, 8–9; cf. *For My People*, 86.

20. See Cone, *Black Theology and Black Power*, 47: "Whites are thus enslaved to their own egos. Therefore, when blacks assert their freedom in self-determination, whites too are liberated." Cf. *God of the Oppressed*, 139: "It is the same for the oppressors: they never recognize that the struggle of freedom is for all, including themselves. . . . As bearers of liberation—of the realm of health in a sick society—the oppressed must therefore fight against the oppressors in order to fight for them."

21. See Cone, *Black Theology and Black Power*, 46: "The white structure of this American society, personified in every racist, must be at least part of what the New Testament meant by the demonic forces."

22. Cone, *Black Theology and Black Power*, 169–170.

23. See Cone, *A Black Theology of Liberation*, 114: "Most whites, some despite involvement in protests, do believe in 'freedom in democracy,' and they fight to make the ideals of the Constitution an empirical reality for all. It seems that they believe that, if we just work hard enough at it, this country can be what it ought to be. But it never dawns on these do-gooders that what is wrong with America is not its failure to make the Constitution a reality for all, but rather its belief that persons can affirm whiteness and humanity at the same time. This country was founded for whites and everything that has happened in it has emerged from the white perspective. The Constitution is white, the Emancipation Proclamation is white, the government is white, business is white, the unions are white. What we need is the destruction of whiteness,

which is the source of human misery in the world"; cf. 21: "To be black is to be committed to destroying everything this country loves and adores."

24. Cone, *Black Theology and Black Power*, 163; cf. 19: "Black Power seeks not understanding but conflict; addresses blacks and not whites; seeks to develop black support, but not white good will."

25. Cone, *Black Theology and Black Power*, 48: "Again, this is no easy life; it is a life of suffering because the world and Christ are in constant conflict. To be free in Christ is to be against the world"; cf. 74; Cone, *A Black Theology of Liberation*, 86.

26. See esp. Cone, *A Black Theology of Liberation*, 114: "Christianity believes that the answer to the human condition is found in the event of Jesus Christ who meets us in our wretched condition and transforms our nonbeing into being for God. If that is true, then black confrontation with white racism is Jesus Christ meeting whites, providing them with the possibility of reconciliation."

27. See Matthew M. Harris and Tyler B. Davis, "'In the Hope That They Can Make Their Own Future': James H. Cone and the Third World," *Journal of Africana Religions*, Volume 7, Number 2, 2019, 189–212. The central argument of the piece is that scholarly interpretation of Cone has been overly focused on his first four books. If one looks to later materials (beginning in 1977) that reflect Cone's commitment to global dialogue, a theology emerges that is focused not so much on black assertion in the U.S. (as a reductive standard narrative of Cone interprets his significance) as it is on forging international solidarity amongst the oppressed of the world.

28. Harris and Davis provide a helpful map of occasions of dialogue: "Prior to the 1977 addresses, Cone spent significant time in Tanzania (1971), Ghana (1974), Korea (1975), Japan (1975), Trinidad (1976), and Mexico (1977). He also had heated dialogues with Latin American liberation theologians such as Beatriz Melano Couch (Uruguay), Hugo Assman (Brazil), Paulo Freire (Brazil), and Gustavo Gutiérrez (Peru) in Geneva, Switzerland (1973), and Detroit, Michigan (1975, and again in 1980). Cone's internationalism deepened in the decade following 1977 as he engaged in extended deliberation with subjugated peoples and theologians in Sri Lanka (1979), Cuba (1979), Korea (1979), Japan (1979), Jamaica (1979), Brazil (1980), India (1981), Switzerland (1983), South Africa (1985), China (1986), and Mexico (1986)" ("Cone and the Third World," 194).

29. James H. Cone, *For My People*, 142; cf. 146. Harris and Davis summarize the turn toward solidarity in Cone's work as follows: "These dreams of liberation situate Cone within what Cedric Robinson called the Black radical tradition, a collective intelligence that viewed the context of struggle as the globe. Such dreams of freedom are part of a fighting spirituality, one that refuses to invest in the pragmatic securities of citizenship on the terms of this world and, with others, demands the impossible: a new world" ("Cone and the Third World," 203).

30. See Cone, *For My People*, 152, where "capitalism" is listed as one of the "demons" that must be destroyed: "Racism, sexism, colonialism, capitalism, and militarism must be comprehensively analyzed so that these demons can be destroyed."

31. See Cone, *For My People*, 146: "Third World theologians urged us to analyze racism in relation to international capitalism, imperialism, colonialism, world poverty, classism, and sexism. For the first time, black theologians began to seriously

consider socialism as an alternative to capitalism." Among his recommendations for the future of black liberation, Cone says: "The new social order should be democratic and socialist, including a Marxist critique of monopoly capitalism" (*For My People*, 204). Regarding the relation between socialism and dialogue with the Third World, see *My Soul Looks Back*: "I have been convinced that the black church cannot remain silent regarding socialism, because such silence will be interpreted by our Third World brothers and sisters as support for the capitalistic system, which exploits the poor all over this earth." Thus, for Cone, explicit advocacy of socialism is connected to accountability toward the Third World; black Christians must prove to the rest of the world that they are not simply out to get a slice of the American capitalistic pie. Cf. Harris and Davis, "Cone and the Third World," 197–200, 203.

32. On the racialized nature of capitalism, see Cedric J. Robinson, *Black Marxism: The Making of the Black Radical Tradition* (Chapel Hill: University of North Carolina Press, 2020 [1983]), especially chapter 1, "Racial Capitalism: The Nonobjective Character of Capitalist Development," 9–28.

33. For a broader history of Third World movements during this period, which is attentive to socialism and solidarity, see C. L. R. James, *A History of Pan-African Revolt* (Oakland: PM Press, 2012 [1969]). For the reception of Third World movements by black radicals in the U.S. (with particular attention to the Revolutionary Action Movement [RAM] and the supplementary role of China), see Robin D. G. Kelley, *Freedom Dreams: The Black Radical Imagination* (Boston: Beacon Press, 2002), "'Roaring from the East': Third World Dreaming," 60–109.

34. Cone, *For My People*, 204. With regard to this vision of socialism led by the concerns of the people (and with respect to how such a vision might be practically implemented), see especially Marta Harnecker, *A World to Build: New Paths toward Twenty-First Century Socialism* (New York: Monthly Review, 2015).

35. Cone, *For My People*, 145; cf. 200. Cone thus rejects those who assume "that the problem of racism can be solved in the United States without a socialist transformation in the political economy" (*For My People*, 175–176). Cf. *For My People*, 94–95, 155; also cf. Harris and Davis, "Cone and the Third World," 198.

36. Cone warns: "If African-American churches do not wake up and seriously take note of the signs of the times in the world, they will find themselves oppressors of their brothers and sisters in the Third World" (*For My People*, 141).

37. Cone, *For My People*, 141.

38. See Cone, *For My People*, 141.

39. Cone, *For My People*, 143.

40. It should be noted that these financial resources are understood to come from black Americans in order to fund organizations separate from white interference and overdetermination: see Cone, *For My People*, 143.

41. Claude McKay, *Harlem Shadows: The Poems of Claude McKay* (New York: Harcourt, Brace and Company, 1922), "America," 6.

42. See Paul Holmer, "About Black Theology," in *Black Theology: A Documentary History* (Maryknoll: Orbis, 1979), ed. Gayraud S. Wilmore and James H. Cone, 185.

43. Cone, *Said I Wasn't Gonna Tell Nobody*, 79–80.

44. Cone, *Said I Wasn't Gonna Tell Nobody*, 123.
45. Cone, *Said I Wasn't Gonna Tell Nobody*, 93.
46. Cone, *Said I Wasn't Gonna Tell Nobody*, 93.
47. Cone, *Said I Wasn't Gonna Tell Nobody*, 93.
48. Cone, *God of the Oppressed*, 225.
49. Cone, *Said I Wasn't Gonna Tell Nobody*, 102.
50. Cone, *My Soul Looks Back*, 60; cf. *Said I Wasn't Gonna Tell Nobody*, 94–95.
51. Cone, *My Soul Looks Back*, 107.
52. Cone, *My Soul Looks Back*, 129.
53. On the tradition of democratic socialism, which could be described as the achievement of democracy within the economic realm, see for example Gary Dorrien, *Social Democracy in the Making: Political & Religious Roots of European Socialism* (New Haven: Yale University Press, 2019) and *American Democratic Socialism: History, Politics, Religion, and Theory* (New Haven: Yale University Press, 2021).
54. "The women of Union and elsewhere, especially black, are the best judges regarding my openness to feminist issues. I have tried to listen and to learn from my sisters and have attempted to implement the consequences of my listening and learning in what I teach, write, and do" (Cone, *My Soul Looks Back*, 119).
55. Cone, *My Soul Looks Back*, 115.
56. For an example, see above, 125.
57. Cone, *My Soul Looks Back*, 120.
58. On Williams as Cone's student and eventual colleague at Union Theological Seminary, and his developing dialogue with her, see *Said I Wasn't Gonna Tell Nobody*, 119–125.
59. See Delores S. Williams, *Sisters in the Wilderness: The Challenge of Womanist God-Talk* (Maryknoll: Orbis, 1993), 143–148.
60. Cone, *Said I Wasn't Gonna Tell Nobody*, 135: "believing that if God was with Jesus, God must be with us, because we are also on the cross."
61. Cone, *Said I Wasn't Gonna Tell Nobody*, 131; for the explicit parallel with Rome and the cross, see ibid., 133.
62. See James Cone, *The Cross and the Lynching Tree* (Maryknoll: Orbis, 2011). For Cone's explicit reflections on Williams, see ibid., 149–151.
63. I take it that Williams is essential to Cone's recognition that "The cross can heal and hurt; it can be empowering and liberating but also enslaving and oppressive. There is no one way in which the cross can be interpreted" (*The Cross and the Lynching Tree*, xix).

Conclusion

The Attack as a Work of Love: Kierkegaard and Contemporary Political Theology

CONCLUDING AIMS

By grappling with the work of James H. Cone, the previous chapter established the relative nature of Kierkegaard's ascetic theology of attack. With some qualification, it is useful for those who write and speak from a particular perspective, to a particular audience: namely, from the ruling class to the ruling class. Despite his appeals to the common man, Kierkegaard's emphases on renunciation and destruction make sense as themes preached to those in power. We saw in Cone's work a different and equally valid approach to the destruction of society. Yet the fact that Cone's approach is different does not invalidate Kierkegaard's work. We need someone who speaks for the oppressed, and Cone does an exemplary job. But we also need someone who speaks to the powerful: who reminds them of the true nature of their religious commitments, and calls them to the renunciation of their position and the destruction of the society which gave them such a position. Kierkegaard does an admirable job with this latter task, as has been the burden of my argument throughout this book.

In this closing chapter, I want to claim a distinctive place for Kierkegaard in contemporary political theology. In order to make this point, I will argue for the interpretation of the attack upon Christendom as an invitation to suffering that is at the same time a work of love. In fact, Kierkegaard's attack is a loving act toward his neighbors precisely insofar as it calls them to suffering. In order to arrive at this conclusion, I must turn to material that precedes the attack (especially *Works of Love*), and I must triangulate Kierkegaard amongst Augustine and Hegel. Doing so will illuminate the peculiarity of Kierkegaard's ascetic logic within modernity. He comes to us as a voice who asks us to refuse flourishing in favor of suffering, and thus as a very strange voice indeed.

LOVE AS A WORK OF UPBUILDING IN AUGUSTINE AND KIERKEGAARD

The key definition of love in Kierkegaard is found, not surprisingly, in his magisterial text *Works of Love* (1847). The definition is located in discourse IIIA of the first series, titled "Love is the Fulfilling of the Law." It reads as follows: "*To love God is to love oneself truly; to help another person to love God is to love another person; to be helped by another person to love God is to be loved*" (WL 107/SKS 9:111; emphasis original). To love the neighbor is to draw forth her love for God. True love for the neighbor is, in this sense, always upbuilding; that is, it builds the neighbor up out of her everyday, temporal concerns into existence *coram Deo* (before God).

What this means in a practical sense is a matter of some debate. Some, like Theodor Adorno, hold that Kierkegaard's exclusive concern for the eternal good of the neighbor leads to an abstract and otherworldly ethic.[1] Others, such as M. Jamie Ferreira, argue that this is a misinterpretation of what Kierkegaard is saying. *Works of Love* simply presumes that one is giving material gifts; it then focuses on interrogating one's inner attitude in the giving of those gifts, the result being an ethic that is concrete and this-worldly.[2]

Both of these interpretations miss the mark because they fail to see the fundamentally Augustinian character of Kierkegaard's doctrine of love. Material gifts can be given or withheld depending on whether such a gift would be upbuilding to the neighbor's God-relationship. One should give with the following question in mind: can this gift be used by my neighbor to increase her attachment to God?

Implicit within that question is Augustine's dynamic of use and enjoyment (*uti/frui*). In *De doctrina christiana*, he defines that dynamic as follows: "Enjoyment, after all, consists in clinging to something lovingly for its own sake, while use consists in referring what has come your way to what love aims at obtaining."[3] The human task is thus to order one's love correctly: to love God as the absolute—the one true end-in-itself—and all other things as means for cultivating love for God. This renders the value of all things other than God relative to whether they help one to love God or not.

Later in *De doctrina*, Augustine takes this general principle and applies it to love of the neighbor. First, Augustine speaks to one's own role in this dynamic: one is to love the neighbor not as an end-in-herself, but only as a conduit for increasing one's love of God.[4] Second, in loving the neighbor one should try to inspire in her the same approach toward use and enjoyment to which one has oneself subscribed. Augustine summarizes this second conception of love as follows: "all who love their neighbors in the right way ought so to deal with them that they too love God with all their heart, all their soul, all their mind. By loving them, you see, in this way as themselves, they are relating all their love of themselves and of the others to that love of God, which allows no channel to be led off from itself that will diminish its own flow."[5] This is love of the neighbor conceived as the upbuilding of the neighbor in her God-relationship. Whatever one does for the neighbor should be for the neighbor's upbuilding. The goodness of any material gift given to the neighbor is always relative to whether or not it meets such a goal.

Another way to phrase this Augustinian dynamic is to say that the spiritual always has priority. Any temporal, physical, material reality will always be subject to judgment and interrogation. It will be queried to see if it contributes to spiritual development and judged accordingly. Thus, that which is of material benefit to a particular individual is not always right for that person. It all depends on whether that benefit is upbuilding. The singular ethical question in Kierkegaard and Augustine is the same: will this action lead my neighbor to grow closer to God?

When it comes to love, Kierkegaard's mind thinks in Augustinian patterns. Love is building the neighbor up in her love of God, leading her to desire God more and grow in her attachment to the eternal. This is a formal principle that can incorporate any number of concrete actions as appropriate: "everything can be upbuilding [*Alt kan være opbyggeligt*]" (WL 215/SKS 9:218). From providing comfort to allowing suffering to continue, or even prodding the neighbor to take on more suffering in imitation of Christ—all of these are possible loving responses to the neighbor. With the above formal principle in mind, one must simply use one's judgment as to what will be most conducive to the neighbor's upbuilding. Such is also the case in Augustine, but it is not the case in that old sparring partner, Hegel, nor in those who follow him, as I will now demonstrate.

KIERKEGAARD'S DOCTRINE OF LOVE AND HEGELIAN SOCIAL ETHICS

While I have emphasized only one text so far, Kierkegaard's doctrine of love should not be gleaned solely from *Works of Love*. In fact, *Works of Love* should be read in tandem with *Upbuilding Discourses in Various Spirits*, as Kierkegaard himself prescribed (KJN 4:86/SKS 20:86). The interplay between these two texts is critical to understanding Kierkegaard on the topic of love.

According to the discourse "You Shall Love *the Neighbor*," there are always two moments involved in any act of love for the neighbor. First, one isolates oneself as a single individual before God. Then, one goes out of one's isolation to meet and to love the neighbor whom one has been commanded to love in that prior moment of isolation where one is *coram deo*.[6] With the whole of *Works of Love* in mind, such directions are surprising. There is not much material in this text on isolating oneself. Kierkegaard does offer an explanation for such a lack: "In this little book, we are continually dealing with the works of love; therefore we are considering love in its outward direction" (WL 282/SKS 9:280). Everywhere in *Works of Love*, the first moment of isolation before God is presumed, while at the same time focusing on the second moment of going out of one's isolation to one's neighbor. This is why it is essential to read *Works of Love* in tandem with *Upbuilding Discourses in Various Spirits*, for isolation before God is what this previous text is all about.

Upbuilding Discourses in Various Spirits begins with the occasion of confession, in which one actively places oneself as a single individual before God. Confession requires "[t]hat the person making the confession is beyond comparison, that he has withdrawn from every relation in order to concentrate on his relation to himself as a single individual and by doing this to become eternally responsible for every relation he is in ordinarily" (UDVS 152/SKS 8:248). During confession, the individual suspends all social relations and all social constitution of the self (wherein the self would gain its identity only through its social role), focusing only on the self's relation to itself.[7]

Once isolated with oneself and therefore before God, one will be able to will the Good for the sake of the Good, without any thought for positive or negative consequences for one's own self. This is purity of heart, and it prepares the newly minted single individual to perform works of love, for these are what the God one meets in isolation bids one to do.

Once purity of heart before God is achieved, one can act directly for the neighbor's good. Acting directly for the neighbor's good is what is laid out in *Works of Love*, where, through outward actions, one helps the neighbor find herself as a distinct individual before God.[8] This is not the end of the story, however. As *Works of Love* makes clear, such outward action for the neighbor's good then increases one's own attachment to God.[9] In a strange way, then, *Works of Love* is always moving back toward the focus of *Upbuilding Discourses in Various Spirits*, which is always moving forward toward *Works of Love*. This is the dialectical movement in Kierkegaard's doctrine of love, which constantly loops from the individual to the neighbor back to the individual: one's own love for God is increased as one acts to build up the neighbor in her love of God. Each stage of the dialectical movement enriches the next.

In setting up such a dialectical movement, Kierkegaard is engaging a Hegelian pattern of thought and undoing it from within.[10] The foundational text for understanding Hegel's ethical teaching is his *Philosophy of Right*. This text also has a dialectical movement, which unfolds over time. The ethical subject first understands himself as a single individual,[11] committed to universal duties to which he owes absolute allegiance, without regard for consequences; this is what Hegel calls *Moralität*, and the debts to Kant should be clear.[12] Yet the ethical subject in Hegel must press beyond this first Kantian moment, in which one realizes the reality of moral obligation, to something less abstract. Kantian *Moralität* abstracts the ethical subject from the social ties that bind him and which constitute the only stage on which he can act morally.[13] Hence, Hegel proposes his theory of *Sittlichkeit*, or social ethics, which takes these obligations into account. The ethical individual moves from realizing himself as a creature of universal obligations (e.g., to tell the truth) to realizing himself as a creature of specific obligations to those around him (e.g., to tell the truth in a variety of particular circumstances and social roles, each with their own distinctive shape of truth-telling, from father to husband to civil servant); he moves from inward noumenal identification of himself as an ethical subject to outward identification as a contributing moral member of *this* society.[14]

There are several parallels and differences that can be noted when comparing Kierkegaard's *Upbuilding Discourses in Various Spirits/Works of Love* to Hegel's *Philosophy of Right*, but one parallel and one difference stand out as most important.

First, the parallel: there is dialectical movement in each of these thinkers, such that one does not get a proper handle on their respective ethical theories if one isolates only one moment of this dialectic. This has generally been understood fairly well when it comes to Hegel—less so with Kierkegaard.

Now, the difference: in Hegel, the ultimate sphere for moral action is always society.[15] The ethical subject is the person who contributes to the flourishing of his society. In Kierkegaard, society is at best a preliminary consideration. The ultimate sphere is always eternity (WL 6, 252–3/SKS 9:14–5, 252–3). Ethics in Kierkegaard is all about increasing attachment to the eternal sphere, whether our own attachment or that of others. In Kierkegaard, it is possible that at times the good of society must take a back seat to the flourishing of individual souls before God, a flourishing that can happen even amidst the devastation or dissolution of human society.

When it comes to love, then, Kierkegaard uses a pattern of thinking similar to Hegel's, yet he ends up with a much different result. Kierkegaard takes the Hegelian interplay of *Moralität* and *Sittlichkeit* and makes it subservient to spiritual goods. All temporal societal goods are made relative to the eternal good of each individual before God, such that even if a societal good contributes mightily to the temporal flourishing of a given people group, it is to be dropped immediately if it is seen to be harmful to human souls. This is because all temporal goods or ills are only to be made use of for the purposes of increasing our enjoyment of God. In sum, Kierkegaard takes a modern pattern of thought—Hegelian dialectics—and pushes it in an Augustinian direction, undoing its basic premises in the process.

KIERKEGAARD AND AUGUSTINE AGAINST HEGEL AND AUGUSTINIAN LIBERALISM

The recovery of an ancient, Augustinian conception of love within a situation of regnant Hegelianism is a significant achievement,[16] and the potential uses of Kierkegaard's doctrine of love are many. Here, I will focus on one of the potential ramifications of this recovery: the critique of contemporary Augustinian liberalism (an influential school in modern political theology, mainly based out of Princeton University). Whereas Kierkegaard appropriates Hegelian patterns of thought and pushes them in an Augustinian direction, I will argue that Augustinian liberals appropriate Augustinian patterns of thought and push them in a Hegelian direction.

Eric Gregory is one of the most sophisticated representatives of Augustinian liberalism, a group that includes philosophers and theological ethicists such as Reinhold Niebuhr, Jean Bethke Elshtain, Oliver O'Donovan, Jeffrey Stout, and Charles Mathewes. Gregory's *Politics and the Order of Love* is particularly notable for the purposes of this chapter precisely because its focus is on love. His book is an attempt to utilize Augustine's thought in order to inspire the sort of love for liberal democratic ideals that results in civic virtue.[17] In so doing, Gregory shifts the focus of Augustinian liberalism from sin to love.[18]

This is a doctrine of love that, from the start, must fit within the governing presuppositions of liberal political order. Although he does not precisely define what the liberal political order is, I take Gregory's meaning to be consonant with what John Locke proposes in *A Letter Concerning Toleration*, namely that the first duty of government is to protect and promote the material well-being of its citizens, with the further proviso that whatever spiritual interests a government may have, those may not contravene government's first duty.[19] This is an understanding of political governance that Hegel fully upholds, as *Sittlichkeit* only extends the commitment to individual material flourishing into society as a whole, in addition to providing spiritual benefits that complete without contravening material benefits.[20] In this respect,

Hegel fits comfortably within the lineage of political liberalism.[21] In short, liberal political order is defined by its aim of promoting the material welfare of citizens and, concomitantly, the elimination of the material suffering of those citizens: this is the rather uncontroversial definition of liberalism that Gregory endorses. Gregory does not ask whether Augustine might be critical of the project of liberalism in general; rather, he asks how the use of Augustine might be beneficial to the modern liberal political project.[22] To his credit, Gregory explicitly admits that his goal is not faithfulness to the historical Augustine.[23] I do not object to the creation of a modern political ethic that is inspired by an ancient figure, even if it is not entirely faithful to that ancient figure. Rather, what Kierkegaard's more historically faithful Augustinianism demonstrates is that Gregory has not considered the power of certain objections the historical Augustine would make to the ideals of liberal democracy. These objections still bear considering, and Kierkegaard presses us to do exactly that.

In essence, Gregory argues that Augustine grants us a "Christian humanism" that inspires us "to revisit the moral and religious sources of liberal commitments."[24] The ethical subject is henceforth motivated to enthusiastically embrace principles such as tolerance, non-violent conflict resolution, and just distribution of material goods. That is to say, the liberal citizen inspired by Augustine will not just formally subscribe to these principles as an abstract condition for living a private life, but actively embrace them; furthermore, she will often be critical of her society for not meeting these ideals.[25]

This is fine as far as it goes, and it certainly is an interesting variant upon previous Augustinian liberalisms (such as that of Reinhold Niebuhr), which is just what Gregory intends it to be. The problem is that amongst the ideals of liberalism—and perhaps implicitly present in all of them—is the elimination of material human suffering as an unqualified and unquestionable good.[26] This view of material suffering and its elimination would be anathema to Augustine and to Kierkegaard.

Why? Who could be so callous as not to wish human suffering a long overdue goodbye? These outraged questions reveal precisely how pervasive the ideals of liberalism are amongst Western readers. Augustine and Kierkegaard believe that whatever is useful for upbuilding should be what is sought out or allowed to happen, both for oneself and for one's neighbor. Sometimes, this does involve the elimination of suffering, especially in cases where human dignity is at stake.[27] At other times, an increase in suffering is recommended;[28] the attack, in which Kierkegaard asks his readers to ostracize themselves from the comfortable society of which they are a part, is a clear case in point (more on this below). In this understanding of love, one cannot decide in advance whether one should do everything one can to eliminate the neighbor's suffering or if one should encourage one's neighbor to embrace yet more suffering than she now experiences. Such a view is certainly disturbing in the possibilities it enables; for example, should one withhold food from a hungry neighbor if one has good reason to think the withholding of one's gift will draw the neighbor closer to God? As Stephen Minister has put it, "ambiguity" is at the heart of Kierkegaard's conception of love; there is an undecidability built in to the structure of material gifts.[29] Rather than explaining away the disturbing possibilities Kierkegaard and Augustine enable, those readers who choose to follow these thinkers in formulating their own ethical beliefs should admit, as Minister does, that there is an ineradicable element of "ethical risk" involved in taking this standpoint.[30]

For Augustine and Kierkegaard, there is something truly more important than the elimination of material pain, and that is the good of the soul. If there is a case in which suffering would clearly lead to the good of the soul, then that is what they will recommend. Love, on their understanding, would require it.

In Gregory's quasi-Augustinian schema of love-infused liberal values, it is not clear that suffering could play any positive role in the Christian life. Insofar as that is a problem for the reader, she will also have a problem with Gregory. *Politics and the Order of Love* may not be an attempt to remain faithful to the historical Augustine, and one may grant Gregory's point that this need not be a goal for contemporary Christian ethicists. But in occluding these dynamics that are part of the historical Augustine, Gregory's constructive project fails to consider the potential good of suffering for the Christian. Just as in a non-Augustinian, standard liberal account of politics such as Locke and Hegel's, suffering is only an aberration awaiting its final demolition. The wisdom of ascetic Christianity—Augustine and Kierkegaard included—is left behind, on account of an *a priori* acceptance of liberal ideals. To the extent that Christians want to make sense of suffering as potentially contributive to spiritual good, Gregory's project is left wanting. The potential spiritual usefulness of material suffering is a reality for which he simply cannot account.

Like Locke and Hegel after him, Gregory is committed to the material flourishing of human society as a first principle of political governance. In opposition, Kierkegaard and Augustine allow that material human flourishing can coincide with spiritual degradation. Concomitantly, the solution to such spiritual degradation may involve the dismantling of a flourishing human society. To show what this might mean, we can finally return to the attack.

THE ATTACK UPON CHRISTENDOM AS A WORK OF LOVE

Kierkegaard did not want his society to flourish. He wanted it to dissolve, at least insofar as it was constituted in his age. This was an age in which material human flourishing and Christianity were equated; as Julia Watkin writes: "To be an evangelical Lutheran was part of being a Dane; the temporal and spiritual formed one realm of God in which the godly citizen was expected to enjoy earthly prosperity as well as spiritual well-being."[31] The solvent Kierkegaard applied to this combination of worldly and eternal benefit was the New Testament, which teaches that the true Christian inevitably receives unmitigated hatred from the world (TM 22–3/SKS 14:143). With this teaching in mind, one must choose: either the comfortable, secure life of a flourishing modern society, or Christianity. Thus, the society Kierkegaard faced, which tried to draw these two incompatible identities together, cannot stand; already it is not the Christian society it claims to be. The belief that one can have it all, that one can be happy in this life and the next, is a delusion.

With this incompatibility in mind, Kierkegaard takes direct aim at the crowning achievement of modern society, the comfortable life, as an anti-Christian ideal.[32] This comfortable life bears close resemblance to an ideal realization of Hegelian *Sittlichkeit*: each person in society is perfectly in her place, is performing her unique contribution for the good of all and is accorded recognition and respect by the other participating members. This is a life of secure temporal happiness (TM 20/SKS 14:143).

The comfortable life modern society affords at least some of its members is a significant achievement. It is also precisely what Christianity calls one to renounce. One should note here, in connection with the theme of ethical risk mentioned above, that Kierkegaard's attack literature is primarily directed to those comfortable members of Danish society who do in fact have something to renounce. If one is disturbed that Kierkegaard's doctrine of love cannot rule out acts generally considered horrific, such as deliberately withholding bread from the hungry, perhaps this disturbance can be somewhat mollified by observing how Kierkegaard himself applied the Augustinian principle of upbuilding love: he attacked not the poor but the comfortable, the latter being a group he considered especially characteristic of his time. Commenting on Christ's statement that "[t]he way is narrow" (Matthew 7:14), Kierkegaard writes: "That was a severe *nota bene*; the comfortable—precisely that in which our age excels—cannot be brought into any relation at all to an eternal happiness [. . .] the eternal is obtained only in the difficult way" (TM 110/SKS 13:152–3)—that is, the way of suffering.

This way of suffering is in fact what God's providence wants to arrange for people, as Kierkegaard makes clear in the eighth issue of *The Moment*:

> We human beings are by nature inclined to view life as follows: we regard suffering as an evil that we strive in every way to avoid. And if we succeed, we then one day on our deathbed think we have good reason to be able to thank God that we were spared suffering. We human beings think that the point is merely to be able to slip happily and well through this world; and Christianity thinks that all terrors actually come from the other world, that the terrors of this world are childish compared with the terrors of eternity, and that the point is therefore not to slip happily and well through this life, but rightly to relate oneself to eternity through suffering . . .
>
> [T]he God of love is in heaven fondly loving also you. Yes, loving; that is why he would like you finally to will what he for the sake of eternity wills for you: that you might resolve to will to suffer, that is, that you might resolve to will to love him, because you can love him only in suffering, or if you love him as he wills to be loved you will come to suffer. Remember, one lives only once; if it is neglected, if you do not come to suffer, if you avoid it—it is eternally irreparable. (TM 293–294/SKS 13:352)[33]

In the sharp rhetoric of the attack, Kierkegaard calls upon his neighbors to will to suffer so that they might imitate Christ and thereby earn the blessing of eternal comfort. This is a harsh and unpleasant call—but that does not mean it fails to be an act of love.

Even though the attack upon Christendom is written not to take away the neighbor's suffering, but instead to prod the neighbor toward an increased embrace of suffering, it is still a work of love according to Kierkegaard's definition.[34] The attack literature is an attempt to take an illusion away from the neighbor and, in so doing, enable her to grow closer to God. Precisely in this way, the attack upon Christendom is a preeminent example of Christian love-in-action; it is Kierkegaard's attempt to step forth into society and direct people toward greater attachment to God (TM 91–2/SKS 13:129–30). The attack is a building up of the neighbor out of her comfortable society into a direct confrontation with the rigorous call of God; it is therefore, quite simply, a work of love.

Sometimes love for the neighbor can take the form of recommending he give up a life of meaningful contribution to society; for example, Kierkegaard explicitly calls upon his fellow Danes to stop attending church, thus interrupting the this-worldly-other-worldly continuum so central to Danish Christendom (TM 71–78/SKS 13:113–124). Such a recommendation of renunciation holds even if one's society is progressing toward a more just distribution of material goods and would benefit from one's participation in that project. That is to say: if refusing to attend church excepts one from this grand progressive project, leads to social ostracization, brings suffering upon one, and brings no material benefit to any other person—well, so be it. Recommending such a course of action can only be a work of love if one has a conception of love as upbuilding—that is, if love for the neighbor is doing for the neighbor whatever will draw her closer to God. As I have argued, both Kierkegaard and Augustine hold to precisely such an account of love.

This account departs from a modern liberal preoccupation with material flourishing, a preoccupation shared by Hegel and by Augustinian liberals, where works of love are those actions intended to help the neighbor live a better temporal life (which includes but is not limited to material flourishing). Hegel and Eric Gregory aim to reform modern liberal societies, to make them more just and tolerant; there is of course nothing intrinsically wrong with this, not even in Kierkegaard and Augustine's conception. The problem arises when something more than reform is seen to be necessary for the good of human souls residing in a given society. Kierkegaard and Augustine can affirm that a society should be dissolved, even if such dissolution causes suffering, if such a society is causing harm to human souls. Hegel and Augustinian liberals can only articulate a logic of reform that aims toward the elimination of human suffering in a progressive realization of human flourishing.

In sum: the ancient, ascetic conception of love in Kierkegaard and Augustine is able to make sense of lives lived in renunciation as lives of love in a way that liberalism is not. This conception is able to see suffering as a good, if it is being used by an individual to draw closer to God. And it is able to see suffering as a good both for oneself as a single individual (*Upbuilding Discourses in Various Spirits*), and—more controversially—for one's neighbor in her God-relationship (*Works of Love*). And sometimes it is a preeminent act of love to attack the very society that has made the neighbor's life so pleasant. On this, Kierkegaard and Augustine agree, and they continue to call into question the validity of any doctrine of love that cannot admit such a proposition. When reflecting back on the attack, then, I propose that we offer Kierkegaard a word of thanks for his work of love.

NOTES

1. T. W. Adorno "On Kierkegaard's doctrine of love," *Zeitschrift für Socialforschung / Studies in Philosophy and Social Science*, 8, no. 3413–29 (1939), 413–429.

2. M. J. Ferreira, "Other-worldliness in Kierkegaard's *Works of Love*," *Philosophical Investigations*, 22, no. 1 (1999): 65–79.

3. Augustine, *Teaching Christianity* (Hyde Park, NY: New City Press, 1996), trans. Edmund Hill, 107. Cf. WL 40/SKS 9:47: "The despair is due to relating oneself with infinite passion to a particular something, for one can relate oneself with infinite passion—unless one is in despair—only to the eternal."

4. Augustine, *Teaching Christianity*, 114.
5. Augustine, *Teaching Christianity*, 115.
6. Kierkegaard uses the image of the closet, taken from Matthew 6:6: "There is indeed a big dispute going on in the world about what should be called the highest. But whatever it is called now, whatever variations there are, it is unbelievable how much prolixity is involved in taking hold of it. Christianity, however, immediately teaches a person the shortest way to find the highest: Shut your door and pray to God—because God is surely the highest. If someone goes out into the world to try to find the beloved or the friend, he can go a long way—and go in vain, can wander the world around—and in vain. But Christianity is never responsible for having a person go even a single step in vain, because when you open the door that you shut in order to pray to God and go out the very first person you meet is the neighbor, whom you *shall* love" (WL 51/SKS 9:58).
7. See, for example, Kierkegaard's description of the apostle: "An apostle [. . .] leaves out everything else, forgets everything else, does not see it, does not hear it, does not sense it, but has his sights on God alone [. . .] No, for this humble martyr people simply are not present" (UDVS 336/SKS 8:426).
8. See WL 271/SKS 9:270: "The small-minded person has never had the courage for this God-pleasing venture of humility and pride: *before God* to be oneself—the emphasis is on "before God," since this is the source and origin of all distinctiveness. The one who has ventured this has distinctiveness; he has come to know what God has already given him, and in the same sense he believes completely in everyone's distinctiveness. To have distinctiveness is to believe in the distinctiveness of everyone else, because distinctiveness is not mine but is God's gift by which he gives being to me, and he indeed gives to all, gives being to all."
9. See WL 384/SKS 9:376: "The direction is inward; essentially you have to do only with yourself before God." It is important to see this statement in its context, located in the conclusion to a text that has been focused on outward works.
10. See further Thomas J. Millay, "Concrete *and* Otherworldly: Reading Kierkegaard's *Works of Love* alongside Hegel's *Philosophy of Right*," *Modern Theology*, 34, no. 1 (2018): 23–41.
11. Hegel's understanding of political participation is exclusively masculine. See G. W. F. Hegel *Elements of the Philosophy of Right*, xxix.
12. Hegel, *Philosophy of Right*, 105–41.
13. See Hegel, *Philosophy of Right*, 135: "However essential it may be to emphasize the pure and unconditional self-determination of the will as the root of duty—for knowledge [*Erkenntnis*] of the will first gained a firm foundation and point of departure in the philosophy of Kant, through the thought of its infinite autonomy (see 133)—to cling on to a merely moral point of view without making the transition to the concept of ethics reduced this gain to an *empty formalism*, and moral science to an empty rhetoric of *duty for duty's sake*. From this point of view, no immanent theory of duties is possible. One may indeed bring in material *from outside* and thereby arrive at *particular* duties, but it is impossible to make the transition to the determination of particular duties from the above determination of duty as *absence of contradiction*, as *formal correspondence with itself*, which is no different from the specification of

abstract determinacy; and even if such a particular content for action is taken into consideration, there is no criterion within that principle for deciding whether or not this content is a duty. On the contrary, it is possible to justify any wrong or immoral mode of action by this means."

14. Hegel, *Philosophy of Right*, 146–57.

15. Hegel, *Philosophy of Right*, 257.

16. On the specific Danish Hegelianism Kierkegaard is combating in *Works of Love*, see Millay, "Concrete *and* Otherworldly," 27–30.

17. Eric Gregory, *Politics and the Order of Love: An Augustinian Ethic of Democratic Citizenship* (Chicago: The University of Chicago Press, 2008), 1–10, 262–3, 383.

18. Previous exponents of Augustinian liberalism tend to focus on how due recognition of human sin should cause us to chasten our expectations of what the political order can do. See especially the work of Reinhold Niebuhr, e.g., "Augustine's political realism," in *The Essential Reinhold Niebuhr: Selected Essays and Addresses* (New Haven, CT: Yale University Press, 1986), 123–41.

19. John Locke, *Locke on Toleration* (Cambridge: Cambridge University Press, 2010), ed. Richard Vernon, 6–7. "Liberalism" is a contested term, but the debates (such as on how active or intrusive the government should be in achieving its aim of material benefit) do not challenge the fundamental principle above summarized (see Alan Ryan, *The making of modern liberalism* [Princeton, NJ: Princeton University Press, 2012] 21–44). Locke is often taken to be a "founding father" of liberalism (Ryan, *Making of Modern Liberalism*, 233), and even accounts that challenge how this liberalism is to be defined do not dispute this moniker (John Baltes, *The Empire of Habit: John Locke, Discipline, and the Origins of Liberalism* [Rochester, NY: The University of Rochester Press 2016]). I have attempted to provide as broad and inclusive a definition of liberalism as possible, *via* a figure who is indisputably important to its intellectual heritage.

20. Hegel, *Philosophy of Right*, 41–53, 160–171.

21. Marek N. Jakubowski and Torun Bydgoszcz, "Hegel's non-Liberal Liberalism," *Hegel Jahrbuch 2014*, 237–241.

22. Gregory, *Politics and the Order of Love*, 2.

23. Gregory, *Politics and the Order of Love*, 7.

24. Gregory, *Politics and the Order of Love*, 371.

25. Gregory, *Politics and the Order of Love*, 383.

26. Gregory, *Politics and the Order of Love*, 71, 349.

27. See Kierkegaard on the elimination of slavery: UDVS 242–3/SKS 8:341–2.

28. See FSE 80/SKS 13:101: "Harder sufferings! Who is so cruel as to dare say something like that? My friend, it is Christianity, the doctrine that is sold under the name of the gentle comfort, whereas it is eternity's comfort, yes, truly, and for all eternity—but it certainly must deal rather severely."

29. Stephen Minister, "An Ethics for Adults? Kierkegaard and the Ambiguity of Exaltation," in Stephen Minister, J. A. Simmons, and Michael Strawser (eds), *Kierkegaard's God and the Good Life* (Bloomington: Indiana University Press, 2017), 153.

30. Ibid.

31. Julia Watkin, *Historical Dictionary of Kierkegaard's Philosophy* (Oxford: Scarecrow Press, 2001), 4. Here I use the terms temporal and worldly interchangeably, and equate them with concern for material goods, in line with Kierkegaard's usage. I do not mean to claim that there is a univocal sense for these terms in Kierkegaard's writings, as there is not (especially not for 'temporal'; see William McDonald "Time/Temporality/Eternity," in KRSRR, Vol. 15, Tome 6, 163–168). I only mean that these terms come to be associated (amongst other things) with the egocentric, selfish pursuit of material benefit. See Watkin, *Historical Dictionary*, 77.

32. See further Thomas J. Millay, "The Late Kierkegaard on Human Nature," in R. Králik et al., eds., *Acta Kierkegaardiana Vol 6: Kierkegaard and Human Nature* (Toronto: Kierkegaard Circle, 2013), 144–51.

33. Cf. TM 213/SKS 13:267: "[God] makes you unhappy, but he does it out of love."

34. In *Efterföljelsens Teologi hos Sören Kierkegaard* (Stockholm: Svenska Kyrkans Diakonistyrelses Bokförlag, 1956), Valter Lindström argues that persecution from the neighbor replaces self-denying love for the neighbor as Kierkegaard's authorship develops (136–162). Obviously, I believe this to be a deeply mistaken argument.

Bibliography

Adorno, Theodor W. "On Kierkegaard's Doctrine of Love," *Studies in Philosophy and Social Science*, vol. 8, 1939–1940, 413–429.

Agacinski, Sylviane. *Aparté: Conceptions and Deaths of Søren Kierkegaard.* Tallahassee: Florida State University Press, 1988. Kevin Newmark, trans.

Anderson, Benedict. *Imagined Communities*. London: Verso, 1983.

Anderson, Hans Christian. *The Annotated Hans Christian Andersen.* Edited by Maria Tatar. Translated by Maria Tatar and Julie K. Allen. New York: W. W. Norton & Company, 2008.

Augustine. *Teaching Christianity*. Translated by Edmund Hill. Hyde Park, NY: New City Press, 1996.

Backhouse, Stephen. *Kierkegaard's Critique of Christian Nationalism*. Oxford: Oxford University Press, 2011.

———. "State and Nation in the Theology of Hans Lassen Martensen," in *Hans Lassen Martensen: Theologian, Philosopher and Social Critic*. Copenhagen: Museum Tusculanum Press, 2012. Jon Stewart, ed. 293–318.

Baltes, John. *The Empire of Habit: John Locke, Discipline, and the Origins of Liberalism*. Rochester: The University of Rochester Press, 2016.

Barnett, Christopher B. *From Despair to Faith: The Spirituality of Søren Kierkegaard.* Minneapolis: Fortress Press, 2014.

———. *Kierkegaard, Pietism and Holiness*. Burlington and Farnham: Ashgate, 2011.

Barrett, Lee C. *Eros and Self-Emptying: The Intersections of Augustine and Kierkegaard*. Grand Rapids: Wm. B. Eerdmans, 2013.

Berman, Patricia G. *In Another Light: Danish Painting in the Nineteenth Century*. New York: Vendome, 2007.

Bernard of Clairvaux. *Selected Works (The Classics of Western Spirituality)*. Translated by Gillian R. Evans. Mahwah: Paulist Press, 1987.

Brown, Peter. *Treasure in Heaven: The Holy Poor in Early Christianity.* Charlottesville: University of Virginia Press, 2016.

Bukdahl, Jørgen. *Søren Kierkegaard and the Common Man*. Translated by Bruce H. Kirmmse. Eugene: Wipf and Stock, 2001.
Casey-Pariseault, Matthew. "Old Religious Tensions Resurge in Bolivia after Ouster of Longtime Indigenous President," *The Conversation*, November 19, 2019.
Chatterji, Angana P., Thomas Blom Hansen, and Christophe Jaffrelot, eds. *Majoritarian State: How Hindu Nationalism is Changing India*. Oxford: Oxford University Press, 2019.
Christensen, Dan Ch. *Hans Christian Ørsted: Reading Nature's Mind*. Oxford: Oxford University Press, 2013.
Chrysostom, John. *On Virginity, Against Remarriage*. Translated by Sally Rieger Shore. New York: Edwin Mellen Press, 1983.
Coates, Ta-Nehisi. *Between the World and Me*. New York: Spiegel & Grau, 2015.
Cone, James H. *Black Theology and Black Power*. Maryknoll: Orbis, 2018 [1969].
———. *A Black Theology of Liberation*. Maryknoll: Orbis, 2020 [1970].
———. *The Cross and the Lynching Tree*. Maryknoll: Orbis, 2011.
———. *For My People: Black Theology and the Black Church*. Maryknoll: Orbis, 1984.
———. *God of the Oppressed*. Maryknoll: Orbis, 1997 [1975].
———. *Said I Wasn't Gonna Tell Nobody*. Maryknoll: Orbis, 2018.
Connell, George B. *Kierkegaard and the Paradox of Religious Diversity*. Grand Rapids: Eerdmans, 2016.
Denvir, Daniel. *All-American Nativism: How the Bipartisan War on Immigrants Explains Politics as We Know It*. London: Verso, 2020.
Ditlevsen, Tove. *The Copenhagen Trilogy*. Translated by Tiina Nunnally and Michael Favala Goldman. New York: Farar, Straus and Giroux, 2021.
Dorrien, Gary. *American Democratic Socialism: History, Politics, Religion, and Theory*. New Haven: Yale University Press, 2021.
———. *Social Democracy in the Making: Political & Religious Roots of European Socialism*. New Haven: Yale University Press, 2019.
Du Mez, Kristin Kobes. *Jesus and John Wayne: How White Evangelicals Corrupted a Faith and Fractured a Nation*. New York: W. W. Norton, 2020.
Fenger, Henning. *The Heibergs*. Translated by Frederick J. Marker. New York: Twayne Publishers, 1971.
Ferreira, M. J. "Other-worldliness in Kierkegaard's *Works of Love*," *Philosophical Investigations*, 22, no. 1 (1999): 65–79.
Garff, Joakim. *Søren Kierkegaard: A Biography*. Translated by Bruce H. Kirmmse. Princeton: Princeton University Press, 2005.
Gellner, Ernest. *Nations and Nationalism*. Oxford: Blackwell, 1983.
Gregory, Eric. *Politics and the Order of Love: An Augustinian Ethic of Democratic Citizenship*. Chicago: The University of Chicago Press, 2008.
Hampson, Daphne. *Christian Contradictions: The Structures of Lutheran and Catholic Thought*. Cambridge: Cambridge University Press, 2001.
Harnecker, Marta. *A World to Build: New Paths toward Twenty-First Century Socialism*. Translated by Fred Fuentes. New York: Monthly Review, 2015.

Harris, Matthew M., and Tyler B. Davis. "'In the Hope That They Can Make Their Own Future': James H. Cone and the Third World," *Journal of Africana Religions*, Volume 7, Number 2, 2019, 189–212.

Haugbolle, Sune. "Did the Left Really Win in Denmark?" *Foreign Policy*, June 7, 2019.

Hegel, G. W. F. *Elements of the Philosophy of Right*. Edited by Allen W. Wood. Translated by H. B. Nisbet. Cambridge: Cambridge University Press, 1991.

Heiberg, Johan Ludvig. *Heiberg: "On the Significance of Philosophy for the Present Age" and Other Texts.* Edited and translated by Jon Stewart. Copenhagen: C.A. Reitzel, 2005.

Hobsbawm, Eric. *Nations and Nationalism since 1780: Programme, Myth, Reality.* Cambridge: Cambridge University Press, 1990.

Hughes, Carl. *Kierkegaard and the Staging of Desire: Rhetoric and Performance in a Theology of Eros*. New York: Fordham University Press, 2014.

Jakubowski, Marek N., and Torun Bydgoszcz. "Hegel's non-Liberal Liberalism," *Hegel Jahrbuch 2014*, 237–241.

James, C. L. R. *A History of Pan-African Revolt*. Oakland: PM Press, 2012 [1969].

Kangas, David J. *Errant Affirmations: On the Philosophical Meaning of Kierkegaard's Religious Discourses*. London: Bloomsbury, 2018.

———. *Kierkegaard's Instant: On Beginnings*. Bloomington: Indiana University Press, 2007.

Kant, Immanuel. *Religion within the Bounds of Mere Reason and Other Writings*. Cambridge, Cambridge University Press, 1998. Edited and translated by Allen Wood and George di Giovanni.

Kelley, Robin D. G. *Freedom Dreams: The Black Radical Imagination*. Boston: Beacon Press, 2002.

Kempis, Thomas à. *The Imitation of Christ.* Translated by Richard Whitford. New York: Harper and Brothers, 1943.

Khawaja, Noreen. *The Religion of Existence: Asceticism in Philosophy from Kierkegaard to Sartre*. Chicago: University of Chicago Press, 2016.

Kirkpatrick, Matthew D. *Attacks on Christendom in a World Come of Age: Kierkegaard, Bonhoeffer, and the Question of "Religionless Christianity."* Eugene: Pickwick, 2011.

Kirmmse, Bruce H. *Kierkegaard in Golden Age Denmark*. Bloomington and Indianapolis: Indiana University Press, 1990.

Kirmmse, Bruce H., ed. *Encounters with Kierkegaard*. Translated by Bruce H. Kirmmse and Virginia R. Laursen. Princeton: Princeton University Press, 1996.

Lepore, Jill. *This America: The Case for the Nation.* New York: Liveright, 2019.

Lindström, Valter. *Efterföljelsens Teologi hos Sören Kierkegaard*. Stockholm: Svenska Kyrkans Diakonistyrelses Bokförlag, 1956.

Lippitt, John, and George Pattison, eds. *The Oxford Handbook of Kierkegaard*. Oxford: Oxford University Press, 2013.

Locke, John. *Locke on Toleration*. Edited by Richard Vernon. Cambridge: Cambridge University Press, 2010.

Lorentzen, James, and Gordon Marino, eds. *Taking Kierkegaard Personally: First Person Responses*. Macon: Mercer University Press, 2020.
Lowrie, Walter. *A Short Life of Kierkegaard*. Princeton, NJ: Princeton University Press, 1942.
McGinn, Bernard. *Thomas Aquinas's "Summa Theologica": A Biography*. Princeton: Princeton University Press, 2014.
———. *The Varieties of Vernacular Mysticism (1350–1550)*. New York: The Crossroad Publishing Company, 2012.
Mahn, Jason. *Becoming a Christian in Christendom: Radical Discipleship and the Way of the Cross in America's 'Christian' Culture*. Minneapolis: Fortress, 2016.
Malantschuk, Gregor, and N. H. Søe (eds). *Søren Kierkegaards Kamp mod Kirke*. Copenhagen: Munksgaards Forlag, 1956.
Marsh, Charles. *Strange Glory: A Life of Dietrich Bonhoeffer*. New York: Penguin Random House, 2014.
Martens, Paul. *Reading Kierkegaard I: Fear and Trembling*. Eugene: Cascade, 2017.
Martens, Paul, and C. Stephen Evans, eds. *Kierkegaard and Christian Faith*. Waco: Baylor University Press, 2016.
Martensen, Hans Lassen. *Christian Ethics: Special Part. Second Division: Social Ethics*. Edinburgh: T&T Clark, 1892. Sophia Taylor, trans.
———. *Den christelige Daab betragtet med Hensyn paa det baptistike Spørgsmall*. Copenhagen: C. A. Reitzel, 1843.
Marx, Karl. *Capital, Vol. 1*. Translated by Ben Fowkes. London: Penguin Books, 1990.
Maximos the Confessor. *On Difficulties in Sacred Scripture: The Responses to Thalassios*. Translated by Maximos Constas. Washington, D.C.: The Catholic University of America Press, 2018.
McKay, Claude. *Harlem Shadows: The Poems of Claude McKay*. New York: Harcourt, Brace, and Company, 1922.
Millay, Thomas J. "Against Flourishing: The Continuing Relevance of Kierkegaard's Asceticism," in *Taking Kierkegaard Personally*. Edited by Jamie Lorentzen and Gordon Marino. Macon, GA: Mercer University Press, 2020, 147–153.
———. "Conceptual Clarity: Kierkegaard's Dialectical Method as a Response to the Religious Crisis of Golden Age Denmark," in *The Crisis of the Danish Golden Age and Its Modern Resonance*. Edited by Jon Stewart and Nathaniel Kramer. Copenhagen: Museum Tusculanum Press, 2020, 109–120.
———. "Concrete *and* Otherworldly: Reading Kierkegaard's *Works of Love* alongside Hegel's *Philosophy of Right*," *Modern Theology* 34:1 (January 2018), 27–41.
———. "Kierkegaard, Hegel, and Augustine on Love," in *The Kierkegaardian Mind* (Abingdon: Routledge, 2019), eds. Adam Buben, Eleanor Helms, and Patrick Stokes, 446–456.
———. "Kierkegaard, Imitation and Contemporaneity: The Importance of the Double Danger," *The Heythrop Journal*, LXII (2021), 21–24.
———. "The Late Kierkegaard on Human Nature," in *Acta Kierkegaardiana Vol. 6*. Edited by Jamie Turnbull. Toronto: Kierkegaard Circle, 2013, 137–151.

———. "You Must Change Your Life: Kierkegaard and Augustine on Reading," in *Augustine and Kierkegaard*. Edited by John Doody, Kim Paffenroth, and Helene Tallon Russell. Lanham: Rowman & Littlefield, 2017, 169–177.

———. *You Must Change Your Life: Søren Kierkegaard's Philosophy of Reading*. Eugene, OR: Cascade Press, 2020.

Minister, Stephen, J. A. Simmons, and Michael Strawser, eds. *Kierkegaard's God and the Good Life*. Bloomington: Indiana University Press, 2017.

Minna Stern, Alexandra. *Proud Boys and the White Ethnostate: How the Alt-Right is Warping the American Imagination*. Boston: Beacon Press, 2019.

Moretti, Franco. *The Bourgeois: Between History and Literature*. London: Verso, 2013.

Niebuhr, Reinhold. *The Essential Reinhold Niebuhr: Selected Essays and Addresses*. Edited by Robert McAfee Brown. New Haven: Yale University Press, 1986.

O'Toole, Fintan. *The Politics of Pain: Postwar England and the Rise of Nationalism*. New York, NY: Liveright Publishing Company, 2019.

Pedersen, Mikkel Venbord, et al. *Danmark og kolonierne*. 5 volumes. Copenhagen: Gads Forlag, 2017.

Poddar, Prem, Rajeev S. Patke, and Lars Jensen, eds. *Postcolonial Literatures: Continetnal Europe and Its Empires*. Edinburgh: Edinburgh University Press, 2008.

Podmore, Simon D. *Kierkegaard and the Self before God: Anatomy of the Abyss*. Bloomington: Indiana University Press, 2011.

Pupper, John. *De quatouor erroribus circa legem evangelicam exortis et de votis et religionibus factciis dialogus*, ed. Christian W. F. Walch in *Monumenta Medii Aevi*. Göttingen: n.p., 1760.

Pyper, Hugh. *The Joy of Kierkegaard*. Sheffield: Equinox, 2011.

Robinson, Cedric J. *Black Marxism: The Making of the Black Radical Tradition*. Chapel Hill: University of North Carolina Press, 2020 [1983].

Rochester, Stuart T. *Self-Denial: A New Testament View*. Eugene: Cascade, 2019.

Ryan, Alan. *The making of modern liberalism*. Princeton: Princeton University Press, 2012.

Schlegel, Friedrich. *Friedrich Schlegel's "Lucinde" and the Fragments*. Translated by Peter Firchow. Minneapolis, MN: University of Minnesota Press, 1971.

Stewart, Jon. *The Cultural Crisis of the Danish Golden Age: Heiberg, Martensen and Kierkegaard*. Copenhagen: Museum Tusculanum Press, 2015.

———. *A History of Hegelianism in Golden Age Denmark, Tome I, The Heiberg Period: 1824–1836*. Copenhagen: C.A. Reitzel's Publishers, 2007.

———. *A History of Hegelianism in Golden Age Denmark, Tome II, The Martensen Period: 1837–1842*. Copenhagen: C.A. Reitzel's Publishers, 2007.

Stewart, Jon (ed). *A Companion to Kierkegaard*. Oxford: Blackwell Publishing, 2015.

———. *Hans Lassen Martensen: Theologian, Philosopher and Social Critic*. Copenhagen: Museum Tusculanum Press, 2012.

———. *Kierkegaard and His Contemporaries: The Culture of Golden Age Denmark*. Berlin and New York: Walter de Gruyter, 2003.

Swartley, Willard M. "The 'Imitatio christi' in the Ignatian Letters," *Vigilae Christianae* 27 (1973), 81–103.

Taylor, Mark C. "Journeys to Moriah: Hegel vs. Kierkegaard," *The Harvard Theological Review*, Vol. 70, No. 3/4 (Jul–Oct. 1977), 305–326.

Thompson, Curtis. *Following the Cultured Public's Chosen One: Why Martensen Mattered to Kierkegaard.* Copenhagen: Museum Tusculanum Press, 2008.

Tudvad, Peter. *Kierkegaards København.* Copenhagen: Politiken, 2004.

Van Engen, John. *Devotio Moderna: Basic Writings (Classics of Western Spirituality).* Translated by John Van Engen. Mahwah: Paulist Press, 1988.

———. *Sisters and Brothers of the Common Life.* Philadelphia: University of Pennsylvania Press, 2008.

Vanaik, Achin. *The Rise of Hindu Authoritarianism: Secular Claims, Communal Realities.* London: Verso, 2017.

Walsh, Sylvia. *Kierkegaard and Religion: Personality, Character, and Virtue.* Cambridge: Cambridge University Press, 2018

———. *Kierkegaard: Thinking Christianly in an Existential Mode.* Oxford: Oxford University Press, 2009.

———. *Living Christianly: Kierkegaard's Dialectic of Christian Existence.* University Park: The Pennsylvania State University Press, 2005.

Watkin, Julia. *Historical Dictionary of Kierkegaard's Philosophy.* Lanham: Scarecrow Press, 2001.

———. "The Logic of Søren Kierkegaard's Misogyny, 1854–1855," *Kierkegaardiana* 15 (1991), 79–93.

Westphal, Merold. *Kierkegaard's Critique of Reason and Society.* Macon: Mercer University Press, 1987.

Whitehead, Andrew L., and Samuel L. Perry, *Taking America Back for God: Christian Nationalism in the United States.* Oxford: Oxford University Press, 2020.

Williams, Delores S. *Sisters in the Wilderness: The Challenge of Womanist God-Talk.* Maryknoll: Orbis, 1993.

Wilmore, Gayraud S., and James H. Cone, eds. *Black Theology: A Documentary History. Volume One: 1966–1979.* (Maryknoll: Orbis, 1979).

Wilkerson, Isabel. *Caste: The Origins of Our Discontents.* New York: Random House, 2020.

Index

AAR (American Academy of Religion), ix–x
Anderson, Benedict, xiv, 111–112, 114
ascetic, xi–xv, 3, 11, 13, 34, 36, 38–43, 50n98, 66, 70, 83n12, 89–92, 97, 102n52, 117–118, 141, 148, 151
asceticism, xiv, 13, 38–39, 78, 91, 97–98, 102n52, 118
askēsis, xii, xiv, 14, 34, 36, 38, 41, 86n35, 91, 116–118, 130–131
Augustine, 94, 142–143, 146–148, 151
Augustinian liberalism, 146–148, 151

Backhouse, Stephen, xiv, 45n18, 107–112, 115–116, 120nn24–25, 121n45
Barth, Karl, 124, 133
Black Power, 125
Bolivia, 104
Bonhoeffer, Dietrich 70, 82n4, 117
boredom, 26–27, 30

cannibals, pastors as xv, 12
capitalism, 128, 130, 134, 138n30
chastity, xii–xiii, 91–93, 97–98, 99n7, 117
Christendom, ix–xv, 1–8, 13–14, 23–24, 41–43, 56, 58, 60–61, 65, 69, 70, 73, 76–77, 81, 83n15, 84nn25–26, 85nn28–29,32, 86n38, 89, 91, 103–104, 116–117, 123–124, 150
clergy, 71–72, 78–80, 83nn10–11, 18, 20, 85n29
Coates, Ta-Nehisi, 123
colonialism, xi, 20–21, 47n51, 90
comfort, xi–xii, 2–3, 13–14, 16, 20, 30–31, 36, 38, 59, 63–64, 66, 71–72, 78, 90, 94, 96, 115–116, 143, 147, 149–150, 153n28
Cone, James H., xiv, 118, 123–141
confession, 2–4, 34–37, 75–77, 79, 84n26, 86n33, 95–96, 144

Davis, Tyler B., 127–130
Denmark, x–xi, 12, 14, 18, 62–66, 72–73, 77–79, 81, 109, 124
destruction, 13, 56, 77, 124–127, 130, 136, 141
devotio moderna, 91–97, 99n14, 100n16–29, 101nn31–51
Dorrien, Gary, 140n53
Du Mez, Kristin Kobez, 114–115, 121n43

England, x
ethical, the, 29–34, 50n88

Golden Age Denmark, xi–xii, 16, 19–23, 33
Gregory, Eric, 146–148, 151
Grundtvig, N.F.S., 109–111, 116, 120nn27, 32

Harnecker, Marta, 139n34
Harris, Matthew M., 127–130
Hegel, G.W.F., 9, 32, 67n12, 145–148, 151, 152–153n13
Holy Spirit, the, 40–41

India, x, 104–105

James, C. L. R., 139n33
Jesus Christ, 7, 73, 82, 95, 108, 110–111, 124, 126, 138n26

Kant, Immanuel, 32, 49n85
Kelley, Robin D. G., 139n33
Kierkegaard, Søren, *Concluding Unscientific Postscript*, ix, 12, 33–34, 56, 64, 91; *Either/Or, Part I*, 26–29, 48nn72–74; *Either/Or, Part II*, 29–31; *Fear and Trembling*, ix, 31–33, 49n84, 87n41; *For Self-Examination*, 3, 40–42, 52n119, 76, 153n28; *On the Concept of Irony*, 25–26, 30, 48n69; *Practice in Christianity*, xi, 1–3, 7–8, 40, 45n13, 46n40, 70–71, 74–75, 77; *Stages on Life's Way*, 30; The Corsair *Affair*, xivn6, 2, 44nn2, 7, 78; *The Moment and Late Writings*, 1, 3, 7–8, 12–14, 46n25, 51n114, 55–68, 71–89, 91, 149–150; *The Sickness unto Death*, 23; *Upbuilding Discourses in Various Spirits*, 13, 34–37, 50nn101–102, 51nn103–105, 78, 90, 116, 144, 151, 152n7; *Works of Love*, ix, 12, 23, 37–40, 51n110, 52n117, 90, 142, 144–145, 151–152;
Kirmmse, Bruce H., 4, 6–7, 13, 21–22

Locke, John, 146, 148, 153n19
love, 37–40, 127, 141–152

Luther, Martin, 84n27

Martensen, Hans Lassen, xiii, 4–11, 18–19, 33, 45n19, 60–61, 65, 77–78, 81, 87nn45–46, 108–111, 120n32, 131
martyrdom, 69–70, 82, 98
Marx, Karl, 82n8, 134
Mez, Kristin Kobez du, 114–115, 121n43
Mynster, Jakob Peter, xiii, 3–4, 7–8, 11, 15–19, 22, 43–44, 44nn5,7, 55, 57–59, 65, 69–71, 73, 76–77

nationalism, x–xi, xiv–xv, 1, 41, 62–65, 81, 104–121, 124
New Testament, the, 8, 51n114, 58–62, 65–67, 71–73, 75, 77, 83n20, 84n25, 106, 117, 126, 131, 137n21, 149

obedience, xii, 32, 34, 39, 90–93, 97–98, 117, 126

persecution, 10, 39–40, 91, 96, 98, 117, 154n34
pleasure, 17, 22, 25–31, 41, 56, 77, 125
political theology, xi, xv, 141, 146
poverty, xii, 19, 57, 64, 83n12, 91–94, 97–98, 117

Robinson, Cedric J., 139n32

Schlegel, Friedrich, 25–26, 30
self-affirmation, 124–127
self-assertion, xi, xiv, 17, 41, 104, 106, 113–117, 121n50, 125–126, 137n15
self-denial, xiv, 2, 17, 38–39, 92, 117, 154n34
self-renunciation, xi, xiv, 117, 124, 127–129
selfishness, 39–41, 50n101, 52n118–119, 98
Sibbern, F.C., 82n3
Sittlichkeit, 31–34, 42, 50n88, 56, 145–146, 149; *See also* the ethical

socialism, 120n26, 128, 134, 138–139n31
Socratic, 78, 86n38, 89, 98
Spencer, Richard B., xiv, 113–115, 118, 121n39
state church, 24, 70, 78, 80–81, 87n45
suffering, xii, xiv–xv, 2, 16, 35–36, 39, 41–43, 55–62, 70, 72, 90–91, 93, 95, 97, 115–116, 121n45, 127, 132, 135–136, 138n25, 141–143, 147–151, 153n28

truth-witness, 5, 8–10, 45n16, 55–59, 64, 66, 71–72, 83nn14, 18, 131

United States of America, x–xi, 104–106, 125–130, 134, 137n23

Walsh, Sylvia, 23–24, 41–42, 48n65, 52n118, 87nn42–43
Williams, Delores S., 134–136, 140n63

About the Author

Thomas J. Millay is a senior research fellow at the Hong Kierkegaard Library, St. Olaf College, and the author of *You Must Change Your Life: Søren Kierkegaard's Philosophy of Reading* (Cascade Press, 2020).

www.ingramcontent.com/pod-product-compliance
Lightning Source LLC
Chambersburg PA
CBHW020122010526
44115CB00008B/934